A Colder Fire

VICTOR H. STRANDBERG

A Colder Fire
The Poetry of
Robert Penn Warren

GREENWOOD PRESS, PUBLISHERS
WESTPORT, CONNECTICUT

Library of Congress Cataloging in Publication Data

Strandberg, Victor H
    A colder fire.

    Reprint of the ed. published by the University
of Kentucky Press, Lexington.
    Includes bibliographical references and index.
    1. Warren, Robert Penn, 1905-   --Criticism
and interpretation. I. Title.
[PS3545.A748Z87 1975] 811'.5'2   73-15319
    ISBN 0-8371-7180-6

Reprinted in 1975 by Greenwood Press,
a division of Williamhouse-Regency Inc.

Library of Congress Catalog Card Number 73-15319

ISBN 0-8371-7180-6

Printed in the United States of America

To My Father

and with many thanks
to Professor James F. Beard, Jr., of Clark
to Professor Hyatt H. Waggoner, of Brown
and to my wife, Penny

Preface

ROBERT PENN WARREN . . . has been so badly read, when read at all, that *Selected Poems, 1923–1943,* may really need . . . a little elementary unheroic plumbing." So said an early reviewer of Warren's poetry, W. P. Southard, in an article in the autumn, 1945, number of the *Kenyon Review,* and though Warren has emerged since then into obvious eminence in American letters, the need for elementary plumbing, at least so far as Warren's verse is concerned, still remains as strong as ever.

The incomprehension of readers faced with Warren's poetry is understandable, for the originality of his imagery and themes and the density of his verse texture are certainly not calculated for immediate lucidity. But obscurity has been a prime characteristic of much modern literature, and it is only through outside critical help that many readers have been able to fully appreciate the richly tapestried world of Joyce, Yeats, Eliot, Faulkner, or even Hemingway. Such help has been precious little as concerns the art-world of Robert Penn Warren, and even less than little as concerns his poetry. The only full-length study of Warren's work which has appeared to date, Leonard Casper's *Robert Penn Warren: The Dark and Bloody Ground*, devotes just thirty of its two hundred pages to a consideration of Warren's verse.

And so a critical analysis of Robert Penn Warren's total body of poetry seems needed. In this study, I hope to meet that need in such a way that both the individual poems and the body of verse as a whole may be better understood and appreciated.

MY GREATEST DEBT is owed to Hyatt H. Waggoner, who suggested this book to me and contributed generously to it, not only by guiding, combing, and improving the text but also by providing a large and permanent broadening of the mind's horizons for myself and many others in his seminars. For their many constructive suggestions and a meticulous editorial eye, I also extend my sincere thanks to Patricia O'Brien Smylie of Baton Rouge, Louisiana, and to John B. Gardner of Brown University.

I am indebted to Random House, Inc., for permission to quote from *Brother to Dragons*, copyright 1953 by Robert Penn Warren, *Promises*, copyright 1955, 1957 by Robert Penn Warren, and *You, Emperors, and Others*, copyright 1958, 1959, 1960 by Robert Penn Warren; and to the William Morris Agency for permission to quote from Warren's earlier volume, *Selected Poems: 1923–1943*, copyright 1944 by Harcourt, Brace and Co. Much of the chapter on *Brother to*

Dragons was published in the September, 1964, number of *PMLA* under the title, "Theme and Metaphor in *Brother to Dragons.*" Let me finally note a debt of scholarship to Leonard Casper, whose *Robert Penn Warren: The Dark and Bloody Ground* provides an excellent bibliography of writings about Warren over the decades.

V.H.S.

Contents

The Themes of
Robert Penn Warren

MORE THAN TWENTY-FIVE years ago, in an article called "The Present State of Poetry in the United States," Robert Penn Warren saw the central issue in modern literature as growing out of this question: "Can man live on the purely naturalistic level?" [1] He might also have observed, had he cared to, that that question has been his own major concern in poetry. Defined simply, naturalism is the concept that nature is a sort of giant machine, impersonal and without a discoverable purpose, whose "heartless secrets" (as Joseph Conrad called them) are made known by the scientific method. Associated with the naturalistic view of life are such philosophies as materialism, logical positivism, and nihilism, with their various responses to the dilemmas that naturalism poses. Man, in this view, is but a weak, transitory part of nature's total machinery, and his dominant mood must therefore be fear of his own extinction.

In literature, manifestations of the naturalistic outlook have been many and powerful: in Hemingway's sleepless men obsessed with "nada"; in Eliot's definition of man as "fear in a handful of dust" (Section I of *The Waste Land*); in Kierkegaard's view of despair as "the sickness unto death"; or in Melville's momentary atheism in "The Whiteness of the Whale," when the whiteness of the Milky Way "shadows forth the heartless voids and immensities of the universe, and thus stabs us from behind with the thought of annihilation." Clearly, many writers have found naturalism hard to live with.

In his earliest volume, *Thirty-six Poems*, Warren likewise finds naturalism hard to live with, and his saying so constitutes much of the substance of these poems, where the speaker's attitude ranges from moods of despair, culminating in a death wish, to stoical endurance, and even occasionally to flickers of religious hope. In *Eleven Poems on the Same Theme*, however, Warren begins to develop that synthesis of psychology and religion which was to become his fundamental and lasting solution to the dilemma of naturalism. The idea of an unconscious, undiscovered self beyond the reach of naturalistic extinction evolves here and points ahead to the serpent-self in *Brother to Dragons* and to the vision of a collective self in *Promises:* "all Time is a dream, and we're all one Flesh, at last." This concept of a collective self bears striking parallels to Jungian psychology, as the chapters on these poems will illustrate. Both Jung and Warren see the unconscious as a primary source of religious experience, and both therefore look upon modern man's repression and repudiation of the unconscious as a grave error, or even "sin." Much of *Eleven Poems* and *Brother to Dragons* thus treats the relationship between the conscious ego, consigned to naturalistic oblivion, and the unconscious self, who for all his brutelike and loathesome appearance holds the secret of ultimate identity.

Readers of Warren's fiction may find, under various guises of plot, imagery, and character, the undiscovered self to be a major recurrent theme. It exists in the ambiguities of self-definition in *Night Rider;* in the search into the cave of self (or of other people's selves) in *The Cave;* and in Jack Burden's discovery of his bastardy in *All the King's Men.* The unknown self is further elaborated in the search for identity in *Wilderness* (a title that, like *The Cave,* is in part a metaphor for self) and is implicit in such episodes as the trip to Big Hump's island in *World Enough and Time* or the slave raid into the African interior in *Band of Angels,* episodes that appear to function as revelatory of self in dredging out the cesspool of collective consciousness. In *At Heaven's Gate*—a strangely neglected masterpiece—Slim Sarrett writes (Chapter 27) of his undiscovered self (made known now because of Slim's act of betrayal and murder) with a mournful irony resembling that of Warren's own poetry: "It came from your mother's womb, and she screamed at the moment of egress . . . [and] the old nurse washed it and washed it, without complete success. . . . In hired rooms he sits by your side and in dark dreams. . . ." And in Warren's most recent novel, *Flood*—which gathers most of its author's previous themes under the groundtheme of "blessedness"—we find this familiar animal metaphor for the undiscovered self (Chapter 31):

Then, in the inner darkness of himself . . . the black beast
heaved at him. . . . But he had . . . come to a grim
acceptance of that black beast with cold fur like hairy ice that
drowsed in the deepest inner dark, or woke to snuffle about, or
even, as now, might heave unexpectedly at him and breathe upon
him. No, he had come to have more than acceptance; in the long
nights . . . he had even come to have an affection for that
black beast. For in the hours before dawn the beast, weary with its
own heaving and snarling, would lie down beside him and snug-
gle, as though trying piteously to warm itself from whatever
warmth there was in Bradwell Tolliver.

In *Promises* the answer to the problem of naturalism
becomes more explicitly religious in a metaphysical way. The
chief "promise" in this volume appears in "Rumor Unverified . . . Can You Confirm," in which "there's a rumor
astir / That the woods are sold, and the purchaser / Soon
comes" to transform his fallen creation: "and subdues to
sweetness the pathside garbage. . . ." The attitude towards death in *Promises* is generally one of turning to nature
to find models of quiet acceptance, without fear or protest. To
Rosanna, the speaker points out how the sea gull "sank on
unruffled wing" from evening's "last light" into darkness
("The Flower"), and to Gabriel, in "The Necessity for
Belief," the speaker brings a novel analogy: although light fails
at evening ("the sun is red"), the "sky does not scream" in fear
of the darkness. Later the moon rises, indicating that belief is
justified: "The moon is in the sky, and there is no weeping. /
Much is told that is scarcely to be believed."

In *You, Emperors, and Others*, Warren restates his key
ideas with increased emphasis. There is the undiscovered self,
the "brute trapped in your eye," in "The Self That Stares,"
and there is the collective identity that ties "you" and the

Roman emperors (not to mention the "others") in a oneness of time and flesh. And there are the vivid intuitions of religious mysticism, some of which appear in the "Nursery Rhymes" like "The Bramble Bush"—"And I now saw past the fartherest stars . . . and I heard the joy / Of flesh singing on the bone"—and some of which are offerings of the unconscious self, as is the case in "Prognosis," where a woman dying of cancer slept and "at last . . . past despair, / Dreamed a field of white lilies wind-shimmering, slow, / And wept, wept for joy. . . ." Against these hopeful intuitions stands, as usual in Warren's poetry, the argument for naturalism, a view shared by (among others) the Roman Emperor Tiberius, a nihilist ("All is nothing, nothing all"), and the speaker in "Nightmare of Man," who represents both the success and the failure of scientific naturalism: "I assembled, marshaled, my data . . . [and] My induction was perfect . . . / But the formula failed in the test tube, despite all my skill, / For I'd thought of the death of my mother, and wept; and weep still."

In his four volumes to date, then, Warren's major theme has focused on his own question whether man can live on the purely naturalistic level, and his major subthemes have consisted of answers that range from the death-wish at one extreme to intuitions of supernatural redemption at the other. This whole experience of confronting naturalism and seeking alternatives may be thought of as constituting the modern "dark night of the soul," an image which will bear further discussion in the following chapter, on *Selected Poems* and its sources.

CHAPTER ONE

The Emerging
of Vision and Voice:
Selected Poems: 1923-1943
and Its Sources

MAN IS PRECARIOUSLY balanced in his humanity between the black inward abyss of himself and the black outward abyss of nature." Robert Penn Warren was writing about Joseph Conrad when he made this statement in his Introduction to *Nostromo*,[1] but he might as well have been writing about himself or, for that matter, about a whole range of writers of the past century who have been caught up in that crisis of belief which constitutes the naturalistic dark night of the soul. As Warren's statement indicates, this modern dark night of the soul has two dimensions, one external to the self and the other internal. The external, "the black outward abyss of nature," has been at the heart of much modern literature, usually embodied in the fear that death means the extinction of the self. This was the dominant fear that Tennyson wrestled with in "In Memoriam," and was later a conviction contributing substantially to Quentin Compson's suicide in *The Sound and the Fury*. Perhaps the most powerful expression of this feeling is found in T. S. Eliot's irony when, at the end of "The Burial of the Dead," Eliot lists three ways in which the dead may be resurrected naturalistically: "That corpse you planted last year in your garden, / Has it begun to sprout? Will it bloom this year? / Or has the sudden frost disturbed its bed? / Oh keep the Dog far hence . . . / Or with his nails he'll dig it up again!"

The internal dimension of the dark night of the soul, that which Warren calls man's "black inward abyss of himself," defines the self as inherently degraded, rife with guilt, bestiality, and moral pollution. The compulsive fornicators in *The Waste Land* or the obsessive seekers of wealth in Dreiser and Norris might fit this description. Ultimately, this sense of a dark animalism within man is likely to come to rest in a concept of psychological determinism. Thus, if we trace the inner and outer dimensions of the modern dark night of the soul to their source, we are apt to find Darwin and Freud as seminal influences. Darwin's diminishment of human dignity to the status of an evolving animal would apply mainly, in its denial of individual immortality, to the naturalistic darkness external to man, whereas Freud's reduction of all human ethics and motives to animal self-interest would relate primarily to man's inner darkness. The ideas of these men and their associates and followers, buttressed by all the evidence that scientific logic and method have been able to produce in more than a century, not only made the modern dark night of the soul inevitable but also conditioned its literary responses and alternatives. Thus, Eliot's slow, tortuous path to orthodoxy, Robert Frost's "Prayer in Spring" that God "give us not to think so far away / As the uncertain harvest," and Wallace Stevens' escape into the creative imagination all have a common basis in the naturalistic view of reality. And like these, Robert Penn Warren has sought in his poetry to find or construe some kind of light, not fallacy or delusion, by which the human soul might find its way out of naturalistic darkness, and so make its world meaningful and habitable.

In his early verse, Warren's main concern is the darkness external to the self, "the black outward abyss of nature" in relation to which the self appears of infinitesimal and transitory significance, as the naturalistic view of final reality would have it. For at least twenty years, which is to say, from Warren's undergraduate days at Vanderbilt University into the early years of World War II, his verse clings tenaciously around that central problem of the ultimate meaning of one's existence. Only with the scene of Billie Potts' bowing his head to the father in the evening dusk, to accept, unresisting, his annihilation, is there a release from that long obsession.

Because of its perception of pattern and purpose in nature, with all living nature sharing Billie's quest for identity, and because of its acceptance of death as concluding this quest, "The Ballad of Billie Potts" is something of a watershed in Warren's poetry. Naturalism was to seem much less of a dark night once this sense of possibility had registered. Death might now be viewed in a mood of acceptance or even anticipation, as is the case in some recent poetry where Warren speaks of death as "graduating from time's school."

Our present consideration, however, concerns the poetry **written prior to "The Ballad of Billie Potts."** All but three entries in *Selected Poems* are drawn from Warren's two earlier publications, *Thirty-six Poems* (1935) and *Eleven Poems on the Same Theme* (1942). For some reason, Warren scrapped the continuity of the latter volume in compiling *Selected Poems*, but all eleven of these poems are included, as are thirty-four of the original *Thirty-six Poems*. For both logical and chronological reasons, I have thought it best to discuss the entries in *Selected Poems* according to their original order of appearance in either *Thirty-six Poems* or *Eleven Poems*, and to follow up a discussion of each of these two parent volumes with a treatment of the three "new" entries in *Selected Poems*: "Variation: Ode to Fear," "Mexico Is a Foreign Country: Five Studies in Naturalism," and "The Ballad of Billie Potts."

Thirty-six Poems: The Dark Night of Naturalism

THE EXTERNAL dimension of darkness, or man's relation to "the black outward abyss of nature," is almost exclusively the topic of *Thirty-six Poems*. The first poem of this volume, "The Return: An Elegy," makes the young poet's position on the final meaning of existence unmistakably clear. It is the naturalistic position, such as T. S. Eliot held until the writing of "The Hollow Men," but unlike Eliot, Warren dispenses with side issues like ethics and culture. No Prufrocks or Sweeneys or indiscreet typists can distract this speaker from the essential anguish of time and death:

> Slow film of rain creeps down the loam again
> Where the blind and nameless bones recline.
>
> they are conceded to the earth's absolute chemistry
>
> .   .   .   .
>
> calcium phosphate lust speculation faith treachery
> it walked upright with habitation and a name.   .   .   .

To this poet, Phlebas the Phoenician would represent the crucial problem in *The Waste Land*, Tiresias and his moral anguish being irrelevant in a world without ultimate meaning. Awareness of time is the only valid obsession to the traveler who, looking through the pane, can see the real present vanish into the unreal past:

> The wheels hum hum
> The wheels: I come I come
> Whirl out of space through time O wheels
> Pursue down backward time the ghostly parallels
>
> .   .   .   .
>
> Pursue down gleaming hours that are no more.
> The pines, black, snore.   .   .   .

Intimations of immortality are not particularly encouraging upon a closer look at the evergreens which form the setting of this poem. Surrounding the graveyard beside which Warren had concocted his definition of man as "calcium phosphate lust faith treachery," these pines are dark, sleepy, submissive to wind and storm:

> The pines, black, like combers plunge with spray
>
> .   .   .   .
>
> The boughs like hairy swine in slaughter squeal
> And lurch beneath the thunder's livid heel.
> The pines, black, snore.   .   .   .

Influence of Eliot is seen in the method as well as in the content of "The Return: An Elegy." The hard-bitten humor of some of Eliot's allusions to mass culture ("O O O O that Shakespeherian Rag" and the like) is paralleled by Warren's sarcasm towards the concept of time in a famous sentimental poem:

> turn backward turn backward in your flight
> and make me a child again just for tonight
> good lord he's wet the bed come bring a light

This is the only humor that Warren's grimness of mood permits in this poem, and even this touch of humor is strictly functional: such an escapist view of time, Warren implies, is the intellectual equivalent to wetting the bed.

A more significant Eliot influence is seen near the end of the poem, when the speaker, grieving over the death of his mother, seeks in vain some spiritual sustenance whereby he might bless her, much as Eliot sought to lift the curse in *The Waste Land* ("if there were water . . . But there is no water"):

> honor thy father and mother in the days of thy youth
> for time uncoils like the cottonmouth
>
> .   .   .   .
> Could I stretch forth like God the hand and gather
> For you my mother
> If I could pluck
> Against the dry essential of tomorrow
> To lay upon the breast that gave me suck
> Out of the dark the dark and swollen orchid of this sorrow.

The imagery, the rhythm, the Biblical allusion, and the theme of anguished striving of spirit in this passage are all obviously reminiscent of *The Waste Land*. But the poem is Warren's

own, nevertheless, and some of the images we see here—
particularly the animal image: "for time uncoils like the
cottonmouth"—indicate the original direction that Warren's
technique will take. The desperate wish that suffering may be
efficacious ("If I could pluck   .   .   . / Out of the dark the
dark and swollen orchid of this sorrow") likewise foreshadows
Warren's future development as a thinker, though it will be
years before he will positively state that from evil can come the
possibility of human good.

Warren's resemblance to Eliot continues in "Kentucky
Mountain Farm," notably in the partitioning of this poem
into seven sections, each with its own title and Roman
numeral, and also in some of the imagery; but in the strictly
provincial setting and the general reliance on local nature
imagery one may watch Warren's true character as an artist
taking shape. These characteristics have distinguished his
subsequent output of verse; they have remained constant
through whatever changes or development of outlook have
ensued.

Perhaps indicative of this growing independence of voice is
the fact that Warren rids himself of most of the Eliot
influence in his first section, entitled "Rebuke of the Rocks."
Here may be found definite echoes of *The Waste Land*. Just as
Eliot began with the ironic renewal of life in the springtime—
"April is the cruellest month, breeding / Lilacs out of the dead
land"—so "Kentucky Mountain Farm" begins with the rocks,
secure in their "sweet sterility," observing with irony the
springtime rejuvenation of plant and animal life in the
immediate surroundings:

> Now on you is the hungry equinox,
> O little stubborn people of the hill,
> The season of the obscene moon whose pull

Disturbs the sod, the rabbit, the lank fox,
Moving the waters, the boar's dull blood,
And the acrid sap of the ironwood.

Being lifeless and inanimate, the rocks have an immense
advantage over the living side of nature, trapped in an endless
cycle of reproduction and death as "the obscene moon"
dictates. In contrast to these transient creatures, the rocks have
prevailed over the reproductive cycle, "Renouncing passion by
the strength that locks / The eternal agony of fire in stone."
The rocks have not only survived but prevailed over the fiery
processes of their creation; their once' mutable substance has
gained, so they think, permanence of form. Secure in this
triumph, they warn living nature to give up its futile reproductive cycle and become also as stone:

Then quit yourselves as stone and cease
To break the weary stubble-field for seed;
Let not the naked cattle bear increase,
Let barley wither and the bright milkweed.

Nor is this wisdom reserved for subhuman nature only.
Human beings suffer the tragic futility of the reproductive
cycle as much as the rest of animate nature, and so the rocks
aim their message of emancipation a little higher. The graveyard is a place rocklike enough to bestow the rocks' blessed
state of deliverance even upon humankind:

Instruct the heart, lean men, of a rocky place
That even the little flesh and fevered bone
May keep the sweet sterility of stone.

The phallic connotations of "the little flesh and fevered
bone"—another possible influence of *The Waste Land*—
convey so pitying and contemptuous a tone as apparently to

clinch the argument of the rocks against living nature, but surprisingly, such is not the case. In Section II, entitled "At the Hour of the Breaking of the Rocks," the rocks receive their own final rebuke. Here even the seemingly ageless, changeless rocks are subject to the immutable laws of change and destruction. They, too, are broken into "fractured atoms" and cast into the deeps of eternity—the agent of mutability being frost in this instance—along with the "lean men" and lesser creatures to whom they had rendered advice a short time ago:

> The hills are weary, the lean men have passed;
> The rocks are stricken, and the frost has torn
> Away their ridgèd fundaments at last,
> So that the fractured atoms now are borne
> Down shifting waters to the tall, profound
> Shadow of the absolute deeps.   .   .   .

Here are the beginnings of several motifs that will recur importantly throughout all of Warren's poetry. Most important is this early articulation of Warren's time-mysticism, the feeling that time is the supreme mystery of existence: it gathers in all things and holds within itself—hidden from human gaze—the ultimate meaning of existence. Only by peering down the corridors of time, dark and interminable as they seem to be, can the individual find the meaning of his own existence, and with it, his true identity. The use of water imagery ("down shifting waters") to describe time in the above excerpt prefigures similar usage in Warren's later work, where various figures peer into inscrutable, shifting waters of time in an effort to find some basic identity beyond the reflected image of self.

As it turns out, Warren's eventual answer to the search for

identity is prefigured here also in the image which concludes Section II. Here the river of time, by emptying all its load—men, redbuds, stone—indiscriminately into the deeps of eternity, brings about an ultimate oneness of all things; and only by drawing on this ultimate oneness can the individual— man, bud, or stone—find his bedrock identity. This idea of oneness will mean an acceptance of universal complicity in later poems, such as *Brother to Dragons*, and will mean shedding the sanctity of the self in every case, but such implications of the search for identity are undeveloped at this point. Nevertheless, it is a remarkable presence of vision that enables Warren to perceive a spiritual unity from which all emanates and to which all returns:

> .   .   .   the absolute deeps,
> Wherein the spirit moves and never sleeps
> That held the foot among the rocks, that bound
> The tired hand upon the stubborn plow,
> Knotted the flesh unto the hungry bone,
> The redbud to the charred and broken bough.   .   .   .

The images of rejuvenation which had seemed so ironic and futile in the section on the rocks' triumph take on higher meaning here in the section on the breaking of the rocks. Because the spirit which "moves and never sleeps" in the "absolute deeps" of eternity holds all cycles of time in its keeping, the new life it effects (it has "Knotted the flesh unto the hungry bone, / The redbud to the charred and broken bough") is at least as meaningful as the extinguishing of this' new life at the end of its cycle. Temporal life partakes, however minutely, of eternity, and so has some meaning at this point in Warren's career. Though this meaning is not very comforting to the isolated self in fear of annihilation, at least it can justify the insistence, which undergirds so much of Warren's later art, that nothing is ever lost. Later, in *Promises*, the conception of the keeper of time, the spirit which moves and never sleeps, assumes a personal dimension whereby the individual self may be redeemed from annihilation.

In Section III of "Kentucky Mountain Farm," however, the spirit of the absolute deeps is decidedly impersonal, and so the thinking mind in search of ultimate meaning must contemplate its own extinction: "There are many ways to die." The death imagery in this section is delicately beautiful, so much so as to imply a death-wish in the speaker, who desires oneness with ultimate reality above all else. Untimely death— the new grass of May being printed by the "hound's black paw" (signifying death), or the "laurel" (human fame?) and sycamore being flooded out to sea—takes on a quality of desirability climaxed in the image of a human body deliciously submissive to death in the rush of time's waters to the ocean of eternity:

> Think how a body, naked and lean
> And white as the splintered sycamore, would go
> Tumbling and turning, hushed in the end,
> With hair afloat in waters that gently bend
> To ocean where the blind tides flow.

This is Warren's version of Phlebas the Phoenician, who beyond the fury of the burning and the pettiness of profit and loss rests in enviable peace: "A current under sea / Picked his bones in whispers. As he rose and fell. . . ." Or we might turn to Faulkner for an analogue—to Quentin Compson contemplating his imminent death by water: "in the caverns and grottoes of the sea tumbling peacefully to the wavering tides." In Warren's poem the "ocean where the blind tides flow" suggests the impersonal nature of the spirit of the absolute deeps, but the "hushed" state of the body "in waters that gently bend" is nonetheless all that the naturalistic mind can hope for.

In contrast to this submissive human body, the cardinal in Section IV knows how to live so as to seize from passing time a sustaining meaning. "Lover of cedar, lover of shade," this bird finds joy of existence although it lives among emblems suggesting the limitation of that existence. Its very redness sets it flagrantly apart from its background of "slumberous green," denoting death:

> At the hour of noon I have seen
> The burst of your wings displayed,
> Vision of scarlet devised in the slumberous green
> . . . Lover of cedar and shade.

Because the cardinal does not share the death-wish of the human body—does not seek to merge itself with its surroundings (as the body merged with the waters)—it gains a sort of immortality on its own terms. Its spontaneous acceptance of life as given by the spirit of the deeps enables the cardinal to live untroubled in the world of death and time. The poet appears to be setting up an opposite polarity to his own death-wish here; constructing and synthesizing such opposite polarities of attitude was to constitute a major part of Warren's vision and art as his career unwound:

> Here is a bough where you can perch, and preen
> Your scarlet that from its landscape shall not fade,
> Lapped in the cool of the mind's undated shade,
> In a whispering tree, like cedar, evergreen.

In its spontaneous joy of life, this cardinal makes an obvious contrast to the lizard in this poem, who, described in ironic imagery of orthodox religion ("devout as an ikon," having an "altar"), blends fearfully into his background and so disappears:

> What if the lizard, my cardinal,
> Depart like a breath from its altar, summer southward fail?
> Here is a bough where you can perch, and preen. . . .

Such use of animal imagery shows Warren's true voice emerging, and more important, it shows the poet's essential humility coming forward. Warren's conception of oneness in nature is so genuine, as is apparent in "The Ballad of Billie Potts," *Promises*, and *You, Emperors, and Others*, and elsewhere, that he does indeed accord every creature its inviolable importance and sanctity of self, even aside from all considerations of imagery. Like Hemingway, Warren insists that man is only a part of nature, having by no means exclusive dominion over the mystery of self.

The jay, hero of Section V, also promotes humility, though in a manner different from the cardinal's. "Bright friend of boys, troubler of old men," he reminds older human observers of time and death as he chases autumn leaves to their rest—"outrageous sergeant in the summer's rout." A third bird image, in "Watershed" (Section VI), is most humbling of all. High up over the mountain watershed, the "sunset hawk now rides / The tall light," serenely unaffected by the darkness covering the landscape below and enjoying a totality of vision not given to man:

> . . . His gold eyes scan
> The crumpled shade on gorge and crest
> And streams that creep and disappear, appear,
> Past fingered ridges and their shrivelling span.
> Under the broken eaves men take their rest.

This contrast between far-seeing bird and short-visioned, earth-bound man appears elsewhere in Warren's verse—most crucially in the opening section of *Promises*, where it dominates the five poems dedicated to Rosanna. In this later sequence, the narrator is able at last to gain for himself, through an arduous ascent up a mountain peak, something akin to the bird's comprehensive vision. But here in "Kentucky Mountain Farm," the narrator already stands on the highest mountains available—the watershed—and, by contrast with the hawk, to no avail. All the narrator can obtain in this poem is some idea of what he needs—transcendent vision, like the hawk's, which might perceive total reality with absolute certainty of truth. Sufficient "certitude" of perception would sustain the perceiver even through the death of self and all the mutability of earth:

> . . . Not love, happiness past, constrains,
> But certitude. Enough, and it remains,
> Though they who thread the flood and neap
> Of earth itself have felt the earth creep. . . .

This demand or cry for absolute certitude bespeaks a very insistent sort of mysticism indeed. It goes beyond the naturalistic mysticism of Hemingway, who said in *Across the River and into the Trees* that love and bravery were the only mysteries he could believe in. Not satisfied with such limited certainties, Warren specifically rejects both love and courage as they are commonly defined; here he says, "Not love . . . constrains," and in a later poem, "Ransom," he asserts that "Our courage needs, perhaps, new definition." What Warren's new definition of love and courage will be comes clear in various later works, but most impressively in *Brother to Dragons*, where the kind of courage Warren espouses is the courage to see the self accurately, and the kind of love that is needed is the love of self, even when the self is seen in all its foulness and depravity, whether personal or—through the oneness of all things—vicarious.

Aside from technical considerations, it is this unrelenting craving for the absolute (impossible to satisfy, of course)—for seeing total reality with final certainty—that makes Warren so intense and powerful an artist. His is a poetry of vision, and though his perceptions into ultimate reality may be rejected for lack of proof, they can never be dismissed as trivial. It is, however, this same insistence on striving for the unattainable, for all-embracing vision and absolute certainty, which has in an essentially classicist age isolated Warren from his fellows, and particularly those from the schools of poetry contemporarily popular, like the poets of social protest or of esthetic consolation.

Section VII, entitled "The Return," which concludes "Kentucky Mountain Farm," shows what direction this newly announced search for ultimate reality will take: inward, into the isolated self. "The Return" is a peculiarly difficult poem to understand. In one way, its structure is lucidly simple, for its two stanzas establish a perfect correlation of thought between an analogy drawn from nature (Stanza 1) and the application of this analogy to a human relationship (Stanza 2). The main obscurity arises in the second stanza, because the human relationship under consideration is never adequately defined. Is it a relationship between mother and son or is it the quite different relationship between husband and wife?

Whether one or the other, the important thing about this human relationship is that it is ultimately a failure. The contact between selves has broken down. Such contact, it seems, can never be permanent or ultimately effectual, in view of which fact the self has only its inner resources to rely upon. The title image of "The Return" refers not to the ostensible return of husband to wife or son to mother, but rather to the return of the self to its source in time, wherein the self's true identity lies locked in secrecy. The image of the dying leaf thus returning to its deeper self in time—an image repeated in "The Hazel Leaf" in *Promises*—is beautifully rendered, time being represented here as *still* waters:

> .   .   .   Again the timeless gold
> Broad leaf released the tendoned bough, and slow,
> Uncertain as a casual memory,
> Wavered aslant the ripe unmoving air.
> Up from the whiter bough, the bluer sky,
> That glimmered in the water's depth below,
> A richer leaf rose to the other there.
> They touched; with the gentle clarity of dream,
> Bosom to bosom, burned on the quiet stream.

This conjoining of the temporal self, through death, with the eternal self ("A richer leaf rose to the other there") is an exquisitely tender, moving scene, one which intensifies the speaker's death-wish in his hope and desire for self-completion. By contrast with this ultimate return of self to deeper self, the return of self to a different self on a temporal level, such as the return of a son to his mother, is marked by disappointment and superficiality.

At this point in Warren's development, before he has evolved, from his rudimentary concept of the ultimate oneness of Nature, a tenet concerning the oneness of Flesh, the self is effectively isolated; its true meaning and identity cannot be found in its relationship to other people, but only by looking inward. Thus this final subpoem of "Kentucky Mountain Farm" concludes with the following sense of estrangement between the two main characters (apparently mother and son):

> . . . And he, who had loved as well as most,
> Might have foretold it thus, for long he knew
> How glimmering a buried world is lost
> In the water's riffle, the wind's flaw;
> How his own image, perfect and deep
> And small within loved eyes, had been forgot,
> Her face being turned, or when those eyes were shut
> Past light in that fond accident of sleep.

"The water's riffle, the wind's flaw," in contrast to the perfectly still waters that had received the leaf, indicate the movement of time which (until that movement is stopped in death) conceals or distorts identity even from those who had once known and loved it. On a surface level, this lack of recognition on the part of the mother shows that the son has changed since his departure, as any intelligent boy will in later adolescence and early manhood. The old image of his identity —"perfect and deep / And small within loved eyes"—has lost its accuracy with the youth's internal changes, and in any case has been forgotten in his long absence ("her face being turned"). Personal biography is implicit here, these poems themselves indicating what sort of estranging growth in the youth the "water's riffle" refers to. But more significant than these personal meanings is the effect of this experience on the poet's future development. For some time yet this poet's voice will speak of a self in isolation, whose only hope of self-completion must rest in the eventual return of the self to the oneness of Nature. That such a return comes through death, which at this point means eternal annihilation, only strengthens the death-wish, rather than diminishes the desire to rejoin ultimate reality. Death was always to remain the doorway into final reality in Warren's verse, but seldom would it be portrayed in such neurotically attractive terms as in this early period of his career.

By the time "Pondy Woods" was written, Warren had effectively rid himself of T. S. Eliot's influence and had found his own true voice. It was to be a voice full of subtle modulations—irony, grim humor, both academic and provincial dialects—and it would always be recognizably original. It was to be, moreover, a voice of extraordinary technical resources, a voice that could summon many levels of rhetoric to its service or evince, when it chose, a great range in tone and richness of sound texture. Above all, it was to be a voice insistent on propagating its own vision, regardless of the opacity, indifference, or outright hostility of the audience, if such had to be the price of independence from the "schools" of poetry.

"Pondy Woods" reworks the central image of "Watershed," the all-seeing hawk, towards a particularly bizarre effect. Replacing the hawk, whose "gold eyes scan," are two buzzards with similarly golden eyes and with similar freedom from the human limitations of these "Pondy Woods":

> In Pondy Woods in the August drouth
> Lurk fever and the cottonmouth.
> And buzzards over Pondy Woods
> Achieve the blue tense altitudes,
> Drifting high in the pure sunshine
> Till the sun in gold decline;
> Then golden and hieratic through
> The night their eyes burn two by two.

These buzzards don't need the golden sun, as men do; their eyes are lit by golden fires from within that glow even during

the human night in Pondy Woods. They can see into the
darkness encompassing man's lifespan.

What they see is not especially encouraging to the runaway
Negro whom the posse is seeking on charges of murder ("But a
buzzard can smell the thing you've done"). The buzzards
realize that the Negro is not so resourceful as the white man in
conjuring up ways to evade the reality of death ("Nigger, your
breed ain't metaphysical"), but just in case he has any
borrowed misconceptions, they take care to divest runaway Jim
of these. Here at the hour of his death he is given to
understand that not gods, but buzzards, hold the true vision of
reality. The buzzards eat such gods, the Christian man-
god included:

> "But we maintain our ancient rite,
> Eat the gods by day and prophesy by night.
> We swing against the sky and wait.
>   .   .   .   .   .
>
> "The Jew-boy died. The Syrian vulture swung
> Remotely above the cross whereon he hung
> From dinner-time to supper-time, and all
> The people gathered there watched him until
> The lean brown chest no longer stirred,
> Then idly watched the slow majestic bird
> That in the last sun above the twilit hill
> Gleamed for a moment at the height and slid
> Down the hot wind.   .   .   ."

After imparting such knowledge, the voluble buzzard suddenly
withdraws into inscrutable silence whereby the Negro knows
he is doomed: "Jim understood, and was about to speak, / But
the buzzard drooped one wing and filmed the eyes."

One further point in this poem is worth our attention.

Towards the conclusion of "Pondy Woods," Warren reiter-
ates his vision of total mutability, much as we had seen it at
the beginning of "Kentucky Mountain Farm." Here, too, the
rocks have disintegrated—this time into loam—and the fires
that once burned within stone are transmuted into the "yellow
flame" of a wheat field:

> At dawn unto the Sabbath wheat he [Jim] came,
> That gave to the dew its faithless yellow flame
> From kindly loam in recollection of
> The fires that in the brutal rock once strove.

It is interesting to note that Warren is the kind of poet who
keeps exploring the implications of his imagery. It is as though
the scrutiny of the self at the center of his verse has a technical
counterpart on the surface, the images themselves undergoing
continual exploration.

"Eidolon," the fourth of the *Thirty-six Poems*, describes an
entirely different kind of hunt from that for the runaway
Negro. Whereas that poem forecast the extinction of self, this
one appears to put forth an opposite polarity of thought. The
"eidolon" of the title apparently refers to the phantom-
self which escapes from the hounds though they have slain
their quarry:

> Dogs quartered the black woods: blood black on
> May-apple at dawn, old beech-husk. And trails are lost
> By rock, in ferns lost, by pools unlit.
> I heard the hunt. Who saw, in darkness, how fled
> The white eidolon from fangèd commotion rude?

The principle of self in the slaughtered prey, probably a
raccoon, has returned to the dark, still waters of time ("in
ferns lost, by pools unlit"), thereby eluding the "fangèd

commotion rude," much as the human body had eluded time's anguish in "Kentucky Mountain Farm." The effect of this image of an escaping "eidolon" is not resoundingly affirmative—no Elysian fields throw open their splendor to receive the self into eternity. On the contrary, the image of eternity as an unlit pool sheds little light as to where the "white eidolon" has disappeared. But in the distinction between the temporal self, the body, and the phantom-self, the "white" eidolon which returns to eternity, Warren at least leaves ajar the door through which he may enter to perceive greater things later on.

"Letter of a Mother" begins with a matter-of-fact scene of a young student-poet receiving a letter from his mother, but by the poem's end this mother-son relationship has been transformed into an elaboration of the recurrent death-wish in these early poems. The real mother of the self, towards which the poet yearns with filial tenderness, is the primal oblivion from which he came, the darkness whose womb shall reclaim him as his worldly mother's womb cannot:

> But still the flesh cries out unto the black
> Void, across the plains insistently
> Where rivers wash their wastage to the sea . . .
> The mother flesh that cannot summon back
>
> The tired child it would again possess
> As shall a womb more tender than her own
> That builds not tissue or the little bone,
> But dissolves them to itself in weariness.

Death is the ultimate, most tender mother here, almost precisely as Whitman conceived it in his splendid "When Lilacs Last in the Dooryard Bloom'd": "Dark mother always gliding near with soft feet, . . . Approach, strong deliveress."

What is most important about "Letter of a Mother" is that it rejects the mystical possibilities present in the last poem, "Eidolon." Whereas that poem envisioned a principle of self, a "white eidolon," that eluded the "fangèd commotion" causing physical death, this poem derides such ideas as an "illegal prodigality of dream," which will certainly prove false when the "escheat heart" that spawns such folly has stopped beating:

> "So hunger is bred in the bitter bone
> To cleave about this precious skeleton
>
>   .   .   .   .
>
> ... a subtile engine, propped
> In the sutured head beneath the coronal seam,
> Whose illegal prodigality of dream
> In shaking the escheat heart is quick estopped."

Such dreams of immortality are not only vain but unnecessary, the poet asserts. Rather than dream of immortality, one should really be grateful to his natural mother for providing the "gift of mortality" whereby we are all assured of rejoining our ultimate mother, primal oblivion:

> "Such is the substance of this legacy:
> A fragile vision fed of acrid blood,
> Whose sweet process may bloom in gratitude
> For the worthier gift of her mortality."

In the tension of opposites which ties the nihilism of this poem together with the mystical possibilities of the "white eidolon," one sees precisely the manner of intellectual development which will characterize Warren's whole career, regardless of what outlook he might hold at any one period. The very comprehensiveness of the vision that he seeks means that he will have to perceive and synthesize opposites if—as he asserts—he wants to remain true to reality. Consequently, his work will always have to synthesize good and evil, hope and despair. The artistic polarizing of such internal tensions will make them appear like double stars, whirling about a common center, until at length after painful deliberation some sort of resolution evolves.

"Genealogy," one of the two entries of *Thirty-six Poems* not included in *Selected Poems,* carries the death-wish of "Letter of a Mother" to such a bitterly personal extreme as to explain its deletion from the later collection. Here the poet's grandfather, Gabriel (Warren's own son would later be his namesake), responds with premature enthusiasm to the birth of Warren's father:

> But swollen ran the river, the hills were brown,
> And a wind in the east, when a son was born.
> "A fine little bastard," Gabriel said,
> But Martha lay in a strict high bed,
> No breath in her body or trouble in her head.

The death of his grandmother in childbirth was the lesser tragedy, in the poet's estimation, when compared to the intolerable irony of fate that made the baby, Warren's father, survive long enough to bring him, Robert Penn Warren, into a ruined world:

> Gabriel, Gabriel   . . .
>   .   .   .   .   .
> Your grandson keeps a broken house.
> There's a stitch in his side no plasters heal,
> A crack in the firmament, maggots in the meal;

There's a mole in the garden, fennel by the gate,
In the heart a curse of hell-black hate
For that other young guy who croaked too late.

Perhaps as a consequence of his above reference to Grandfather Gabriel, whose one observation ("A fine little bastard")
reveals a certain lack of refinement in not only himself but his
whole generation, the next poem, "History," sets the speaker's
death-wish in a historical perspective. Those rough, lusty
fellows of grandfather's day lived hard, suffered much, sacrificed greatly—but had no death-wish:

We came bad ways,
The watercourses
Dry,
No herbs for horses.
(We slew them shamefastly,
Dodging their gaze.)
Sleet came some days,
At night no fuel.

.   .   .

Much man can bear.

Such sufferings in the wilderness gave meaning to the lives
of the pioneer grandsires, but after Canaan has been possessed,
observe what happens to the new generation gorged with milk
and honey:

In the new land
Our seed shall prosper, and
In those unsifted times
Our sons shall cultivate
Peculiar crimes,
Having not love, nor hate,
Nor memory.

Though some,
Of all most weary,
Most defective of desire,
Shall grope towards time's cold womb.   .   .   .

The New World Canaan for which the grandsires sacrificed so much has evolved into Warren's own sort of waste land, a world so utterly devoid of meaning as to have no values, proper or improper ("neither love, nor hate"), and no tradition ("nor memory"). Warren's future probings into the nature of love and hate and the meaning of the past will eventually restore these missing values to his art, but at this point in his development it is not at all surprising to find that everything his speaker sees in the world external to the self serves only to strengthen the reasons for his death-wish ("some   .   .   . most weary, / Most defective of desire, / Shall grope towards time's cold womb").

Some modification of this overriding despair is evident towards the end of this poem when the speaker tries to find some modern substitute for the values that sustained his grandsires:

We seek what end?
The slow dynastic ease,
Travail's cease?
Not pleasure, sure.   .   .   .

The crucial problem of life, he decides, is not to obtain ease and security, as the grandsires had supposed, but is rather to perceive what Warren has all along been seeking—an ultimate purpose of one's existence. A mysticism of "the way down" appears to be Warren's answer in this poem to the search for ultimate meaning—a calm and resolute probing of time and experience before death cuts off both:

What name
Sustains the core of flame?

.   .   .   .   .

Time falls, but has no end.
Descend!

The gentle path suggests our feet;

.   .   .   .   .   .

We shall essay
The rugged ritual, but not of anger.
Let us go down before
Our thews are latched in the myth's languor,
Our hearts with fable grey.

"History" shows a subtle but very significant shift in the poet's perspective. The concluding resolution to use the gift of life in an active search for meaning, rather than to yearn passively for that meaning through the death-wish, will falter and fail before it really bears fruition, but it will eventually produce Warren's very best work. The tone of resignation and humility wherein Warren undertakes this search for ultimate meaning ("the gentle path," "We shall essay / The rugged ritual, but not of anger") is particularly reminiscent of the beginning of "Ash-Wednesday," where Eliot deliberately renounces his former bitterness of despair, though the despair itself may linger.

Following "History" in *Thirty-six Poems* is "Resolution," a poem that further articulates the poet's determination to probe ultimate reality, with particular respect to the sovereignty over reality vested in "Grape-treader Time." The first stanza shows one way to resist Time's sovereignty: to live so intensely as to attain momentary timelessness. This attitude may remind us of Hemingway's fiction:

> Time's secret pulse
> The huddled jockey knows;
> Between the bull's
> Horns, as the cape flows,
> The matador;
> The pitcher on his mound,
> Sun low, tied score.   .   .   .

Of all such possibilities of timelessness, sexual love, in Stanza 2, offers most promise. But the exponent of this idea is not the speaker, but a lover with whom the speaker disagrees:

> I spoke of Time. You said:
> *There is no Time.*
> Since then some friends are dead;
> Hates cold, once hot;
> Ambitions thewless grown;
> Old slights forgot:
> And the weeper is made stone.

The climax of the speaker's argument that Time is real comes with his observation that Time has even separated the two people most involved in the poem—the speaker, "I," from his interlocutor, "You": "We, too, have lain / Apart, with continents / And seas between."

The speaker's resolution—the title motif—asserts that there is Time, then; and full of respect for its existence and power, he will pursue his inquiry into Time's meaning without fear of whatever truth—even if it involves annihilation of self—may come clear:

> *Old winnower!*
> *I praise your pacèd power:*
> *Not truth I fear.*
> How ripe is turned the hour.

One of half-a-dozen "Letter" poems appears at this point in *Thirty-six Poems*, this one entitled "Letter from a Coward to a Hero." As the title indicates, the main function of this "Letter" is to celebrate the bravery of an unnamed friend who died in war and at the same time to comment sarcastically on the speaker's own fear of death, which paradoxically coexists with his death-wish:

> Empires collide with a bang
> That shakes the pictures where they hang
>
> .   .   .   .
>
> And the time is out of joint:
> But a good pointer holds the point
> And is not gun-shy;
> But I
> Am gun-shy.
>
> .   .   .   .   .
>
> Rarely, you've been unmanned;
> I have not seen your courage put to pawn.

Probably the most significant feature of this poem, aside from the fact that it reveals yet another facet of Warren's attitude towards death, is the emergence towards the poem's end of the uniquely tender irony that identified Warren's voice among those of his fellow poets. This tenderness shows through first from behind a facade of sarcasm in the middle of the poem when the speaker, unable to sleep because of his awareness of time and sudden death ("clocks that tick all night, and will not stop"), offers some advice on how to combat insomnia: "For sleep try love or veronal, / Though some prefer, I know, philology." This ironic reference to "philology" is explained in the following line, where newspaper euphemisms are insufficient to assuage the speaker's vision of horror: "Does the

airman scream in the flaming trajectory?" The word "trajectory"—Latinate, impersonal, scientific-military—appears to be
the philological euphemism which Warren rejects as inadequate for describing the real horror of the situation.

By the end of the poem, the speaker's tenderness breaks
through the facade of irony almost completely. Here is a tone
and a rhythm that—as will be seen in "The Ballad of Billie
Potts"—invariably signifies the release of Warren's most
moving, most distinctly original lyric voice:

> At the blind hour of unaimed grief,
> Of addition and subtraction,
>
> .   .   .   .   .
> At the hour to close the eyes,
> At the hour when lights go out in the houses . . .
> Then wind rouses   .   .   .
>
> .   .   .   .   .
> What is that other sound,   .
> Surf or distant cannonade?

This piling up of death images, all tied together by a common
phrase of introduction ("At the hour   .   .   .") and culminating in the audible nearness of the ocean of eternity
("Surf   .   .   ?"), provides increasing emotional power.
The final image of death, as a parting salute to the speaker's
friend, is gentle, understated, and dignified:

> No doubt, when corridors are dumb
> And the bed is made,
> It is your custom to recline,
> Clutching between the forefinger and thumb
> Honor, for death shy valentine.

Next in *Thirty-six Poems*, is "Late Subterfuge," a bitter
poem which uses the seasonal setting of winter to demonstrate

yet once again the endless human capacity for survival through
self-deception—hence the title motif "subterfuge." Like the
various animals we see in the poem—the grackles flying south,
the "fox in ground," the "snake cold-coiled"—human beings
find ways to hide themselves from unpleasant realities, the
most obvious reality at this juncture being the prevalence of
the season of death ("the winter's rot begun"). One way to
evade such realities is to water down one's values, one's sense
of need:

> The year dulls toward its eaves-dripping end.
> We have kept honor yet, or lost a friend;
> Observed at length the inherited defect;
> Known error's pang—but then, what man is perfect?

In contrast to this slough of despond at the year's end, the
year had begun with the usual folly of hope and resolution:

> This year was time for decision to be made.
> *No time to waste,* we said, and so we said:
> *This year is time.*   .   .   .

But of course all this was nonsense, like the big words that in
Hemingway's *Farewell to Arms* came to be associated with the
phrase, "in vain." What had really occurred in this, as in every
year, was the resorting to the old makeshift protections that
men have always erected against the intolerable realities—
protections like thickening of the skin through inurement or
huddling in the artificial warmth of an unwarranted faith:

> .   .   .   Our grief can be endured,
> For we, at least, are men, being inured
> To wrath, to the act unjust, if need, to blood;
> And we have faith from evil bloometh good.

Universally common is yet another device whereby men seek to evade the realities of their environment, and this is the most delusory of all: sexual love, the most intimate mode of alliance of selves, and yet how ineffectual:

> In pairs we walk, heads bowed to the long drizzle—
> With women some, and take their rain-cold kiss;
> We say to ourselves we learn some strength from this.

So strong is Warren's dismay concerning this last "subterfuge," and so reminiscent of Frederick Henry's situation at the end of A *Farewell to Arms* (rain and all) is the scene, that one might indeed suspect that Warren has been influenced here by his readings of Hemingway. His introductory essay to that novel shows that it profoundly affected him, so much, in fact, that he deemed it Hemingway's greatest novel. But aside from this possible external influence, "Late Subterfuge" is an important poem for reemphasizing with considerable power one of Warren's own recurrent themes, the absolute isolation of the self in a hostile environment. Looking ahead to Warren's later work, we may note as a measure of his development that two of the motifs he treats here with great irony—"from evil bloometh good" and "we learn some strength from this [kiss]"—he later treats with utmost seriousness. The one theme is Willie Stark's major premise in *All the King's Men* and the other, concerning the isolation of the individual self, is rebutted by the major theme of *Promises*: "we're all one Flesh, at last." But at this point in his thought, such notions are mere "late subterfuges."

The next poem, "Ransom," like "Letter from a Coward to a Hero," seems to have been occasioned by news of international bloodshed. It, too, cuts through the impersonal remoteness of newspaper accounts with an insistence on the concrete

immediacy of faraway butchery: "What wars and lecheries!
. . . ere dawn in rosy buskins laced / Delivers cool with
dew the recent news-story." Such speculations on human
depravity as we see in Stanza 2 foreshadow the concept of total
human complicity—and thereby total human redeemability
—in *Brother to Dragons*, though here the diction is stiff and
inflated:

> The mentioned act: barbarous, bloody, extreme,
> And fraught with bane. The actors: nameless and
> With faces turned (I cannot make them out).
> Christ bled, indeed, but after fasting and
> Bad diet of the poor; wherefore thin blood came out.

The references to Christ in these early poems are laced
with a heavy irony calculated to emphasize modern deprivation and anxiety. In "Pondy Woods," the "Jew-boy" became
food for the vultures in a naturalistic eucharist ("we maintain
our ancient rite, / Eat the gods by day. . . .") intended to
instruct runaway Jim of his similar transubstantiation, now
imminent. Here in "Ransom" the crucifixion allusion underscores the greater crucifixion going on in modern times,
victimizing men whose blood is not thin like Christ's but is
thick with the milk and honey of secular Canaan and is thus
desperately anxious to retain its temporary content of life.

More significant to Warren's future development than
such references to Christ is the description of the modern
crucifiers as "actors: nameless and / With faces turned (I
cannot make them out)." Much of Warren's future poetry,
and particularly *Brother to Dragons*, was to represent a
strenuous effort to "make out" the identity of these nameless,
faceless actors, both the crucifiers and those crucified. When
those faces finally do turn towards the poet, in Warren's later

work, a bizarrely unexpected recognition will take place: there amongst both victims and afflicters will appear Warren's own face, together with such innocent countenances as Thomas Jefferson's or perhaps the reader's own, or the face of the character Warren calls "you." In such random vignettes as this one, often appearing as of marginal interest, Warren's major themes lie dormant and waiting.

The title motif of this poem, "Ransom," has rather obscure application to the poem proper. In a poem dealing with universal rapacity—"What wars and lecheries!"—the only hope of "ransom" is the thin hope offered in the final stanza, which calls for a redefinition of courage, not in terms of the international military battlefield, but in reference to the confrontation of self. Poems like "Ransom" and "Late Subterfuge" point to a wounded innocence that is central to Warren's artistic motivation. He *does* think, as he says in *Promises*, that the human need is for perfection, both ethical and metaphysical; and the death-wish and violence and horror in these early poems are nothing more than the revulsion of a sensitive, idealistic observer to realities he cannot bear. His continuing obsession with extremes of violence and horror, such as the human vivisection in *Brother to Dragons*, results from the artist's perverse honesty of intellect which insists that whether bearable or not, such infamies of past (*Brother to Dragons*) or present ("Ransom") *are* real, and, what is more, must be confronted within the darksome labyrinth of the self as well as in the comfortably faraway world of newspapers. An increasingly intense skepticism towards the virtue of the self, however pious a front the self may maintain, takes rudimentary form in these early poems and assumes central importance in *Eleven Poems on the Same Theme* and in nearly all of Warren's later works. A valid idealism, in an age

of unprecedentedly destructive idealism (fascism, commu-
nism, etc.), must begin with the courage to recognize the less
attractive attributes of the self. Such courage is the only hope
of "ransoming" the self from those attributes, Warren observes, though the "Ransom" is very tentative indeed as the
poem ends:

> Defeat is possible, and the stars rise.
> Our courage needs, perhaps, new definition   .   .   .
> .   .   .   .
> Though frail as the claspèd dream beneath the blanket's wool.

Of the several poems of psychological terror in this volume,
"Aged Man Surveys the Past Time" is one of the most
effective. The imminence of death in the face of a hostile
environment had, in earlier poems, offered a certain amount of
comfort in that it brought the termination of suffering, but
there is no comfort here. Because this speaker is a broken old
man rather than a self-conscious youth, not even the harsh
comfort of irony is permitted; the old man frankly weeps for
the fearful imminence of his death: in "tears he stands
.   .   .   in diminished light"; "By fruitful grove, unfruited
now by winter"; "Light fails beyond the barn and blasted oak."
Unlike the youthful speaker whom we have seen imagining his
own death in attractive images of submission and peace, this
old man cannot indulge the luxury of a death-wish. He
confronts the real thing, and without the mitigating presence
of personal volition.

The old man's tears bespeak a true and touching humility,
but the humility is not enough. What he really needs is
indicated in the two references to Christian and classical myth,
Christ's death and Orpheus' descent to the underworld. His

need, obviously, is for a strong religious faith wherewith he, too, might confront and surmount the terrors of the underworld. Sadly enough, he has no faith—he is "adept, too late, at art of tears"—and the victory of Orpheus holds no promise for him: "Could Orpheus map / The rocky and bituminous descent?" As though all this were not enough, he is mocked in his unbearable anxiety by a "secular" and "well-adapted" catbird, who represents the fallacies of modern positivism and who seems unaware of the intolerable barrenness of his surroundings:

> By fruitful grove, unfruited now by winter,
> The well-adapted and secular catbird
> Whimpers its enmity and invitation.
> Light fails beyond the barn and blasted oak.

In this rejection of modern positivism Warren shows once again his tenacious honesty, which will not permit easy, delusory answers to man's predicament. Although he specifically rejects the orthodox religious answers in this poem, which concludes with terms negative to religious mysticism (the "trifoliate strumpet spray of green" of April and its "godless summer"), he rejects with equal fervor the pain-killers of secular optimism: adaptability or psychological "adjustment" to realities one cannot bear. The metaphysical as well as the ethical nature of man may fall desperately short of the poet's desire for perfection, but he will not accept secular tranquilizers for the lack of Balm of Gilead. The honesty, compassion, and humility—the basic rudiments of the religious attitude—which Warren reveals in "Aged Man Surveys the Past Time" again foreshadow Warren's future development. These essential religious virtues are the "fragments he will shore against his ruins," to use T. S. Eliot's phrase, until, like

Eliot, he finally breaks a path out of the waste land of naturalism.

Although "Aged Man Surveys the Past Time" and "Toward Rationality" both deal with the same subject, confronting the fact of self-annihilation, and although both poems have identical form (blank-verse quatrains), the latter poem evinces a markedly different tone. Warren's voice assumes its typical irony in "Toward Rationality"—an irony that is typical, at least, when Warren's attention is focused on mankind in general rather than on particular individuals. "Toward Rationality" passes from geological imagery at the beginning ("Brothers, stones on this moraine of time, / And I, a stone") to an image of card-playing at the conclusion ("Shuffle the picturecard mind / And deal") in an effort to show the inadequacy of "rationality" for solving the ultimate problem, annihilation of self. History, philosophy, heroism, and all the glories of the past cannot avail against the fact of extinction, which has transformed the illustrious figures of antiquity into "stones" on time's moraine. The valiant stand at Salamis or Thermopylae, regarded in this hard light, diminishes to a "littoral picnic by the unfettered sea" for "Xerxes' guests." The reader may choose other examples as he pleases from the noblest names the past offers:

> Ransack your backward calendar for sages,
> Their architectural and russet names,
> Or kings who sat with liberal, sunny brow. . . .

The "kings with liberal, sunny brow," the "sages," and the reference to Xerxes make clear what epoch of "Rationality"— the title motif—the poet has in mind as the supreme example: the Golden Age of ancient Greece, the time of Socrates and

Pericles and the great men of letters. Time has lent a diabolic leer of ultimate wisdom to faces once nobly at ease in Zion. What manner of rationality is this?

> Too happy, happy gentlemen, you freeze
> Downward. Shuffle the picturecard mind
> And deal: while your kind faces all reflect
> The rude Abhorson's spittlebearded grin.

True rationality, by contrast with the grand hallucinations of a Golden Age, is readily available in every man's backyard, where a traditional symbol of immortality bends to the wind (an east wind likewise meant death in "Genealogy"): "The cedar standing close to my house wall / Groans in the long drag of the east wind."

Two more of the epistolary poems come up at this point, "To a Friend Parting" and "Letter to a Friend." They are quite contrary in tone, mood, and theme. The first of these, "To a Friend Parting," seeks to encourage, while the other undertakes to chill gratuitous courage. Curiously enough, the two friends receiving the letters seem to get just the sort of advice each one would be apt to consider spurious: the friend who lives by faith is warned against losing it and the one who lives by courage (without faith) is urged to be afraid.

The imagery of "To a Friend Parting" is quite lovely, the rhythm strong and lyrical. The central image of faith, of transcendent vision, is the same in this poem as in "The Watershed"—a hawk hovering in high sunlight while evening darkens the landscape below. The friend, his "heart unbraced yet unbetrayed," has access to that vision, it would seem, though the more sophisticated speaker doubts whether such a portent will suffice:

O you who by the grove and shore walked
With us, your heart unbraced yet unbetrayed,
          . . . We saw above the lake
Tower the hawk, his wings the light take.
What answer to our dread?

Speaking from his own experience apparently, the speaker
warns the friend that he is entering a country devoid of any
sustenance of spirit such as the hawk ("rough country of no
birds"), and here his resources and his faith will be really
tested. It may well be in such a crisis that the only sustenance
of real merit will be human friendship, such as the poet
himself is presently extending:

Follow the defiles down. Forget not,
When journey-bated the nag, rusty the steel,
The horny clasp of hands your hands now seal;
And prayers of friends, ere this, kept powder dry.
Rough country of no birds, the tracks sly:
Thus faith has lived, we feel.

The recipient of "Letter to a Friend," unlike the above
wayfarer, is fully experienced. He has been through the "rough
country of no birds," and it has not bothered him a bit. Time
and eternity and the eventual annihilation of self are seen and
encountered by this fellow with cool imperturbability:

Our eyes have viewed the burnished vineyards where
No leaf falls, and the grape, unripening, ripes. . . .

And seen the ever-rounding vaulty-structured
Ocean moveless . . .
     .   .   .   .   .
That voyage, then each to each we said, had rendered

Courage superfluous, hope a burden.

They had been indeed sophisticated and worldly wise thus to find courage and hope superfluous; perhaps, the speaker has since discovered, they had been just a little too knowing. Courage and hope, regardless of what one has seen, remain the only available food for the human spirit: "But living still, we live by them, and only / Thus." Striking up what becomes one of his major themes at this point, Warren asserts that the human heart is unknown to its owner. It needs basic definition that will strike below the postures of intellect, whether nihilism, religious doctrine, or indifference:

> The caterpillar knows its leaf, the mole
> Its hummock, who has known his heart, or knows
> The trigger of this action, set and sprung?

Against the posture of imperturbable calm in his friend ("to you unfrighted yet"), the speaker counsels humility as the only wisdom, as the only genuine courage. That Time has ways of inculcating humility we have already seen in "Aged Man Surveys the Past Time" and "At the Hour of the Breaking of the Rocks." Here likewise the concluding image is chillingly remindful of the limitations of the self:

> In this, the time of toads' engendering,
> I write to you, to you unfrighted yet
> Before the blunt experiment of Time.
> Your triumph is not commensurate with stone.

Since "Letter to a Friend" warns against calling "courage superfluous, hope a burden," we might expect the next poem, "Aubade for Hope," to be reasonably affirmative in tone and content. But it is soon clear that Warren's morning song for hope is not meant to inspire exhilaration. As a matter of fact, its main function is to express the speaker's dismay and resentment at being recalled from the land of "unaimed faceless appetite of dream" into a world less congenial to the heart's desire:

> Dawn: and foot on the cold stair treading or
> Thump of wood on the unswept hearth-stone is
> Comment on the margin of consciousness,
> A dirty thumb-smear by the printed page.

Although the speaker does not repudiate hope completely, he does, like Quentin Compson in *The Sound and the Fury*, prefer to remain in a world where hope, whether it is folly or necessity, is irrevelant by reason of the withdrawal of the consciousness from contact with reality. Sleep, not delusory intellectual postures, is the only release for a mind in torment: "All night, the ice sought out the rotten bough."

Unfortunately, the "rotten bough" of the mind in anguish never gets the freezing of sensibility that it needs. Dawn intrudes upon the dulled consciousness, alerting it heartlessly, as always, to time and pain and the nagging necessity of hope. The speaker's experience in this poem is reminiscent of Milton's dismay at losing the apparition of his deceased wife upon waking: "I waked, she fled, and day brought back my night." For Warren's speaker, day brought back his apparition of Hope, who, unlike Milton's wife, is of a sort to inspire repugnance rather than solace and strength. She is a "block-head grandma" with "merciless great eyes / Blank as the sea" —as the sea of eternity, we may suppose—and as she huddles like a spiritual Scrooge trying to draw warmth from pitifully inadequate embers, she croaks and dribbles feebly. Unlike Milton's wife, moreover, this apparition of Hope derives from this world only; herself feeble and senile, she looks ready to expire at any time. But she is all that reality—the world of the wakened consciousness—offers. Knowing this, the speaker accepts, albeit grimacingly, the coffeespoon dole that the spirit subsists on:

> . . . I name some things that shall
>
> .   .   .   .
>
> . . . bespeak us yet for time and hope:
> For Hope that like a blockhead grandma ever
> Above the ash and spittle croaks and leans.

Warren does not enumerate in the above poem any of the "things that shall . . . bespeak us yet for time and hope," but the next poem in the *Thirty-six Poems* sequence does predicate some grounds, however shadowy and insubstantial, for hope. The occasion of this poem, "Man Coming of Age," is the death of the speaker's childhood self—the death which enabled him to (as the title says) "come of age"—and the cause of hope, in a paradoxical way, is the feeling that that death was not really final. We know from Warren's total production as an artist that he feels "nothing is ever lost." We know likewise that Warren's most urgent application of this principle is to the self in search of its ultimate identity, the value of the principle to the search being that the self may find its identity through probing its own past, its origins and formation. "Man Coming of Age" appears to be a poem of autobiography wherein Warren measures his present self, naturalistically orientated, to a former self that once imparted transcendent meaning to these surroundings:

> Now standing on his own doorsill,
> He views the woods that crest the hill,
>
> And asks: "Was it I who roamed to prove
> My heart beneath the unwhispering grove
> In season greener and of more love?"

To answer this question, the speaker tries to seek out that phantom self of the past in the old familiar places, but the "season greener" of yesteryear has given way to the "snowy bough" of his present nihilism:

> And was it he? Now let him stride
> With crampèd knee the slant hillside,
>
> Pondering what ways he used to know,
> Seeking under the snowy bough
> That frail reproachful *alter ego*.

The speaker bears most unusual reverence here towards his former self. Normally, one feels that as a corollary of his present outlook, his "coming of age," he must put away as a childish thing the misguided self of previous convictions. Not so with Warren's persona. He regards the vanished self of the past with respect and tenderness, so much so that his last word in the poem is a caution to himself against violating the sanctity of that former self by trespassing on sacred ground:

> Walker in woods that bear no leaf,
> Climber of rocks, assume your grief
>
> And go! lest he, before you tread
> That ground once sweetly tenanted,
> Like mist, down the glassy gloom be fled.

It is important to observe that this reverencing of the former self is not merely a childish Romantic yearning after prelapsarian innocence. Warren does not adulate his former self at the expense of the present one. We know from his later works that Warren's search for identity will not be resolved by so simple a device as the dismissing of one self for the sake

of a better one. What his search for identity will finally bring
will be a synthesis of past and present selves, of the naturalist
and the mystic, so that in *Promises,* for example, imagery of
slaughter and dissolution, horrifyingly graphic, will coexist
with imagery of redemption. In "Man Coming of Age,"
Warren foreshadows that synthesis by evincing both a reverence for his former mystic self and a respect for his present
naturalistic self, which has attained a grace of its own through
its unrelenting search and inquiry. Apparently, Warren is
referring to his own verse in the passage below, where a
"brilliance" of "light that glitters out of thought" has given
grace even in a "dark and cold . . . dead world" of
naturalism:

> This brilliance in the night was wrought:
> Of dark and cold a dead world caught
> Such light that glitters out of thought.
>
> So settles on a dying face,
> After the retch and spasm, grace.

We have seen this "retch and spasm" in the earlier poems,
those poems manifesting the great revulsion of a wounded
idealist towards realities he could not bear, those poems
articulating a death-wish. At this transitional stage, before his
reverence and humility towards his former self begin to lead
him out of these "woods that bear no leaf," his art in itself is
balm for the soul. As though to demonstrate this point, "Man
Coming of Age" is, technically speaking, a beautifully wrought
piece of work. In keeping with its subject matter, which is
highly personal, its tender mood, and its reverent tone, it uses
all the devices traditionally associated with lyric emotional
intensity: short lines, a strong and regular rhythmic beat, and a

simple rhyme scheme. The alternation of two- and three-line stanzas is an original device that quickens the pace considerably and adds to the lyric simplicity of design. But beyond these technical considerations, "Man Coming of Age" is a poem evincing beauty of concept, forerunning the magnificent vision of self-unification that will eventually resolve, as far as poetry can resolve anything, Warren's intensive search for identity.

We have seen how urgently the imminence of death has impressed Warren's imagination in a number of poems, sometimes with attractive connotations and at other times, as in "Aged Man Surveys the Past Time," with decidedly fearsome ones. In "Kentucky Mountain Farm" the imminence of death was dramatized through use of springtime imagery; in "Late Subterfuge," by use of a winter setting. We come now to a series of poems where that motif is represented against an autumn background. The first of these, "Croesus in Autumn," imposes upon this autumn setting a perspective ironically drawn from the classical world. Having previously shown misgivings about the Golden Age of Greece in "Toward Rationality," Warren here expresses similar skepticism towards a different sort of classical Golden Age by his reference to the richest man of Roman antiquity. He explicitly rules out any consideration of the higher achievements of Roman classicism, a consideration that will materialize in *You, Emperors, and Others*, by dismissing from view the noblest exponent of those higher achievements. "Though this grey guy be Aurelius," the speaker asserts, Croesus is "more Roman than the doddering emperor." His crassness represents Latin civilization better than does the great Stoic's asceticism, Warren is certain, and moreover, perhaps we underrate Croesus' sensitivity a little bit (Note the spoofing of neoclassic

pomposity of diction in the following lines; Warren does not
share the Augustans' innocent adulation of Latin linguistics or
culture):

> If the distrait verdure cleave not to the branch
> More powerfully than flesh to the fervent bone,
> Should then gruff Croesus   .   .   .
> Lament the absolute gold of summer gone?
>
> Though this grey guy be no Aurelius
>
> .   .   .   .
>
> He might consider a little piteous
> The green and fatal tribe's decline.   .   .   .

Warren's central metaphor is indeed quite graphic in the
first two lines above, where the leaves fall from the trees like
disintegrated flesh from the human skeleton. Croesus might
well consider "a little piteous" the "green   .   .   .   tribe's
decline." But Croesus lived, after all, in a climate where, in
comparison with Warren's Kentucky, everything might have
seemed perpetually green; that is, the vegetation remained
permanently green, whereas all that mattered to Croesus
remained, and still remains, permanently gold. In contrast to
this happy state, Warren's speaker has seen deciduous green
turn to gold, and gold turn to something yet more provocative
of thought:

> But in Kentucky against a dwindling sun
> The riven red-oak and the thick sweet-gum
> Yet hold the northward hills   .   .   .
>
> .   .   .   .
>
> The seasons down our country have a way
> To stir the bald and metaphysic skull.   .   .   .

This little piece of comparative psychology might further explain the buzzard's comment to runaway Jim in "Pondy Woods": "Nigger, your breed ain't metaphysical." Why should his breed be metaphysical when, like the Golden Age breed of Croesus' type, it was surrounded by Africa's eternal greenery? Little wonder that metaphysics has been an obsession of the northern peoples above all others. But in due time metaphysics has a way of thrusting itself into an Age of Gold as well as into the Black Forest. Warren's last word in this poem is to summon Croesus home out of the land of eternal green and permanent gold, and into the world of time's reality:

> I bring you but this broken metaphor;
> So haul your careful carcass home, old fellow,
> More Roman than the doddering emperor
> Now green is blown and every gold gone sallow.

The next poem, "So Frost Astounds," uses the autumn metaphor in an entirely different manner. Here the artist, after deriding false transcendence of time in an Age of Gold and a Land of Green, seeks genuine transcendence through other recourse. The structure of this poem, incidentally, employs a rather novel method of development, one which reaches full maturity in "The Ballad of Billie Potts." A straightforward character portrait of a girl is set forth in ordinary Roman print, but interspersed between portions of this description are lyric passages in italics, offering direct and personal commentary by the narrator concerning what has been described. As in "The Ballad of Billie Potts," moreover, the narrator's commentary occurs in time present, whereas the descriptive portrait is in the past tense.

The central incident of the poem, as the title "So Frost Astounds" would imply, is the death of the girl described:

> *Shut to light—too much of light—the classic lids*
>
> .   .   .   .
>
> *So frost astounds the summer calyxes.*

Like a flower, the girl had been seen in a green setting:

> You were sustained in the green translucence that resides
> all afternoon under the maple trees.
> I observed your hands which lay, on the lap, supine.

The supineness of the hands which the speaker noted above had created an illusion of permanence, a permanence which, though frost may astound, nevertheless offers the speaker the only hope of real permanence that he can find. Not that he has found it yet—his last thought in the poem is *"this will I find"*—but at least this is the best hope a naturalistic world will afford. What this hope turns out to rest upon is the doctrine of the permanence of art, a doctrine that may be supported by Warren's latent conviction that nothing is ever lost.

Previously, Warren had confirmed the sustaining efficacy of art in the autobiographical poem, "Man Coming of Age," where "Such light that glitters out of thought" sustained the poet in a dark and cold "dead world." Here in "So Frost Astounds" the "light that glitters out of thought" imparts the permanence of a still-life painting to what otherwise may have seemed a passing impression. The speaker resumes his description of the girl's supine hands:

> And so was locked their frail articulation
> by will beneath the pensive skin:

as though composed by the will of an artist on dull blue cloth,
forever beyond the accident of flesh and bone,
or principle of thief and rat and moth,
or beyond the stately perturbation of the mind.

The transcendent power of art has made the girl timeless in this scene much as it made the lovers timeless on Keats' Grecian urn: "For ever wilt thou love, and she be fair!" It is important to remember, however, Warren's final comment on this sort of transcendence: "*I have thought: this will I find.*" Whether a thing of beauty is a joy forever is not a matter he is ready to resolve conclusively as yet, because he has yet to know the meaning of the word "forever." As it turns out, defining the meaning of "forever" comes to take considerable precedence in Warren's art to defining the meaning of beauty. It is doubtful that Warren's art would have amounted to much, either in quantity or in lasting significance, had he lingered in the Ivory Tower.

Warren abandons the Ivory Tower of Art without delay in the third and climactic poem that centers upon the autumn metaphor. This poem, "The Last Metaphor," is the most explicitly religious, in the orthodox sense, of any we have encountered so far. The speaker of this poem does indeed attempt to construct "the last metaphor," as the title denotes, with an eye towards deriving from the metaphor of the seasons a stoical strength and forbearance. The death imagery of late autumn at that moment encompasses him, and he confronts it as honestly as any man can, as the first stanzas show:

The wind had blown the leaves away and left
The lonely hills and on the hills the trees;
One fellow came out with his mortal miseries
And said to himself: "I go where brown leaves drift

"On streams that reflect but cold the evening,
    Where trees are bare, the rock is gray and bare,
    And scent of the year's declension haunts the air,
    Where only the wind and no tardy bird may sing."

Lest one should doubt his sincerity or his sensitivity in
applying this sinister imagery to his own condition, the speaker
obligingly rounds out the exemplum: "I am as the tree and
with it have like season."

Up to this point, the metaphor of autumn seems to have
almost exclusively negative implications. There is little ground
for strength and forbearance here. In the next few stanzas,
however, more promising connotations may be seen. The cycle
of springtime rebirth and autumn dissolution, culminating in
the present state of barrenness, has actually produced the
ultimate blessing: the very leaflessness of the trees means that
they are rid at last of those clinging symbols of mortality.
"Unreminiscent" of those leaves now, the trees are not grieved
by their loss. Rather, they are "made strong" by their present
invulnerability; they can lose nothing more:

"Assuredly the planet's tilt will bring
    The accurate convulsion of the year—
    The budding leaf, the green, and then the sere.   .   .   .

        .   .   .   .

"Now flat and black the trees stand on the sky
    Unreminiscent of the year's frail verdure.
    Purged of the green that kept so fatal tenure
    They are made strong; no leaf clings mortally."

Had Warren ended the poem at this point, "The Last
Metaphor" might be classified as a stoical modification of his
frequently unstoical naturalism. The poem goes on, however,

to show in the final stanza that the poet's thoughts are not inclined towards the stoic posture, with its stress on strength and pride and independence of self, after all. Rather, the "final metaphor" in the speaker's mind is one which counsels profound humility, conceived in terms of religious orthodoxy and represented in a scene suggestive of the ending of "The Ballad of Billie Potts":

> [a final metaphor] he gave to the chill air,
> Thinking that when the leaves no more abide
> The stiff trees rear not up in strength and pride
> But lift unto the gradual dark in prayer.

Here once again Warren shows his almost Whitmanesque comprehensiveness of perspective, his own way of being large and containing multitudes. Even during the time when he was most strongly influenced by naturalism, Warren took care not to exclude alternative perspectives entirely. Early and late, he has rejected dogmatism, whether the dogmatism of naturalistic orientation or of Christian doctrine, as intellectual escapism from the human dilemma. Such dogmatism is not only dishonest in its oversimplification of the human predicament, but it can even be downright dangerous, as in the case of the political millennialism that Warren attacks in *Eleven Poems* and in "Mexico Is a Foreign Country." In place of dogmatism, whether political, religious, or philosophical, Warren's poetry relies for its vision on personal experience or intuition, the contributions of tradition being of secondary importance. And the range of Warren's intuition and experience is unusually wide—wide enough to permit the subordinate perspectives of his earlier verse, such as the broadly religious posture of humility at the end of "The Last Metaphor," eventually to come to the fore and, against strong undertows, predominate.

As though to demonstrate this poet's comprehensiveness, "Pacific Gazer" (the poem following "The Last Metaphor") depicts in understanding and perhaps even admiring tones an observer who confronts ultimate reality not in a posture of humility and supplication, as of trees lifting "unto the gradual dark in prayer," but rather with an attitude denoting "wrath" and resistance. The metaphor for final reality in this poem is not the cycle of seasons, but a setting having threefold death imagery: the Pacific ocean at floodtide, a strong wind from the sea, and a deepening darkness of evening:

> Seatide invades   .   .   .
>
>   .   .   .   .
> In churn of the muttering gurge.
> Day's nimb recedes.
>
>
>   .   .   .
> A gazer of saddest intent,
> Coat bulged in the wind's flaw,
>   Stares where light went.

The "saddest intent" on this man's face is the occasion of this poem. The poem's narrator wonders, himself having endured enough grief and despair to motivate (in the earlier poems) a death-wish, what ordeal could have moved this gazer to thus seek solace in so grim a perspective as he is now beholding:

> Can the griding ocean's unease
> Or leaning furious blast
>   Hurt heart appease?

To some extent, all tragic literature is a sublimated scream. Behind the tragedian's discipline and irony and objective paraphernalia—characters, plot, setting, symbolism, and so

on—is a mind which has known and continues to know
unbearable agony—at least, agony that would be unbearable
were it not for the partial release that is accomplished through
art. William Faulkner accomplishes this release through his
Christlike idiot, Benjy, in a number of places in *The Sound
and the Fury,* but the scene where Benjy's moaning and
slobbering and bellowing attains its most explicitly universal
vicariousness occurs some twenty pages along in the final
section of the novel: "Then Ben wailed again, hopeless and
prolonged. It was nothing. Just sound. It might have been all
time and injustice and sorrow become vocal for an instant by a
conjunction of the planets." [2]

Warren's "sound and fury," his sense of intolerable suffering, is not expiated through an idiot persona but is expressed
instead through violence of imagery. All the turbulent fury of
nature which the "Pacific gazer" is looking upon—"Icy and
outbound, his gaze / Bends not to men"—serves not to terrify,
but to release his, so to speak, "tragic scream." The "blind
blast" he hears and the "black night" he sees about him serve
as objective correlatives for his inner "black night" of the soul,
which is of such a magnitude as to render him impassive
towards mere external happenstance, even the threat of
extinction:

> What wrath he owes
> Abides in the water's might:
> Only the blind blast echoes
> His wrath who to black night
> Could night oppose.

The internal perspective of the "Pacific gazer," who stands
unmoved in "black night" by reason of the blacker night
within, represents that part of Warren's vision which sees the
individual as essentially isolated: "his gaze / Bends not to

men." American literature is full of characters who similarly seek ultimate meaning in isolation, from Cooper's Bumppo to Hemingway's Santiago. Warren stands within a major tradition when he asserts that the search for identity is largely a descent into the deep labyrinth of self. But it is not only that. The poem "Calendar" discusses another dimension of this search for identity: not only the individual self but the collective self of all humanity is engaged in this search, and the answer will have to be a collective as well as an individual answer. Just how collective will become clear in later volumes, when Warren reconceptualizes Romantic mysticism by including the plant and animal kingdoms and even inanimate nature in his vision of total selfhood. But for the present, in "Calendar," Warren's concern is with the collective self of mankind.

That which has most irreparably fragmented the collective self of mankind has been time, which continually destroys contact between the generations of past, present, and future. In large measure Warren's art has constituted an attempt to reconstruct that contact, as a necessary prerequisite to finding ultimate identity. At the time of "Calendar," this conception of a collective self is still in the formative stage, but the essential materials are here. The most important issue is the nature of death. If death is a return to nonbeing, as a nihilist would imagine his prenatal condition, then the collective self will remain forever fragmented, and the search for identity forever fruitless:

> Do those dead hear
> Earth lunge in its dark gyre,
> And the grinding orbit veer
> Coldward, from the sun's pyre .   .   . ?
>   .   .   .   .

> Long dead they are:
> Do memories they keep
> Backpace our calendar
> To an age that knew no hap
>   Of coil, nor jar?

If the "memories they keep" are indeed the no memories of prenatal nonexistence ("an age that knew no hap / Of coil, nor jar"), then life, to the individual self at least, must be finally meaningless. But one may question the nihilist's premises. Although Warren is fundamentally a naturalist at this point, he is not dogmatically so, and consequently, he leaves the door open to other alternatives. He does not adopt those alternatives at this time—they are posed here in the form of unanswered questions—but he leaves open the possibility of some kind of mystical answer, upon the basis of which he will later predicate the proposition that "nothing is ever lost," that "all Time's a dream, and we're all one Flesh at last":

> Or is their wrong
> Our wrong in the frost's long dark,
> And all our young rage strong
> Tinct of an elder cark?
>   The wind takes tongue.
>
> In midnight's poise
> Long past our hence-going
> Will our hurt in the wind's voice
> Speak so to men unknowing . . . ?

The urgent, straightforward questioning of this poem leads, because of the unavailability of answers, to an ironic letdown in "Problems of Knowledge," as self-explanatory a title as any in this volume. The insubstantiality of the past, its seeming unrealness, frustrates beyond endurance the seeker who must begin his search for identity by breathing real air into the vanished lungs of skeletons, if the skeletons themselves are not vanished also. A stupendous task of the imagination lies ahead—to reinculcate the tangible immediacy of the present into a phantom past. Unless the past becomes as real as the present, the present must become unreal as the past, and with the passing moments the self must become unreal. This is the essential problem that T. S. Eliot confronts in *Four Quartets*, and the crucial problem that Quentin Compson could not confront in *The Sound and the Fury*. Warren, too, will address himself extensively to this problem of time and identity in later works, but at this point, in "Problems of Knowledge," his speaker finds the problem hopelessly insurmountable:

> What years, what hours, has spider contemplation spun
> Her film to snare the muscled fact?
> What hours unbuild the done undone,
> Or apprehend the actor in the act?
>
> .   .   .   .   .   .
>
> The rodent tooth has etched the bone,
> Beech bole is blackened by the fire:
> Was it a sandal smote the troughèd stone?
> We rest, lapped in the arrogant chastity of our desire.

The last two lines above display an impressive compression of thought into irony and paradox. The sandal in "Was it a sandal smote the troughèd stone?" evokes a scene from the classical world, when sandals were conventional footwear, but both the sandal and its wearer, and the classical world itself, have left in their passing little more than a worn spot in the highway of civilizations. We cannot even be sure if it was they ("Was it a sandal   .   .   .   ?") who wore down the stone;

certainly, nothing commensurate with the original totality of self has remained to contact us. The "arrogant chastity of our desire" is also a rousing use of paradox. Arrogance is usually associated with the successful consummation of desire, but here, since the desire is for ultimate knowledge, the seeker must remain always chaste, innocent, unfulfilled, regardless of the strength and urgency of his "lust." This poem constitutes an admission of the limitations of the self, then, such as we have often seen already in Warren's poetry, though seldom with this wryness of tone.

Perhaps the "chastity" that rewards the "desire" for ultimate knowledge led Warren into less frustrating endeavors in the next group of poems, or perhaps he wanted to demonstrate that his waste land, like Eliot's, has a moral as well as a metaphysical dimension. At any rate, the next three poems, "Cold Colloquy," "For a Self-Possessed Friend," and "For a Friend Who Thinks Himself Urbane," all tell of an intensely resented breakdown of communication between the narrator and several personal friends. The first of these, "Cold Colloquy," is gentler in tone—despite its "chilling" title—than the other two, perhaps because it is addressed to a woman, but more likely because the woman has the capacity, like the narrator himself, to suffer because of their estrangement:

> She turned, a puzzlement on fair features wrought
> That of words so freighted with woe so little she caught.
> She turned; with fair face troubled thus would go   .   .   .
>
> .   .   .   .
>
> To stand apart, pondering, as one who grieves
> Or seeks a thing long lost among the fallen leaves.

Probably because the circumstances are so private, this is not very effective poetry. The phrase "words   .   .   .

freighted with woe" too much resembles a cliche, abstract
and hackneyed, to convince a reader not personally involved.
But the concluding image (above) is interesting in its foreshadowing of similar usage in the exploration of self that will
comprise the motive of *Eleven Poems on the Same Theme*.
Whatever power this poem does contain lies in a candle image
in the first stanza, where the breaking of human contact is
effectively exaggerated:

> She hearkened, eyeless and sunk like the uncarved stone,
> Till the light in his face, an empty candle, was blown:
> She hearkened, and all was something once read about,
> Or a tale worn glossless in time and bandied about.

Whereas the broken relationship in "Cold Colloquy" is
treated mainly in terms of regret, as something beyond human
power to amend, the two "Friend" poems are clearly in the
genre of moral satire. The lack of communication here
described results not from psychological necessity so much as
from psychological perversity, from postures and poses designed to hold the self aloof from the anguish that real involvement with others must at times entail.

The particular target of the narrator's bitterness in "For a
Self-possessed Friend" is the literary dilettante, the bland,
sophisticated type who likes to be titillated by the glitter and
form of art but is too worldly-wise to involve himself in the
artist's suffering:

> Many of us too often now have granted
> Praise for some insolent bright thing.   .   .   .
>
>   .   .   .   .
>
> We praise the word, forget the deed;
> Praise furred gold leaves in April, not the seed
> Tissued of delicate blind agony.   .   .   .

Apparently attacking the excessive objectivity of the New Criticism, Warren includes himself as recipient of the above rebuke. But at least he and the other New Critics, even in their most extreme postures of detachment, could evince some kind of enthusiasm. This self-possessed friend, by contrast, is so unmoved, has such "defect of desire" (as Warren occasionally calls this vice), that even the prospect of his own annihilation is met with indifference:

> But you, my friend . . . you do not praise at all.   .   .   .
>   .   .   .   .
>   .   .   .   some things you do not praise enough;
> For instance now, the perilous stuff
> Of your own youth. It is not long . . . beneath
> The door, the wind . . . the candle gone black out.

The most striking part of this poem is its conclusion, where Warren consigns his self-possessed friend into a hell especially designed for sophisticates. Here the suavely indifferent will encounter egotism enough to crush their own, for even the demons of this nether world are "bored and bland" and "incurious." They are self-possessed, too:

> It is an arrogance to save your breath
> Until the time when, self-possessed, you stand
> With measured approbation where await,
> In darkling kindliness, the bored and bland
> Incurious angels of the nether gate.

The next poem, "For a Friend Who Thinks Himself Urbane," is not a very significant poem in any sense, but it rounds out the trio of character portraits which began with "Cold Colloquy" in such a way as to lighten the bitterness of tone we have been observing. Unlike the self-possessed friend, this fellow is a failure at the game he is playing; he only *thinks* himself urbane—actually, he is not, as the series of refrains, "but cannot," emphasizes. Although "you . . . O resolute . . . will try again," this friend does not have enough callousness or, to repeat the term, defect of desire to attain the perfect detachment he wants:

> [You've] tried to smile when you suppressed
> Some callow gesture of the clumsy heart.
> You've tried but cannot, for the better part
> Pinches the will, and memories constrain
> The ready tongue, bland brow, the careful smile.

Taken together, these three poems on human relationships are significant mainly in their insistence that in moral as well as in metaphysical concerns, humility is the only wisdom. Social falseness and self-containment are to Warren the deadliest of follies, fraudulent defenses of a self in nakedness and need. Certainly, Warren himself has seldom exhibited the careful impersonality that most of his contemporaries have deemed necessary in their art. On the contrary, his poetry has been unusually self-exposing, unusually bare of protective devices such as multiple speakers and manifold allusions (which borrow emotional authenticity from the established masters). Warren's self-exposure is, moreover, thoroughly and perhaps painfully conscious, as he indicates in the reference to his friend's attempt to cast "the pearl before opinion's tushèd snout," in "For a Friend Who Thinks Himself Urbane." Warren's art has indeed been thus hostilely received to a considerable extent, but his last word on the matter insists on the artist's obligation to risk such humiliation: "It is an arrogance to save your breath. . . ."[3]

It is clear from the tone of these three character portraits that Warren has not yet achieved the objectivity necessary to create characters effectively. That is a job that will wait for his fiction and his narrative verse. At this stage in his development he is a lyric poet in the strictest sense, his subject being always himself: his attitudes, his feelings and problems and judgments. And so, even when he is writing about other people, he exposes some very private emotions, such as the resentment or loneliness or other personal grievances motivating these character profiles. Although there is a place for this kind of poetry, it is fortunate, in view of its limitations, that Warren quickly finished up his character portraits and returned explicitly to the subject that was at that time most congenial to his art: himself. The last four poems of *Thirty-six Poems* turn once again to the microcosm, to exploring the interior of the self.

"The Garden," despite its dignity of tone and syntax, is clearly a personal poem, its purpose being to define the present posture of its author. "Now poised between the two alarms / Of summer's lusts and winter's harms," the speaker in this poem stands in the transitional autumn landscape that has become characteristic of *Thirty-six Poems*. Here, in a very skillful and subtle interplay of images, the young poet contemplates his achievement as an artist and his manifest destiny. It is, all in all, quite an accurate assessment. The most striking quality of this poem is its blandly deceptive development. The first two stanzas describe what seems to be an ordinary grove of trees whose natural beauty is enhanced by the first touch of frost:

> No marbles whitely gaze among
> These paths where gilt the late pear hung:
> But branches interlace to frame
> The avenue of stately flame. .   .   .

Upon getting to the third stanza, however, one begins to suspect something extraordinary about this garden. A jay and a cardinal, two important figures in Warren's early poem, "Kentucky Mountain Farm," reappear in this setting to "debate / Like twin usurpers, the ruined state." (Their earlier setting had not been thus "ruined" by frost.) Moreover, the poet himself appears in the third stanza, in the person of a gardener who had tilled and toiled here and enjoyed the fruits of his labors:

> The hand that crooked upon the spade
> Here plucked the peach, and thirst allayed;
> Here lovers paused before the kiss,
> Instructed of what ripeness is:
> Where all who came might stand to prove
> The grace of this imperial grove,
> Now jay and cardinal debate,
> Like twin usurpers, the ruined state.

This grove is the garden of art, it would seem, closely resembling the garden of the mind in which Andrew Marvell took his ease in *his* "The Garden." But although it uses a similarly metaphysical technique, Warren's "The Garden" has quite a different theme. Attractive as this lovely grove may be, it cannot satisfy the poet's deepest needs. After all, Marvell's garden had never known the frost; Warren's knew it all too well. There is no rest in this place for a mind in search of knowledge, vision, transcendence:

> But he who sought, not love, but peace
> In such rank plot could take no ease:
> Now poised between the two alarms
> Of summer's lusts and winter's harms,
> Only for him these precincts wait
> In sacrament that can translate
> All things that fed luxurious sense
> From appetite to innocence.

The syntax of the last four lines above is too ambiguous to allow for certainty of understanding, but it is possible through hindsight to observe a statement of intentions in this passage. In view of Warren's later concern with redefining innocence, and in view of his premise that such a redefinition must begin with an awareness of need, or "appetite," we may have a very significant insight into Warren's artistic motivation here. It is the poet's business, as Warren conceives it, to find a "sacrament that can translate / All things . . . / From appetite to innocence." The sacrament, the appetite, and the innocence will be more clearly defined later on, in such scenes as Billie Potts' kneeling "in the sacramental silence of evening / At the feet of the old man," to receive death and ultimate identity at one blow. Unlike Yeats or Wallace Stevens, Warren could not linger in the garden of art as though it were a Garden of Eden. For him, art was a "rank plot," in a "ruined state," corresponding exactly to the fallen world out of which it originated. His purpose in art, consequently, has been to find "innocence," or some kind of redemption from the fallen condition delimiting the self.

"To One Awake," one of the two poems ("Genealogy" is the other) found in *Thirty-six Poems* but not in *Selected Poems,* is not worth a great deal of attention, but it does reveal the intensity of the emotional crisis the young poet underwent. Like the passage about "the Great Sleep" in *All the King's Men,* this poem seeks respite from a futile existence—and the futility extends even unto the seeking mind—in sleep.

> Shut up the book and get you now to bed
> The cold uncrumpled page will keep
> Without your aid
> The thought of many a better head
> Now drugged and dull in sleep.
> Get you to sleep.

The images of death perceived in sleep are truer, it is felt, than anything known to the waking mind. Sleep, not books, reveals ultimate reality:

> The sifting darkness like the dust again
> Will drift through sockets of the skull, oppress
> The throat, the brain.   .   .   .
>
>   .   .   .   .   .   .
>
> If in the unclean flesh of sleep are caught
> The sightless creatures that uncoil in dream,
> Mortal, you ought
> Not dread fat larvae of the thought
> That in the ogival bone preform
> The fabulous worm.

Influence of Edgar Allan Poe's "The Conqueror Worm" seems strong in the above passage, not only in the phrase "the fabulous worm" but also in other phrases. The "sightless creatures that uncoil in dream," for example, resemble the "vast formless things" of Poe's nightmare world. Probably the most significant thing about "To One Awake," however, is not its debt to Poe so much as its foreshadowing of Warren's later dream allegories, the most spectacular of which is the "Ballad of a Sweet Dream of Peace," which constitutes the climax of *Promises*.

"Garden Waters" and "To a Face in the Crowd," the last two entries in *Thirty-six Poems*, are rather obscure poems, but they contain some strikingly provocative imagery. "Garden Waters" develops two kinds of water imagery. The one kind has appeared in various poems as the waters of time, containing within their depths all the past and the inscrutable secrets of identity:

> Though garden waters are not broad or black
> Within them still sometimes, I think, is hid
> The obscure image of the season's wreck,
> The dead leaf and the summer's chrysalid.

This in itself is a finely developed image, with a control of tone—something not always found in these early poems—resulting from Warren's use of understatement, from his reliance on the minimal (*garden* waters) to imply his major concerns.

But there is another kind of water image in this poem, one which makes the garden waters, suggestive as they are, of lesser significance:

> If in his garden all night fell the stream,
> Noisy and silver over the moon-dark stone,
> It was not so with the voiceless waters of dream,
> Monstrously tumbled, falling with no tone.

Although the comparison may be far-fetched, these "monstrously tumbled," "voiceless waters of dream," taken in contrast with the "noisy and silver" garden stream, resemble nothing so much as the central contrast in Coleridge's "Kubla Khan." There, too, we see the "garden waters" of a pleasant formal landscape, complete with "stately pleasure dome" and "walls and towers . . . girdled round," but counterposed against these "sunny spots of greenery" is imagery of mysterious, chaotic subterranean violence. Whether Coleridge meant his "caverns measureless to man" to represent the unconscious mind, a concept unknown to his contemporary science, is an unanswerable question, but there is little doubt that Warren has this psychological concept in mind. Both the macrocosm, the waters of the external landscape, "calling in kinship to the buried blood," and the microcosm, "the torrent with no song,"

present psychological insights into the nature of the unconscious in this striking passage:

> . . . men by crags have stopped against the loud

> Torn cataract or hollow-bosomed flood
> In solace of that full nocturnal tongue
> Calling in kinship to the buried blood;
> More terrible breaks the torrent with no song.

This complexity of water imagery in "Garden Waters" shows
the deepening complexity of Warren's perspective in his
search for identity. His effort to define the self, as this poem
demonstrates, employs both the inward and the outward look,
both the groping downward through the inner labyrinth,
wherein Warren most affirms the Romantic tradition, and the
venturing into the outer landscape, so as to measure and
evaluate, in the Classical tradition, the civilization that has
shaped the raw material of self.

"To a Face in a Crowd," the concluding poem of *Thirty-
six Poems*, looks both inward and outward quite searchingly.
The imagery of this poem is sometimes obscure—though it is
always powerfully suggestive—and it is not clear as to whose
this face in a crowd might be. The chances are that the face
belongs to some alter ego of the narrator (or poet) himself,
particularly since the itinerary which the narrator associates
with this passer-by is largely the same journey which we have
watched Warren himself undertake in these poems. The
narrator first imagines his "brother" going "among the rocks"
where the "faint lascivious grass / Fingers in lust the arrogant
bones of men," and we are here reminded of the death imagery
among the rocks in "Kentucky Mountain Farm." The next

stanza asks, "Beside what bitter waters will you go . . . ?"
and we are reminded again of Warren's recurrent use of water
imagery—pool, stream, or ocean—to represent time and eternity. Little wonder, then, that he says to the passing face, "In
dream, perhaps, I have seen your face before."

The outward look, or Warren's evaluation of his times and
heritage, assumes importance in "To a Face in a Crowd" by
virtue of imagery patterned after *The Waste Land*, images of a
lost generation futilely striving for values and meaning. It is
interesting that like Eliot, Warren here tries to "renounce the
night," the metaphysical blackness surrounding the waste
land, but having no fragments to shore against his ruins,
Warren concludes this poem in a "desert" of time present that
resembles the setting of "The Hollow Men" more than it does
the terrain of *The Waste Land*:

> A certain night has borne both you and me;
> We are the children of an ancient band
> Broken between the mountains and the sea.
>
> .   .   .   .
>
> Your face is blown, an apparition, past.
> Renounce the night as I, and we must meet
> As weary nomads in this desert at last,
> Borne in the lost procession of these feet.

The inward look, or Warren's intensely personal search
into his own psyche, appears most strongly in the passage
where the narrator recapitulates his experience in confronting
death and eternity. The "taciturn tall stone" in the following
passage resembles perhaps too closely the stone images of "The
Hollow Men" ("Here the stone images / Are raised, here they
receive / The supplication of a dead man's hand . . ."):

Of old I know that shore, that dim terrain,
And know how black and turbulent the blood
Will beat through iron chambers of the brain

When at your back the taciturn tall stone,
Which is your fathers' monument and mark,
Repeats the waves' implacable monotone.   .   .   .

The inward and outward looks will each receive fuller
development later, but the above excerpts from "To a Face in
a Crowd," with their anguished depiction of society ("the lost
procession   .   .   .   in this desert") and the individual
sufferer ("how black   .   .   .   the blood / Will beat through
iron chambers of the brain"), evince as much emotional power
as we are likely ever to see. As the last entry in *Thirty-
six Poems*, "To a Face in a Crowd" gives conclusive evidence
that the central problem in Warren's verse is the same which
he himself had identified as the central problem in Eliot's and,
in fact, in all modern literature: "Can man live on the purely
naturalistic level?" Warren's own answer to this question in
Thirty-six Poems suggests that perhaps man must live in a
purely naturalistic world—although other alternatives are not
presumptuously excluded—but he must certainly have a very
hard time of it. So intolerably hard a time, indeed, has the
speaker of *Thirty-six Poems* that the alternatives to naturalism
which are here available, through humility or desire, must
assume increasing importance in future poems, however
doubtful and insubstantial such alternatives might appear to
be. *Eleven Poems on the Same Theme* and "The Ballad of
Billie Potts," the two more recent sources of material for
Selected Poems, constitute an exploration of those alternatives
with respect to both man's inner and outer darkness. *Eleven
Poems*, concerned primarily with the darkness within, and

"The Ballad of Billie Potts," with its nearly mystical response to naturalism, show a fuller development of the issues raised in *Thirty-six Poems*.

Eleven Poems on the Same Theme: The Undiscovered Self

WITH THE PUBLICATION of *Eleven Poems* in 1942, Robert Penn Warren truly found his own voice and his own vision. As has been noted, Warren's first volume of poems shows a fairly steady development away from external influences, particularly the influence of T. S. Eliot, but that development was hardly of such a magnitude as to prepare us for the remarkable deepening of the current in *Eleven Poems*, where both theme and form take on a strikingly original character. All of Warren's subsequent verse has been affected in a fundamental way by the major shift in form and content which occurred in *Eleven Poems*.

The poet's changing "voice," or his new technique, is not apparent in the first few poems of this sequence, which show a continuation of the conventions apparent in Warren's earlier verse. There is the strict verse pattern, usually the conventional iambic tetrameter with a regular rhyme scheme (*abab* or a close variation), and there is a strong effort at controlling the tone through an impersonal manner (no matter how personal the material may be), as in the new poetic criticism practiced by Warren and his colleague, Cleanth Brooks. There is, in addition, the irony and paradox and ambiguity (calculated to defend the poet from the disgrace of didacticism) which

Warren so much admired throughout the Brooks and Warren textbook, *Understanding Poetry* (1938). There is, finally, the intellectualizing of emotion through use of complicated imagery and symbolism which Eliot had adapted from the seventeenth-century metaphysicals and introduced into twentieth-century poetry.

By conforming to these principles of the New Criticism, Warren had quite effectively followed Eliot's practice of masking the poet's identity in his earlier poems. Towards the middle of *Eleven Poems*, however—in poems like "Original Sin: A Short Story," "Crime," and "End of Season"— Warren's form and manner undergo some drastic changes. The verse pattern gets rougher and more original as the subject matter, the descent into the self, becomes more original and personal. The tone becomes particularly personal as Warren drops the protective mask and, in violation of New Critical doctrine, begins to address the reader more intimately, frequently employing the "you" of direct address. Here for certain Warren breaks away from the influence of modern conventions and begins to assume his "true," independent voice in order to expound his original vision of reality.

What that vision of reality is, naturally enough, constitutes the "Same Theme" mentioned in the title of the sequence. In trying to identify the "Same Theme," critics have been tempted to oversimplify somewhat, I believe—a natural enough propensity in view of the complexity of these poems. Leonard Casper, who does a better job with this sequence, I feel, than he does with any of the other poetry he considers in his chapter on Warren's verse, identifies this "Same Theme" as "those torrents of blinding guilt that drench the conscience." F. O. Matthiessen, in a brief but perceptive treatment, says that Warren's dominant theme is his "protest against the tendency of our scientific age to reduce knowledge to abstraction, and to rob experience of its religious tension by making sin meaningless." And W. P. Southard, in his perceptive but excessively disparaging essay (at one point he calls Warren "the servant of the servants of the servants," and elsewhere he compares Warren's irony to hell, "which has the same inscription on the gates") conceives of the "Same Theme" as entailing a progression from "novelty" to "love." [4]

Although these critical articles are helpful, they are not adequate to explain these poems, mainly because they miss the master metaphor of an undiscovered self—a metaphor that was to occur again and again with crucial importance throughout all of Warren's subsequent poetry. The "face drowned deep under water, mouth askew" in *You, Emperors, and Others* (1960); the skeleton granny who "whines like a dog in the dark" in *Promises* (1957); the monster-self loathed and shunned throughout *Brother to Dragons* (1953); the "sad head lifting to the long return, / Through brumal deeps" in "The Ballad of Billie Potts"—these recurrent metaphors of a repressed unconscious self may be traced to the shadow-self that was slain and buried in the dank cellar of the house of the psyche in *Eleven Poems*. Taken together, these metaphors of an undiscovered self—to borrow Jung's phrase—are of utmost importance because it is this unknown self, rather than the conscious ego, which holds the secret of ultimate identity and which therefore offers the best answer to the modern dilemma of naturalism.

The first three poems of *Eleven Poems* set the stage for this new development by continuing the discussion of naturalism which dominated Warren's earlier poetry, and especially by inquiring anew whether Time the Destroyer does, as they say, render all things meaningless. In "Bearded Oaks," for example, two lovers "practice for eternity" by lying totally silent and motionless—cadavers under the ocean of eternity. Enveloped in "kelp-like" grasses under oaks "subtle and marine," what else can a thinking man do but contemplate his extinction in submarine "voicelessness," though ever so near his ladylove? The present seems still, emotionless, and dead because the past is so. Time resolves everything—even love—into ocean-bottom sediments at the last:

> Passion and slaughter, ruth, decay
> Descend, minutely whispering down,
> Silted down swaying streams, to lay
> Foundation for our voicelessness.

If even lovers can't talk to each other, there is little hope for ordinary friendship. Here is where Warren's religious sense enters: naturalism points towards sin not because it denies orthodox belief but because it renders other people as meaningless as one holds oneself. In fact, even more meaningless. Small as one's image is as reflected in another's eye ("Monologue at Midnight"), that image is even smaller in another's heart:

> The match flame sudden in the gloom
> Is lensed within each watching eye
> Less intricate, less small, than in
> One heart the other's image is.

Ultimately, Warren was to heal this sense of isolation by insisting (in *Promises*) that "we're all one Flesh, at last." But here no communication with others is possible (hence the "monologue") in this naturalistic "midnight." In "Picnic Remembered," too, the exterior darkness of naturalism that ends the picnic ("But darkness on the landscape grew") is accompanied by a growing inner darkness and despair making human communion void and sterile ("As in our bosoms darkness, too").

So the human picnic is soon over, the lovers cannot talk to each other, and one is left talking to oneself in midnight solitude. Time's ocean-bottom in "Bearded Oaks" is the ultimate truth of naturalism: a meaningless, homogeneous murk, without distinction or values. This is the place of "defect of desire," as Warren was later to call absolute and therefore spiritually paralytic despair. Here hope and fear alike are nonsense, as are rage and joy and all the other emanations of "desire":

> All our debate is voiceless here,
> As all our rage, the rage of stone;
> If hope is hopeless, then fearless fear,
> And history is thus undone.

But as we know from Jack Burden, R.P.W., Thomas Jefferson, and others, history is not undone. On the contrary, nothing is ever lost. This is because, regardless of naturalism, there is another direction to turn: inward. The concept of meaninglessness "out there" in the world of time and consciousness is only the setting for Warren's true inquiry—whether all is meaningless within. This inquest is where we are likely to lose our way in the labyrinth, for although naturalism is a familiar modern issue, the undiscovered self is not so clear or familiar—not even to its chief articulators, such as C. G. Jung. Hence, Warren's religious poetry postulates not only an ethic—a sense of sin—but also a metaphysic: a reliance on intuition. Intuition of a divided self is the special hope governing these poems, for though the conscious self appears destined for extinction in time's ocean-bottom, there remains yet the mysterious unconscious to consider. So the final image of "Picnic Remembered" would seem at variance with the naturalistic import of the rest of the poem: the deeper self is a "hawk   .   .   , fled / On glimmering wings," whereas the surface self, "unmanned" and "vacant," remains behind, subject to the well-known limitations of naturalistic reality ("sun is sunk and darkness near").

So we arrive in Jung's territory: intimations of an immortality dependent on an undiscovered self. From here on, the poems bring about a fusion of religion and psychology calculated to break through the barrier of naturalism into a new sense of possibility. Thus, if there is anything eternal within the self, it has nothing to do with the conscious, rational self—which is consigned to naturalistic oblivion—but pertains rather to the unconscious self who is locked out in "Original Sin: A Short Story," is murdered (only to rise again) in "Crime," and is fled from (without success) in "Pursuit," "Terror" and "End of Season."

Before bringing Jung to bear upon these poems, I must make one point perfectly clear: Jungian psychology is by no means to be considered a *source* for Warren's poetry. Indeed, the publication dates alone would refute that: *Eleven Poems on the Same Theme* was published in 1942, fifteen years prior to Jung's *The Undiscovered Self*, which is a chief source of illumination. But although not a source, Jung's writings may still provide a relevant means of clarifying what goes on in Warren's poetry. That is, Warren has responded to a climate of ideas which may date back to Hawthorne and Dostoevski or earlier still, but which Jung epitomizes and defines (for our purposes) better than anybody else.

With this qualification in mind, we may proceed to note some specific likenesses between Jung and Warren, both in general concepts and in specific terminology. Jung's remarks have even more relevance to *Brother to Dragons*, where the unconscious self appears variously as minotaur, serpent, catfish, and Lilburn Lewis, but insofar as *Eleven Poems on the Same Theme* anticipates the later masterpiece, Jung serves to enlighten here also. Consider the following use of the word "shadow," for example, to indicate a subconscious, unrecognized guilt in the psyche. The first excerpt below is from "Monologue at Midnight," the second from the chapter on "Self-Knowledge" in Jung's book:

> And always at the side, like guilt,
> Our shadows over the grasses moved,
>
> Or moved across the moonlit snow;
> And move across the grass or snow.
> Or was it guilt? Philosophers
> Loll in their disputatious ease.

The evil that comes to light in man and that undoubtedly dwells within him is of gigantic proportions, so that for the Church to talk of original sin and to trace it back to Adam's relatively innocent slip-up with Eve is almost a euphemism. . . . The evil, the guilt, the profound unease of conscience, the obscure misgivings are there before our eyes, if only we would see. . . . None of us stands outside humanity's black collective shadow. Whether the crime lies many generations back or happens today, it remains the symptom of a disposition that is always and everywhere present —and one would therefore do well to possess some "imagination in evil," for only the fool can permanently neglect the conditions of his own nature.[5]

There is much more of the same in Jung's discussion, but for now let us note some of the terminology in the above excerpts:

"original sin," "guilt," "unease of conscience," "the *obscure misgivings*" (italics mine), "humanity's black collective shadow," "crime," "imagination in evil." Taken together, terms such as these strike at the very essence of Warren's material. These are certainly his major concerns, once the issue of naturalism is solved—or at least set aside—in all his major volumes of poetry: *Selected Poems, Brother to Dragons, Promises,* and *You, Emperors, and Others.* And certainly, Jung's "guilt," "original sin," "the obscure misgivings"—all those terms which assume the deepest kind of psychological and religious (broadly defined) reality to the possessor of "imagination in evil"—these are the special subject matter of the central group of poems in *Eleven Poems on the Same Theme,* where titles like "Crime," "Original Sin," "Pursuit," and "Terror" indicate clearly the resemblance between Jung's thought and Warren's poetry.

There are two paths to knowledge, then. There is the path opened up by the conscious, rational mind, which leads us into Time's ocean-bottom, the knowledge of naturalism. And, largely ignored by an Age of Reason, there is the path of the unconscious and intuitive—leading to such knowledge by instinct, for example, as draws the entire animal kingdom "home" at the end of "The Ballad of Billie Potts":

> The bee knows, and the eel's cold ganglia burn,
> And the sad head lifting to the long return,
> Through brumal deeps, . . .
> Carries its knowledge, navigator without star. . . .

The bee knows, but rational man does not—nor will he until his "sad head" lifts to unconscious instinct the way the eel's does. Once again, Jung offers a substantiating judgment: "Separation from his instinctual nature inevitably plunges civilized man into the conflict between conscious and unconscious, spirit and nature, knowledge and faith, a split that becomes pathological the moment his consciousness is no longer able to neglect or suppress his instinctual side." [6] A little later, as he begins his chapter on "Self-Knowledge," Jung reemphasizes the importance of intuition by calling the unconscious the "only accessible source of religious experience."

Robert Penn Warren agrees with that. His poetry is profoundly religious in the sense in which Jung uses the word, not in the sense of subscribing to the principles and practices of an organized Church or even to an inherited tradition, for both the Church and the tradition are ineffectual if apprehended only by the conscious, rational self. Warren's poetry undertakes what Jung's philosophy prescribes: the periodic reinterpretation of myths and symbols that give meaning to the self—myths and symbols that once emerged fresh and living from the collective unconscious but have lost the dimension of mystery by too long a sojourn in the conscious mind alone.

What Jung has been talking about in discussing "guilt," "crime," and "humanity's black collective shadow" has been, in the language of the mystics, the journey into perilous interior darkness. Warren's "Crime," "Original Sin: A Short Story," and "End of Season" likewise take "the way down" towards intuitive perception of truth. These poems seek out the black shadow-self residing under the conscious identity, and they seek out this hidden self in a personal, instinctive way. We should not be misled, as some critics have been, by Warren's use of traditional religious terminology. Warren's "original sin" is not Adam and Eve's,[7] nor does his vision of redemption share the strictures, the mode of selectivity, affirmed and codified by orthodox religion. His apprehension of reality has been, as psychology and "true" religion insist it must be, a private undertaking, an ordeal confronted anew and alone by the individual man, not something to be evaded by recourse to prepackaged belief or mass affirmation. The extent to which Warren's perceptions do fall in line with orthodox beliefs—and they do so only very broadly—would indicate something about the nature of the archetypal truths his intuition has discovered, I should think, rather than throw doubt upon his intellectual honesty. If the theories of the collective unconscious are valid—and Jung amassed impressive evidence to support them—then broad similarities should be expected to exist between the visions of reality conceived by authors who vary widely in other respects. And if originality of approach is granted—and none of his detractors consider Warren a mere imitator—we have to accept the results of the poet's search as bona fide, I think, even though similar fruits hang elsewhere in the orchard.

With this understanding of Jung in mind, we find that the crucial poems at the center of *Eleven Poems on the Same Theme*, poems which at first glance may seem very obscure, will yield fairly readily to interpretation.[8] "Crime," the fourth entry of the original sequence, tells us to "Envy the mad killer" who "cannot seem / To remember what it was he buried under the leaves." We should envy him because he, being mad, does not have to remember the other self he buried ("But what was it? . . . / An old woman . . . ?/ The proud stranger . . . ? / Or the child . . . ?"). We the sane are not so lucky. We have killed, too; we have slain and buried the shadow-self within, the dark, hidden self who participates in the collective self of all mankind—the self which Jung locates in the unconscious—but unlike the mad killer, we must remember the other self hid "in the cellar dark":

Yet envy him, for what he buried is buried
By the culvert there, till the boy with the air-gun
In spring, at the violet, comes; nor is ever known
To go on any vacations with him, lend money, break bread.

And envy him, for though the seasons stammer
Past pulse in the yellow throat of the field-lark,
Still memory drips, a pipe in the cellar-dark,
And in its hutch and hole, as when the earth gets warmer,

The cold heart heaves like a toad.   .   .   .

"In its hutch and hole   .   .   .   the cold heart heaves." That hidden self is not so dead after all, or at least it is capable of resuscitation if the memory thaws its corpse a little. Now we see for certain why we must envy the mad killer: "what he buried is buried," whereas our victim distressingly stirs. But perhaps this embarrassment may not be so distressing in the long run, Warren hints in the last stanza, for the resurrected self in the cellar holds the secret of a timeless identity, described in a previous stanza as "the object bright on the bottom of the murky pond," and described here as "that bright jewel you have no use for now."

But there will be use for that bright jewel yet; for high in the attic above this cold, wet "cellar-dark" of the unconscious, something has gone wrong with the surface identity. As long as that deeper self remains unacknowledged, surface identity (the name on the letter) also remains unattainable—the "cold heart" in the cellar and the letter "despised with the attic junk" are inseparable correlatives of a single, unified identity.

So the conscious, rational self in the attic sadly awaits reunion with the buried, unconscious self in the cellar:

> The cold heart heaves like a toad, and lifts its brow
> With that bright jewel you have no use for now;
> While puzzled yet, despised with the attic junk, the letter
> Names over your name, and mourns under the dry rafter.

This is the primary meaning of "Crime," but there are a few other loose ends to touch upon. The motive of the crime, for instance:

> Happiness: what the heart wants. That is its fond
> Definition, and wants only the peace in God's eye.
>   .   .   .   .
>
> Peace, all he asked: past despair and past the uncouth
> Violation, he snatched at the fleeting hem, though in
>   error.   .   .   .

These motives, happiness and peace, explain the action of the mad killer well enough—satisfactorily enough, in fact, almost to make us regret the poor results of his "uncouth violation": having "snatched at the fleeting hem, though in error," he has not achieved happiness and peace after all. Instead, he "lies in the ditch and grieves." But so do we. And our motives have not been so spontaneous and pure. Rather than impulsively snatching at the fleeting hem, we have "gestured before the mind's sycophant mirror" and "made the refusal and spat from the secret side of the mouth." This is the final reason to envy the mad killer, then. Compared with his misdeed, our murder of the "other self" is all the fouler: premeditated, spiteful, done in secret. True, all we wanted, like the mad killer, was happiness and "peace in God's eye," but like the mad killer, again,—and also like the Red and Fascist soldiers killing out of "tidal lust" in "Terror"—we find here that happiness and peace are not to be gained through a frontal assault on what we construe to be the incarnate image (always external to the self, of course) of evil. Whatever happiness and peace Warren's persona may find in this or any other poem sequence will not come through so simple a stratagem. Rather, it will be earned out of fear and toil as the seeker works his way down the inward spiral into the cellar-dark of self, striving thereby to clutch "the object bright on the bottom of the murky pond."

In "Original Sin: A Short Story," the secret self is not only resuscitated, as it was (toadlike) in the cellar-dark of "Crime," but is very much alive indeed—indestructibly alive, in fact. And not only alive, but damnably insistent on keeping company with the surface-self that has been trying so hard to repudiate it. Far from being dead and buried, this shadow-self, for all its lowliness and meekness of demeanor, seemingly cannot be repudiated and perhaps (as Jung has surmised) is immortal:

>   .   .   .   you have heard
> It fumble your door before it whimpers and is gone:
> It acts like the old hound that used to snuffle your door and
>   moan.
>
> You thought you had lost it when you left Omaha,
>
>   .   .   .   .
>
> But you met it in Harvard Yard   .   .   .
>
>   .   .   .   .
>
> And you wondered how it had come, for it stood so imbecile,
> With empty hands, humble, and surely nothing in pocket:
> Riding the rods, perhaps—or grandpa's will paid the ticket.

Little wonder that the narrator, the surface-self, should conclude, resigned to his predicament, that "nothing is lost, ever lost!" But he can afford to be resigned now. Murder hardly seems necessary any longer, on two counts. First, the shadow-self is encouragingly detached from the conscious mind: it will never "shame you before your friends" and has "nothing to do / With your public experience or private reformation." Hence, the surface-self can keep its purity, its sanctity, intact; it will not be humiliatingly contaminated. Second, the shadow-self is thoroughly harmless, after all, and is really—except for its irritating habit of hanging around in the background—not worth a thought. Loyal, dull-witted, and gentle, it offers no menace, certainly, and can be outsmarted in any case—can be locked out, for example, when it comes whimpering for recognition:

> It tries the lock; you hear, but simply drowse:
> There is nothing remarkable in that sound at the door.
> Later you may hear it wander the dark house
> Like a mother who rises at night to seek a childhood picture;
> Or it goes to the backyard and stands like an old horse cold
>   in the pasture.

"Oh, nothing is lost, ever lost!" is the moral of the "short story" which Warren entitled "Original Sin," but perhaps we have not tried hard enough to lose what the surface-self wishes to lose. "End of Season" shows a different way to lose the unwanted self, with its embarrassing guilt and shadow. Go down to the water, "beach . . . or spa, / Where beginnings are always easy," or perhaps even to "the Springs where your grandpa went in Arkansas" and found apparent rejuvenation: "And slept like a child, nor called out with the accustomed nightmare, / But lolled his old hams, stained hands, in

that Lethe. . . ." Jung's depiction of the conscious mind
as "washing our hands in innocence and ignoring the general
proclivity to evil" [9] is particularly relevant to Warren's use of
water imagery, which comes to signify Time, in this and later
poems. Here in "End of Season" Warren summons together
three striking allusions, from the Bible, history, and literature,
in which water acts to free the self from its fallen condition:

> For waters wash our guilt and dance in the sun:
> And the prophet, hairy and grim in the leonine landscape,
> Came down to Jordan; toward moon-set de Leon
> Woke, while squat, Time clucked like the darkling ape;
> And Dante's *duca*, smiling in the blessèd clime,
> With rushes, sea-wet, wiped from that sad brow the infernal
> grime.

But in Warren's eschatology, water (which usually connotes Time) is not sufficient, in itself, to do the work of
redemption. There is that shadow-self to face first, some inner
recognition to concede. Otherwise, the water image offers only
escape, not absolution, and the problem of identity remains,
like the shadow-self, unchanged through changes of place and
season:

> On the last day swim far out . . .
>   . . . or deep and wide-eyed, dive
> Down the glaucous glimmer where no voice can visit;
> But the mail lurks in the box at the house where you live:
> Summer's wishes, winter's wisdom—you must think
> On the true nature of Hope, whose eye is round and does not
> wink.

The "true nature of Hope"—one of those dreadful "religious"
words, like "faith" and "love"—is what the pursuit of the

secret self might reveal. But if such terminology—however originally it is employed—is distasteful to the naturalistic reader, at least he cannot say that he was not warned. In *Thirty-six Poems* (1935), in "Letter to a Friend," Warren described the necessity of courage and hope: "we live by them, and only / Thus." Surely, Warren's own quest in art—such as his search for the shadow-self in *Eleven Poems*—is motivated by Hope, by hope for the happiness and "peace in God's eye" that failed to materialize in "Crime," where the other self was slain and buried.

Hope is a psychological gift, it would seem, and a religious gift, too, in the sense that psychology and religion seek much the same thing—the deepest knowledge of self that is possible. Whether psychological or religious, the gift of Hope is essentially subconscious, intuitive, irrational—and is hence beyond the reach of a conscious philosophy such as naturalism. What Warren appears to imply as he concludes "End of Season" is that Hope is available when least anticipated, when least thought possible. This theme would be further developed in *Promises*, some fifteen years later, but here in *Eleven Poems*, it is already clear enough what Warren is about. Here, after showing the failure of all the wiles and evasions of the conscious self—the other self humbly endures murder, suppression, indifference, and repudiation (being locked out of the house of the psyche)—Warren shows the surface-self undertaking at last the pilgrimage it finds so repugnant but so necessary: the humiliating, fearsome journey downward into the "cellar-dark," where somewhere a darker self awaits embracing. Here one might expect total despair, but here, unexpectedly, irrationally, the gift of Hope is offered; and it is real, constant Hope, not fickle like the hopes of the conscious mind, but unchanging and irreducible, beyond "summer's wishes, winter's wisdom," with an "eye [that] is round and does not wink."

So there is Hope. And then there is Love. The next subgrouping of poems in *Eleven Poems*, the seventh through the tenth in the original order of appearance ("Revelation," "Pursuit," "Question and Answer," and "Love's Parable"), takes us out of the interior labyrinth, where Hope may be lurking, into an outer chaos, the world of other people. And so the poems get explicitly religious now, for as we know, the world of other people means love—a religious idea, thinkable as a serious possibility now that the naturalism of the earlier poems has been supplanted by intimations of a permanent, collective selfhood: no longer need one speak in monologues, nor need lovers lie practicing for eternity, voiceless and paralyzed on the floors of silent seas.

What is this tie that binds? The first of these four poems begins the definition with a "revelation"—about love's paradox: "In separateness only does love learn definition." That's what Billie Potts found out, and so came home even to his crude parents. And Jerry Calhoun likewise, who finally gave up Bogan Murdock in favor of his real father, the stooped and clumsy one. And so too Jack Burden and Amantha Starr: exile and separation from the father, followed by acceptance and return. Ikey Sumter reverses the pattern in *The Cave*, but then Ikey is only a fake Jew, an apostate caricature calculated to sharpen by way of contrast the Isaiahic vision Warren was writing into his poetry at about that time: "You fool, poor fool, all Time is a dream, and we're all one Flesh, at last" ("Go It, Granny" in *Promises*).

"Revelation" being only a precursor of all this, its separation in which love learns definition takes a rather modest form: harsh words between mother and son. But given Jung's "imagination in evil," one does not need a ten-year exile to be instructed. The assertions of Jung's shadow-self—"the obscure misgiving," "unease of conscience"—suffice, with the help of the pathetic fallacy, to make quite a drama of this simple affair:

> By walls, by walks, chrysanthemum and aster,
> All hairy, fat-petalled species, lean, confer,
> And his ears, and heart, should burn at that insidious whisper
> Which concerns him so, he knows; but he cannot make out
> the words.
>
> The peacock screamed,   .   .   .
>
>   .   .   .   .   .   .
>   .   .   .   the buck rabbit stamped in the moonlit glade,
> And the owl's brain glowed like a coal in the grove's combus-
> tible dark.

This is a very powerful sense of guilt, indeed, and perhaps embarrassing to the emotionally detached reader, but it is only through such an awareness of guilt, through such concession to the darker self, that salvation ("love's grace") is attainable. Readers may, if they wish, find some resemblance to religious orthodoxy in this theme.

The resemblance to religious orthodoxy becomes stronger, though it remains only a broad resemblance, in "Pursuit," where love is tentatively defined as "a groping Godward, though blind." Walt Whitman felt this way, too, but he flung filaments like a spider—"Till the gossamer thread you fling catch somewhere, O my soul"—whereas Warren gropes with octopus tentacles: ".   .   .   groping Godward, though blind, / No matter what crevice, cranny, chink, bright in dark, the pale tentacle find."

If the main theme of "Pursuit" is love, "a groping Godward, though blind," it is not encouragingly treated. The groping is quite ineffectual here. Misunderstanding, indifference, and all the other factors leading to isolation are what we encounter. The doctor, representing what modern science offers towards self-knowledge, "bends at your heart; / But cannot make out just what it tries to impart." The hunchback on the corner is equally unhelpful—he "has his own wisdom and pleasures, and may not be lured / To divulge them to you," and so "your appeal for his sympathy" goes in vain. Everywhere we go, people are either withdrawn or stare "stern with authority / Till you feel like one who has come too late, or improperly clothed, to a party." The separateness in which love learns definition, according to "Revelation," is here so extreme as to cast doubt on whether anything but separateness is real. The "I-Thou" relationship is difficult to achieve in a world where every "Thou" is "like a fawn / That meets you a moment, wheels, in imperious innocence is gone."

In the final stanza, the naked self sits alone at last, despite all its desire for human communion, and despite the superficial appearance of opportunity for sociability in the Florida funland where the speaker's "pursuit" has finally taken him:

> Till you sit alone—which is the beginning of error—
> Behind you the music and lights of the great hotel. . . .
> .   .   .   .
> There are many states, and towns in them, and faces,
> But meanwhile, the little old lady in black, by the wall,
> Who admires all the dancers, and tells you how just last fall
> Her husband died in Ohio, and damp mists her glasses;
> She blinks and croaks, like a toad . . . in the horrible
>   light. . . .

What this Florida hotel offers, then, is nothing more than a swank waste land, where the essential isolation of the self is all the more emphasized by the empty forms of social concourse. Meanwhile, this little old lady in black, who blinks and croaks like a toad, may remind us (uncomfortably) of that shadow-self back in "Crime," whose "cold heart heaves like a toad" in the cellar-dark.

So "Question and Answer," the ninth of the *Eleven Poems*, brings the quest which availed nothing in "Pursuit" back to its rightful setting—the interior of the self. There is a difference, though, as a result of the social context we have been scrutinizing. The self is once again dependent on its own resources, it is true, but no longer is the individual self seeking in solitude. The quest for ultimate identity is now seen in the broadest imaginable context, with all men and all nature participating as in "The Ballad of Billie Potts," asking (though without reply) the unanswerable questions:

> What has availed
> Or failed?
> *Or will avail?*

Never demand answer, we are warned, of the sand or the sky or even your true love, "For all— / Each frescoed figure leaning from the world's wall   .   .   . / Demand in truth the true / Answer of you." A discouraging prospect to be sure, but yet there is an answer. One thing there is that may avail: the quest itself. At least it will avail if myth and intuition have any validity. The myth Warren selects is that of the flight from Egypt, when the Chosen People, "stumbling the waste," were led,

> Not to the desert well
> Or green-lipped pool,
> Or where moving waters sang
> .   .   .   .   .

But thirsting and accurst—
Tongue black between the teeth
Whence no sweet spittle sprang—
Under the noon's flame
To the rock came.   .   .   .

So there were other waste lands, after all. Modern man can relax a little bit, taking some consolation. And not only consolation, but hope: for the myth of that ancient waste land had an outcome hardly foreseeable to the blighted wanderers:

And think how the Israelite
Struck
And the riven rock

.   .   .

Gave forth to tongue and gut the living stream's delight.

If perhaps the myth of Moses' striking water from the rock seems inapplicable to our twentieth-century waste land— despite T. S. Eliot's later epiphanies—there still remains that other source of ultimate truth: intuition. The concluding image of "Question and Answer" affirms with increased conviction the value of the quest, the "groping Godward, though blind" which we observed in "Pursuit" and which I compared to Whitman's "Noiseless, Patient Spider." The quest endures, whether the myths of orthodoxy are pertinent or not:

But if not that, then know
At least the heart a bow
Bent   .   .   .

.   .   .

.   .   .   [to] let the arrow fly
At God's black, orbèd, target eye.

The word "know" in the above passage is the big one. It rings with authority and conviction that will brook no gainsay. For the sake of the skeptic, then, a word from Jung might again be in order. The verb "know," says Jung (in effect), is not subject to the skepticism of outsiders if the experience in question involves the unconscious, which is "the only accessible source of religious experience": "Anyone who wants to can at least draw near to the source of such experiences, no matter whether he believes in God or not. . . . That religious experiences exist no longer needs proof. . . . Anyone who has had [one] is *seized* by it and therefore not in a position to indulge in fruitless metaphysical or epistemological speculations. Absolute certainty brings its own evidence and has no need of anthropomorphic proofs." [10] As we near the end of *Eleven Poems*, then, we can observe a progressive expansion in the poet's definition of love. It began with acceptance of the shadow-self in "Crime," "Original Sin," and "End of Season"; expanded into broad social interrelationships in "Revelation" and "Pursuit"; and concluded with intimations of divine love, the heart as a bow at "God's target eye," in "Question and Answer."

"Love's Parable," using imagery of secular love, expands still further the definition of divine love. There has been some controversy over this poem. F. O. Matthiessen admired it as reinvoking the seventeenth-century tradition of Andrew Marvell, but W. P. Southard called it "the only flat silly poem in the book." [11] Howard Nemerov's reading that the lovers here are man and God would appear to be the most profitable reading of the poem. Nemerov speaks of "the reduplication as in a mirror of earthly and heavenly love" in this poem, an effect which reminds him of Donne's use of secular love imagery in his religious poems.[12] The theme of "Revelation," that "in separateness only does love learn definition," undergoes a full circle of experience in "Love's Parable": from the Fall to a "garden state" to the Fall again. Tentatively, as the poem ends, a hope for higher innocence emerges: "For there are testaments / That men, by prayer, have mastered grace."

The poem "Terror," the last of the *Eleven Poems*, brings the curve of experience in this sequence back to where it had begun in "Monologue at Midnight": isolation and guilt. The naturalistic crisis of the first three poems, the question of whether Time renders all things meaningless, and the gropings towards hope and love in the ensuing poems all come back to the same issue at the end: definition of self through Jung's "imagination in evil."

That the lack of such imagination in evil is the major defect of modern man has been a recurrent theme in Warren's art; and within the limits of *Eleven Poems*, by observing the expansion of scope from the individual guilt-shadow ("Or was it guilt?") in "Monologue at Midnight" to the world-wide outpouring of depravity in "Terror," we may see Warren's whole career roughly outlined and foreshadowed. This expansion of scope, however, should not delude us into imagining a comparative lessening of our individual guilt, as Warren construes it. On the contrary, the workings of imagination in evil confirm that all the evil going on "out there," where "the criminal king . . . paints the air / With discoursed madness and protruding eye," where the "face . . . / Bends to the bomb-sight over bitter Helsingfors," where "the brute crowd roars or the blunt boot-heels resound / In the Piazza or the Wilhelmplatz," is directly related to the individual self, who has part ownership in humanity's black collective shadow, though "you now, guiltless, sink / To rest in lobbies. . . ." [13]

It has been the peculiar pride of this age, disburdened at last of the religious opprobrium of original sin, to externalize its guilt, to attack humanity's black shadow as though it were exclusively the property of other people. Encouraged by the millennialist political dogmas of our time, how many, asks Warren, have lost their humanity by attempting to exorcise the shadow-self within so as to murder it in the person of other people?

> So some, whose passionate emptiness and tidal
> Lust swayed toward the debris of Madrid. . . .
>
>   .   .   .   .
>
> They fight old friends, for their obsession knows
> Only the immaculate itch, not human friends or foes.

But of course the shadow-self persists, though we murder the bad people. This is why we are "born to no adequate definition of terror": our age has not prepared us for the ultimate terror, the confronting of the inner shadow-self. That haunting specter which we were able to lock out of the house of the psyche in "Original Sin: A Short Story," and whose image still seems so quaintly harmless in "Terror" ("like a puppy, . . . darling and inept, / Though his cold nose brush your hand . . ."), begins for all its harmless appearance to terrify the conscious self in this poem. For all its innocence and sanctity, the surface-self is shocked aware, at last, that something is missing from the picture so that the self must exclaim, as Warren describes this awareness in "The Ballad of Billie Potts," "Why, I'm not in it at all!"

The awareness of lack of identity, then, is the central terror of the poem; and the final image of "Terror" (and of *Eleven Poems on the Same Theme*) leaves us with that terror, for though in a virtuous domestic setting ("But you crack nuts"), we are implicated by our very isolation. Where we ought to find our identity, that black collective shadow of mankind, we "see an empty chair," and the word "conscience-stricken" can only imply some personal complicity on the part of the conscious self which makes it responsible for the empty chair: "But you crack nuts, while the conscience-stricken stare / Kisses the terror; for you see an empty chair."

What we have seen in *Eleven Poems on the Same Theme*, to conclude this discussion, is a psychological drama with profound insights. The antagonists have been the conscious as against the unconscious self; the setting has moved from naturalistic darkness "out there" through the interior darkness in the house of the psyche (attic to cellar); and the issue at stake has been the redemption of man, the "groping Godward, though blind," through the uniting of self, of all selves, in the attainment of identity. We must turn to Warren's later poetry to witness the outcome—so far as a final outcome is within human reach—of this intensely important drama, but insofar as it defines the issues and equips us for understanding, *Eleven Poems on the Same Theme* is a very important part of Warren's total poetic production. And even if his work had ended there, the *Eleven Poems* is, I think, a masterful achievement—original in its conception, significant in its import, and moving in its presentation—in its own right. The emergence of a major new vision and voice dates from this work.

Three "New" Poems: The Dead End of Naturalism

CRITICAL REACTION towards the "new" poems, those entries in *Selected Poems* not taken from Warren's two earlier volumes, has been mixed. In Leonard Casper's opinion, "The volume is . . . harmed by three new but far from satisfactory poems." [14] By contrast with this extremely negative judgment, F. O. Matthiessen considered these three poems, "Variation: Ode to Fear," "Mexico Is a Foreign Country: Five Studies in Naturalism," and "The Ballad of Billie Potts," very promising indeed, particularly because of their technical innovations: ". . . the most exciting feature of his most recent poems is their breaking away from the intellectualized modes that have often been the mannerism of our generation. In 'Variation: Ode to Fear' he makes a far more loosely colloquial statement of his theme. In 'Mexico Is a Foreign Country: Five Studies in Naturalism' he introduces a hearty and humorous coarseness. And finally, in his 'Ballad,' he enters a new realm by accomplishing the fusion that Yeats urged between the poetry of coteries and the poetry of the folk." [15]

Needless to say, I side with Matthiessen's judgment in this matter, though on thematic as well as on technical grounds. Far from "harming" the volume, as Casper asserts, these three poems bring to a climax (and in "The Ballad of Billie Potts," to a resolution) the crucial issue of Warren's earlier work in *Selected Poems*: the issue of whether man can find meaning (or identity) in a naturalistic world. "Variation" and "Mexico Is a Foreign Country" answer this question with a negative that is almost absolute, but "The Ballad of Billie Potts" gives a different sort of answer, something more akin to classical tragedy than to modern naturalism. Though the setting differs, Billie Potts is driven, like Oedipus, after all evasions fail, to find his identity, and to find it at whatever cost. Oedipus lost his eyes and his kingdom; Billie Potts loses his life, but in each case the loss is outweighed by a spiritual gain at the quest's end.

This is Warren's final answer to the problem of naturalism, then. In the hope of attaining final identity, his persona accepts even annihilation, if need be, kneeling in silent submission "in the sacramental silence of evening" as the poem ends. This has nothing to do with Warren's earlier death-wish, his initial response to naturalistic despair, but is rather a deliberate resignation of will, a yielding of the conscious self to submersion in some dark pool welling up from the unconscious. Much as Eliot's naturalistic irony and bitterness disappear, though sorrow remains, in "Ash Wednesday," so the speaker's submission in "The Ballad of Billie Potts" is total enough to render his voice free of such self-justifying devices as irony and bitter humor (which abound in "Variation" and "Mexico"), though the sorrow at receiving the gift of death is so great as to provide one of the most memorable lines in all Warren's verse: "What gift—oh, father, father—from that dissevering hand?" It is interesting to note, since I have called the ending of "The Ballad of Billie Potts" Warren's "final" answer to the problem of naturalism, that a ten-year lapse separates this poem from Warren's next-published undertaking in poetry, *Brother to Dragons* (1953).

Although "The Ballad of Billie Potts" will be studied more closely in this discussion of *Selected Poems*, the other two "new" poems deserve some scrutiny, especially because they define in detail the naturalistic barrenness whose clutch and toil Warren finally managed to elude in the "Ballad." And they achieve a certain success in their own right.

"Variation: Ode to Fear" has been criticized by Casper and others for treating naturalistic despair too flippantly. It is true that some of the stanzas, such as those treating the narrator's physical or financial identity ("When the dentist

adjusts his drill," "When the surgeon whets his scalpel,"
". . . account $3.00 overdrawn," and so on), seem to
parody the naturalistic terror which we know Warren capable
of. But the images of time and death, beautifully objectified in
concrete detail, which appear in the middle stanzas are
sufficiently effective for an "Ode to Fear":

> When in the midnight's pause I mark
> The breath beside me in the dark,
> And know that breath's a clock, and know
> That breath's the clock that's never slow,
>   *Timor mortis conturbat me.*
>
> O thou, to whom the world unknown
> With all its shadowy shapes is shown,
> Whose foot makes no sound on the floor,
> Who need no latchkey for the door
>   (*Timor mortis conturbat me*) . . .

"Mexico Is a Foreign Country: Five Studies in Naturalism" is about as succinct a statement of the naturalistic
position as can be imagined. And it is convincing enough to
prove that although Mexico is a foreign country, the grim
implications of naturalism are anything but foreign and
faraway. Section I, "Butterflies over the Map," begins like a
short story, with plot (in two senses), setting, and character—
"who wrathless, rose, and robed in the pure / Idea, smote, and
fled. . . . / The black limousine was not detected at La-
redo." The butterflies are apparently the lovely, pure-minded
ideals ("wrathless"), probably derived from some scheme of
political millennialism ("robed in the pure idea"), which
motivated this violence. A map corresponds to reality with
about as much wholeness as these bright ideals correspond to
actual life: "Butterflies dream gyres round the precious flower

which is your head." The falsity of the "pure idea," so
characteristic of our age, is witnessed in the last stanza, where
the butterflies dancing around the idealist's head abruptly give
way to an image more consistent with the real world—flies
buzzing around a dead child's face:

> They lay the corpse, pink cloth on its face, in the patio,
> And bank it with blossoms, yellow, red, and the Virgin's blue.
>
> The pink cloth is useful to foil the flies, which are not few.

So Warren rejects that type of response to naturalism—the
modern delusion of political millennialism, "butterflies over a
map."

Section II, "Siesta Time in Village Plaza by Ruined
Bandstand and Banana Tree," implies in the image of the
"ruined bandstand" what sort of response to naturalism will be
treated here—the hedonist response, the consolation through
sex ("praise the bull, deride the steer") and liquor whereby
Hemingway could endure a nada universe:

> If only Ernest now were here
> To praise the bull, deride the steer,
> And anatomize for chillier chumps
> The local beauties' grinds and bumps;
>
> .   .   .   .
>
> But the toothsomer beauties now are sweating
> On beds in need of mosquito netting,
> While I sweat in the Plaza here
> And meditate on my last beer.   .   .   .

Unfortunately, as the "ruined bandstand" image implies, the
glories of hedonism have long since departed from this place.
Rather than enjoy the carnival atmosphere of Hemingway's

bullfights, this narrator sits alone in the utter hiatus that naturalism ultimately implies, and even sex (or at least companionship) and liquor are so unavailing in this setting ("all the shutters are down tight, / While my head rocks in the explosive light") that the great apostle of sex, companionship, and liquor looks from here like a distant, inaccessible star: "And Ernest twinkles from afar / In his abode where the eternals are."

So oppressive is the atmosphere of desolation in this naturalistic village that even the old, outmoded conventional values, religion ("the Baptists"), politics (Henry Wallace), and economics ("Standard Oil"), would be welcome here— they might at least provide some distraction from this emptiness—but of course they are not available in this place of no values ("Baptists, Wallace, and Standard Oil / Are too engrossed in their proper toil"). But suddenly, at the poem's end, there is a great unexpected burst of excitement. Here, even here in this stagnant outpost of naturalism, something of real value has been found at last! A genuine motivation *can* be had!

> But all at once the peace is shattered,
> And all the tranquil hour is tattered:
> In a sudden burst of energy
> The dog seeks out the banana tree.

Well, to be sure, this is narrowing down the hedonistic response to its bedrock essence of pleasure, but at least it is comforting to know that *some* value in life remains irreducibly available. Or is it available? The final stanza of this section throws doubt even on this simple animal pleasure. Though the narrator watches the dog approvingly ("I watch and applaud the sound idea"), he, alas, cannot participate in even so basic an uplift. Perhaps, he hopes, his mystic consolation—whether

Hemingway's form of hedonism or the dog's—will come tomorrow (although, of course, we know it will not):

> I watch and applaud the sound idea,
> As I meditate on my last beer;
> But here even the bladder achieves Nirvana,
> And so I sit and think, "mañana."

But perhaps the sun also rises. The narrator who sat isolated and absolutely empty (even to the depths of his bladder) in the midnight silence of Section II reappears in broad daylight in the final three sections. If the sun does rise, however, what it reveals is not very encouraging. In Section III, "The World Comes Galloping: A True Story," the sun serves mainly to emphasize a contrast that is central in Hemingway's life-ethic: the contrast between the aware and the unaware. The achievement of awareness is embodied in the person of a ragged old man, someone who has known the futility of existence but has nevertheless endured:

> He stood: old.
> Old, bare feet on stone, and the serape's rose
> Unfolded in the garden of his rags;
> Old, and all his history hung from his severe face
> As from his frame the dignity of rags.
>
> We could not see his history, we saw
> Him.
> And he saw us, but could not see we stood
> Huddled in our history and stuck out hand for alms.

Though "he could give us nothing"—none of the "alms" of meaning we beg of him—at least he "asked for nothing," either. He is completely independent, sustained, like the classical Hemingway hero, by his own inner resources, and sustained, moreover, against all the personal ruin implied by the "dignity of rags" surrounding him.

The contrast to this mature awareness is furnished by a young horseman who, in "fury and fever," raises a singular uproar through the quiet street:

> Horse and horseman, sudden as light, and loud,
> Appeared,
> And up the rise, banging the cobbles like castanets,
> Lashed in their fury and fever,
> Plunged:
> Wall-eyed and wheezing, the lurching hammer-head,
> The swaying youth,   .   .   .
>
>   .   .   .   .   .
>
> Plunged past us, and were gone.

The old man draws a metaphor from this little incident. By contrast with this frenzied youth, he is secure in simpler pleasures (unlike Prufrock, he dares to eat a peach), and so can comment on the frenzy wherein our naturalistic culture seeks escape from vacancy:

> So the old one, dropping his peach-pit, spat;
> Regarding the street's astonishing vacancy, said:
> "Viene galopando,"—and spat again—"el mundo."

"Viene galopando el mundo"—here comes the world, galloping. The old man's awareness, coupled with the strength that enables him to endure awareness, relates him to the stoical rather than the hedonistic side of Hemingway's naturalistic ethic. But although this response to naturalism seems more efficacious—more dignified, at any rate—than either frenzy or hedonism (the dog in Section II and this young horseman both "shatter the peace" ridiculously), there remains a question as to how widely applicable the old man's stoicism is: "But he could give us nothing." The virtue of the stoical response, in fact, turns out to be very limited. Its sustaining grace depends upon a feeling of superiority, a prideful distinguishing of the self, by dint of its higher awareness, from the common rabble. Hence, we have Hemingway's strictly selected inner circle of *aficionados* and nada-initiates; and hence we have the old man in this poem spitting his contempt ("spat . . . and spat again") at the galloping world represented by the young horseman.

We know from Warren's later works what he thinks of such a separation of the self from the rest of humanity, but even aside from such biases, there is a basic deficiency in this stoical response to naturalism: although a sense of superiority may be psychologically uplifting, it does not answer the ultimate problem of naturalism, the problem of self-extinction. The old man's peach might have been Eden's half-eaten apple, as he, "dropping his peach-pit, spat," but clearly his higher knowledge has not made him, any more than his mythical forebears, like the gods. The human need in Warren's work—the need for perfection, as Warren identifies it in "The Flower" (in *Promises*)—can never be satisfied by such trivia as a sense of superiority, any more than it can be satisfied by pious protestations of innocence on the part of various Warren characters. For this reason, the old man, though enviably self-sustained, can "give us nothing"; he can give us no "alms."

Section IV, "Small Soldiers with Drum in Large Landscape," describes yet a fourth response to naturalism. Unlike political millennialism, hedonism, or stoicism, this response takes full account ("*Small* Soldiers . . . in *Large* Landscape") of the minuteness, the trivial insignificance, of the self which is implicit, although not always admitted, in naturalism, for to conceive of the self as absolutely nothing must be psychological death. The other responses to naturalism which I have noted represent last-ditch efforts to maintain at least some dignity and importance of self, regardless of the contrary implications of naturalism. Only this poem gives the enormous perspective, hopelessly dwarfing the individual self, of naturalism's large landscape:

> The little soldiers thread the hills.
> Remote, the white Sierra nods.   .   .   .
>   .   .   .   .
>
> The little drum goes rum-tum-tum,
> The little hearts go rat-tat-tat,   .   .   .
>   .   .   .   .
>
> And the single pine is black upon
> The crag; and the buzzard, absolute
> In the sun's great gold eye, hangs.   .   .   .

Oddly enough—probably because to Warren's mind this perspective is the only one that evinces total intellectual honesty—this poem evinces the first display of partiality on the narrator's part. We cannot call it hope, exactly, but there is something that he admires and finds personally attractive about this group of little marchers. Although they adhere to obviously meaningless forms, they do so with precision and energy, without being pretentious about it. They are cheerful, natural, and unsanctimonious about their little ceremonies, unlike the political millennialist or the old man:

> Their bearing lacked ferocity.
> Their eyes were soft, their feet were splayed,
> And dirt, no doubt, behind the ears
> Did them no credit on parade.

They did not tell me why they march—
To give some cattle-thief a scare
Or make their captain happy or
Simply take the mountain air.

.   .   .   .   .   .

And shrouded in the coats and buttons,
The atoms bounce, and under the sky,
Under the mountain's gaze, maintain
The gallant little formulae.   .   .   .

The important image in the above excerpt is that of the atoms and the "formulae." The men constitute "*gallant* little formulae," I think, precisely because they, though representing individual "atoms," have transcended the fragmentation of the naturalistic landscape, a fragmentation so profound that all identity is self-contained, there being no higher purpose or meaning external to the thing-in-itself:

And I am I, and they are they,
And *this* is *this*, and *that* is *that*,

.   .   .   .   .   .

And leaf is leaf, and root is root   .   .   .

And the wind has neither home nor hope;
And cause is cause, effect, effect.   .   .   .

We know from Warren's other work how deadly he considers such fragmentation of reality and such isolation of the self to be. If there is any meaning at all, he has asserted, it has to be self-transcending, encompassing all that exists (past and present) in so wide an embrace that "nothing is ever lost." Such an embrace is precisely what the other naturalists in "Mexico Is a Foreign Country" found lacking. The political millennialist, the man sitting alone with an empty bladder, and the old man spitting after the horseman are distinguished noticeably by their utter solitude, their exclusive reliance on the resources of the self. For this reason, apparently, there is not the faintest glimmer of hope in these poems, or at least none that the narrator can avail himself of.

But in "Small Soldiers with Drum in Large Landscape" there is self-transcendence—the gathering of these minute "atoms," through voluntary mutual commitment, into "gallant little formulae"—and so, even as they march together into oblivion, there is some hint of permanent meaning here, something which distinguishes this little band from the utterly fragmented landscape around them:

> .   .   .   here I stand and watch them go
> From dawn to dark, from East to West,
>
> From *what* to *what*, from *if* to *when*,
> From ridge to ridge.   .   .   .
>   .   .   .   .   .
>
> Across the high waste of the mind,
> Across the distance in the breast,
> And climbing hazier heights, proceed
> To a bivouac in a farther West.

The final two stanzas of this poem quash any possible Romantic misinterpretations of this scene—Wordsworth's nature mysticism in particular is rejected as a source of strength (naturalism tends to see nature as indifferent or hostile to human needs). But for all their naturalistic limitations, these little men offer something that we have not seen before in these poems—self-transcending unity, a purpose (however simple) higher than the thing-in-itself. To such a possibility—and we shall see this idea expanded in *Promises* (in "Gull's Cry" and elsewhere)—the speaker would like to commit his identity:

> As I remarked, the little men
> Had necks unwashed and manners rude;
> They were no cloud of daffodils
> As once blest William's solitude.
>
> But when upon my couch I lie
> And brood the done, and the undone,
> My heart may seize its hint of pleasure
> And march beside them in the sun.

The little men in their gallant formulae offer some promise or possibility, it seems clear, but it is a promise and a possibility that remains unfulfilled. The marchers follow their little drum to the "bivouac in a farther West" and leave the narrator, as the fifth and last "study in naturalism" comes around, in his familiar isolation. Not only is there isolation in "The Mango on the Mango Tree," but there is, worse than that, outright hatred between the fragments of this shattered world. This poem represents Warren's own peculiar view of naturalism— Hemingway and the other apostles of naturalism have no relevance here.

To Warren, as the last three poems have made clear, the worst effect of naturalism is that it fragments the world, throwing the entire burden of discovering meaning and identity upon the solitary self. Facing obvious and insurmountable limitations (particularly of time), the self must find this an intolerable burden, an impossible necessity. "Solution, perhaps, is public, despair personal," Warren had asserted in "Pursuit," and we see just how "public" the solution to the problem of identity is when we get to the end of "The Ballad of Billie Potts," where even the lower creatures of animate creation are seen engaging in the homeward quest: "The bee knows, and the eel's cold ganglia burn, / . . . the sad head lifting to the long return."

A vision of all-embracing oneness is all that can avail against naturalistic meaninglessness. This is the basic theme we see in "The Ballad of Billie Potts" and in later works, such as *The Cave* and *Promises*. But the very title of "Mexico Is a Foreign Country" clearly demonstrates that no such absolute oneness is as yet imaginable. On the contrary, these "Five Studies in Naturalism" have emphasized fragmentation and solitude. The only exception to this universal condition—the little men marching—offered the one hopeful possibility in this whole waste land, but it was a possibility not (for the narrator) actually realized. They marched out of "the high waste of the mind" and up through "hazier heights" beyond, leaving their envying observer lonelier than ever in his desert solitude.

In view of these observations, it is appropriate that Warren devotes the final study in naturalism, which obviously expounds his own perspective, to a treatment of isolation. Here in Section V, "The Mango," the point is literally that a mango cannot "talk" to a man. If it could, then the fragmentation of the world would cease to exist, and life would gain meaning because of the individual's participation in a larger being that goes on and on. But as any naturalist knows, this is just wishful thinking; the first law of nature is every man—and mango—for himself:

> The mango on the mango tree—
> I look at it, it looks at me.   .   .   .
>   .   .   .   .   .   .

The mango is a great gold eye,
Like God's, set in the leafy sky
To harry heart, block blood, freeze feet, if I would fly.

For God has set it there to spy .   .   .
.   .   .   .

Gumshoe, *agent provocateur*,
Stool, informer, whisperer
—Each pours his tale into the Great Schismatic's ear.

For God works well the Roman plan,
Divide and rule, mango and man,
And on hate's axis the great globe grinds in its span.

This is, we must agree, a most singular form of naturalism, with very extensive moral and metaphysical dimensions implicit in its mention of "hate's axis" and a God. Of course, it is not unusual for a naturalist to inveigh against a God whose existence he denies, but Warren's naturalism in this poem seems extraordinary because his persona actually does appear to believe in the divine entity that he assails, the God whose "primal guilt" is everywhere evident in His ruined, suffering creation:

I do not know the mango's crime .   .   .
.   .   .   .

Nor does it know mine committed in a frostier clime.

But what to His were ours, who pay,
Drop by slow drop, day after day,
Until His monstrous, primal guilt be washed away,

Who till that time must thus atone
In pulp and pit, in flesh and bone,
By our vicarious sacrifice fault not our own?

The most remarkable thing about the above excerpt is not its image of a sinful God (a commonplace notion in naturalism), but rather the assertion of innocence on the part of the narrator (*"fault not our own"*), which is not commonplace (except for purposes of satire) in Warren's art. A feeling of sin and guilt, in direct opposition to such an assertion of innocence, has up to this time been steadily gaining ascendancy in Warren's narrator—and I think we may assume that the narrator of this poem is the same who toiled downward through *Eleven Poems on the Same Theme.*

The explanation of this reversal of attitude lies, I think, in Warren's familiar technique of polarizing opposites. Coming between the reluctant acceptance of guilt in *Eleven Poems* and the absolute submission to the father in "The Ballad of Billie Potts," this protestation of innocence, this throwing the entire blame for sin on God in an outburst of resentment, indicates the dramatic tension still going on within the divided self. Honestly motivated as it is, this instance of naturalistic rebellion is a necessary phase in the ritual of acceptance. It indicates that the curve of spiritual experience which Warren is describing in this period of his development is not a smooth, straight line, like an arithmetical progression. Rather, Warren's poetry continues at this stage to show the same sort of paradox, tension, and irony that we observed in the earlier poems, where hope and despair interlocked in inextricable embrace, leading W. P. Southard to comment dourly that Warren's opposing ideas are calculated to "blow hell out of each other." [16] Although this description of Warren's dialectic may be a bit exaggerated, it is quite true that the conflict of joy and despair in Warren's earlier poems leaves, indeed, a very frail wreckage for the survivor to cling to.

The working of this dialectic is what explains Warren's

"blasphemy" in "The Mango on the Mango Tree." Clearly
the speaker is not ready, as yet—as he will be in "The Ballad of
Billie Potts"—to bow his head under the father's hatchet. But
as this poem ends, he is getting ready. And his first step in this
ritual of acceptance is to qualify his assertion of innocence by
admitting a need *both* to receive and to impart forgiveness.
Only thus can the "Babel curse" of universal isolation be
lifted, and he and "God's eye," the mango, be reconciled:

> For, ah, I do not know the word
> That it could hear, or if I've heard
> A breath like *pardon, pardon,* when its stiff lips stirred.
>
> If there were a word that I could give,
> Or if I could only say *forgive,*
> Then we might lift the Babel curse by which we live.   .   .   .

The general theme of isolation (the "Babel curse"), the
tentative moral resolution (*"forgive"*), and the anguished
tone of unfulfilled aspiration ("If there were a word
.   .   .   ," "if I could only say   .   .   .") all suggest some
close resemblances to *The Waste Land,* but the concluding
scene of the poem is strictly Warren's own. Here we see anticipated the "moment of possibility" in "Gull's Cry" (*Promises*),
the vision of unity where *"gobbo, gobbo's* wife, and us, and
all, take hands and sing: redeem, redeem!" That moment of
possibility is only longed for—is not realized—in "The Mango
on the Mango Tree," for in this fragmented naturalistic world
the word *"forgive"* has not been sounded as yet; but the vision
of what *could* be, man and mango joining in a ritual of brotherhood, strikingly anticipates the poetry of fifteen years later:

> And I could leap, and laugh and sing
> And it could leap, and everything
> Take hands with us and pace the music in a ring

And sway like the multitudinous wheat
In blessedness so long escheat
—Blest in that blasphemy of love we cannot now repeat.

"That blasphemy of love," that ritual of universal oneness which seems to gainsay the decree of a hateful, guilt-ridden, naturalistic God, will eventually become the orthodoxy of love in Warren's later work. The initiate into ultimate reality in "Ballad of a Sweet Dream of Peace" (*Promises*), for example, will discover that "we're all one Flesh, at last." But for both this initiate and the narrator of "The Mango on the Mango Tree," this committing of the self to the universal oneness will require of the individual self a harrowing ordeal. It will require, in fact, the annihilation of the self, or at least of the conscious identity which we call the self.

Such absolute submission of the will must obviously come under the classification of religious (not necessarily Christian) experience, as in fact, the whole quest for identity, when pursued to the extreme of self-annihilation, must be considered a religious matter. "The Ballad of Billie Potts," in this broad sense, is a religious poem. Its answer to the problem of naturalism, which Warren has identified as the central problem of our age, is a tragic answer, with both the negative and affirmative dimensions of that adjective. Given the limitations of the other responses to naturalism—responses which Warren has so elaborately scrutinized and found wanting in "Variation: Ode to Fear" and "Mexico Is a Foreign Country"—his answer to naturalism in "The Ballad of Billie Potts" becomes at least as acceptable as any, I should say.

"The Ballad of Billie Potts" uses one of the older forms of literature known to man, the ballad, to recount one of mankind's oldest themes: the relationship between father and son, or, more generally, the complicity of the generations. In the fact that Billie's search for identity leads him back to his father lie religious and psychological implications having the depth and power of archetype and myth—a depth and power that Warren has exploited time and again in his fiction, where the coming to terms with a father or father-figure is perhaps Warren's most dominant recurrent pattern. Allegorically, too, Billie's return to his father—especially when we consider the father's nature ("evil and ignorant and old")—resembles the search of the conscious ego for its shadow, that unknown deeper self whose absence caused the "Terror" at the end of *Eleven Poems on the Same Theme*.

Although Warren sets his story in the frontier country of America, he evokes the image of a very ancient time—when man was also in the frontier land of civilization—by establishing his setting "in the land between the rivers." Mesopotamia, which translated means "the land between the rivers," has long been regarded in Semitic myths, including the Garden of Eden story, as the birthplace of mankind. So Warren subtly hints as early as Line 2 of this poem the origin (and outcome) of the myth he is recreating in terms of New World innocence and its Fall. The importance of this phrase ("the land between the rivers") is indicated by the fact that it becomes the recurrent refrain throughout the ballad, and it ties in with the water imagery that later emerges predominant in the poem.

In the first stanza Warren depicts Big Billie Potts, an American Adam—already fallen, but not yet aware of the tragedy his sin will entail for his posterity—in the rough, uncouth diction of Kentucky frontier country: "His gut stuck out / Like a croker of nubbins." Big Billie's wife is also described in realistic terms having mythical overtones. Although she may lack the mythical dignity of the first Eve, she has the same feline cleverness as the original ("clever

. . . [with] eyes like a cat") and—Warren abruptly slows down the metrical speed here—"Nobody knew what was in her head." The resemblance between Big Billie's wife and Eve is seen more clearly towards the climax of this poem, when we see that it is the woman who instigates the murder of their disguised son: "And the old woman gave the old man a straight look. / She gave him the bucket but it was not empty but it was not water."

The third stanza describes the third member of this family group—the offspring of the senior Pottses, and the hero of this ballad. Billie Potts is here described in his rather vulnerable adolescent innocence ("And a whicker when he laughed where his father had a beller"). As he had done in describing the two elder Pottses, Warren abruptly halts the pace of the poem towards the end of the third stanza and concludes with a brief and blandly portentous statement establishing the character's role in the narrative: "He was their darling."

Having introduced his three main characters, Warren shifts into a longer, slower moving, parenthetical stanza (Stanza 4), which somewhat ominously describes the setting: "The fetid bottoms . . . / Where no sun comes, the muskrat's astute face / Was lifted to the yammering jay; then dropped." The significance of this particular setting becomes evident later in the poem when Billie, "crouched at the swamp-edge" (Stanza 18), prepares for his initiation in the villainy of his father. Stanza 4 also serves a function that is very important in a great deal of Warren's art: it establishes the time perspective of a time past under scrutiny by a narrator in time present. Hence, Warren creates the effect of esthetic distance and also gives the illusion of time past isolated temporarily into a whole for the purposes of literary integrity. As in World Enough and Time, Warren establishes the reality

of time present by a description of the materials out of which
he will create his fable:

> But the land is there, and as you top a rise,
> Beyond you all the landscape steams and simmers
> —The hills, now gutted, red, cane-brake and black-jack yet.

And as in *Brother to Dragons*, Warren prefaces his journey
into the past with a local incident (the narrator asks directions
of a rustic), pointing up in sharp relief the dimension of time
present against whatever fantasy the poet may conjure up out
of the past:

> "Mister, is this the right road to Paducah?"
> The red face   .   .   .
> .   .   .   with the innocent savagery
> Of Time, the bleared eyes rolling, answers from
> Your dream: "They names hit so, but I ain't bin."

The rustic, of course, never has "bin," and never will be "to
Paducah," at least not in the knowledge in which Warren will
go there, just as Mr. Boyle in *Brother to Dragons* will never
possess his land as fully as R.P.W., with his deep sense of the
history of the place, will (with the reader) possess it.

In Stanza 5, Warren returns briefly to his narrative again,
using his original ballad stanza (in contrast to the subtler
parenthetical style) and showing Big Billie setting up his
business in the New Land. But immediately Warren takes us
into the present again, and in retrospect we see the past as a
sort of dumb show, representing in universal scope the tragedy
of failure and anonymity and meaninglessness in the lives of
American frontiersmen (and preparing for the individual
frontier tragedy that is to follow). Again Warren slows the

meter to a more thoughtful pace by use of a longer stanza,
iambic pentameter rhythm (generally), and a less intricate
rhyme scheme (*aabbcc*, etc.):

> (Leaning and slow, you see them move
> In massive passion colder than any love:
> Their lips move but you do not hear the words
> Nor trodden twig nor fluted irony of birds .   .   .
>
> .   .   .   .
> Their names are like the leaves   .   .   .
> .   .   .   .
>   .   .   . seed
> Flung in the long wind: silent, proceed
> Past meadow, salt-lick, and the lyric swale;
> Enter the arbor, shadow of trees, fade, fail.

The rich texture of these last lines, created largely by allitera-
tion, assonance, and consonance ("salt-lick .   .   . lyric,"
"fade, fail"), admirably suits the grieving mood of the lines,
appropriate to their tragic content. It forms a contrast to the
fast-moving anapaests of the narrative stanzas, in which the
characters, not sharing the poet's awareness of impending
tragedy, act with the naive happiness that success brings.

Warren alternates between past and present again in
Stanza 7, which shows Big Billie happily working at his
avocation of hijacking the guests of his inn, and in Stanzas 8, 9,
and 10, all of which are enclosed by a single pair of parentheses. In these parenthetical stanzas, Warren places this little
incident from the past—the waylaying of a traveler ("he was
already as good as dead, / For at midnight the message had
been sent ahead: / 'Man in black coat, riding bay mare with
star' ")—in a focus suggesting some ultimate significance of
the crime: some untraceable origin of it in time past and some

incalculable implications throughout time future. Thus Warren achieves the secular parallel of a religious perspective on time:

> There was a beginning but you cannot see it.
> There will be an end but you cannot see it.

In delineating the ultimate implications of the crime, Warren does not merely settle the blame upon its immediate perpetrator, nor is he concerned only with the specter of violent death. Rather, he wants to discover (in Billie Potts) the ultimate source of evil in man, beyond any one individual. From the spectacle of Little Billie reenacting the sin of his father (who, we may speculate, had no doubt learned a few things from *his* father), we may infer a concept of original sin: the father molding the son into his own imperfect image, the ancestral (moral) weakness recurring in successive generations. The beginning, or the original violation of moral order, occurred sometime during the obscure infancy of mankind ("There was a beginning but you cannot see it"), and the ultimate consequences of man's moral failure are likewise beyond the present scope of human vision. Warren does share, then, the religious view of time as a meaningful whole in which the pattern of human existence gradually assumes ultimate significance. What that significance is, Warren cannot say, because of the limitation in the human apprehension of time past and time future ("The answer is in the back of the book, but the page is gone"), but he does trace, as far as a man is able, the pattern of human affairs, risking the assumption that there is a final importance to men's lives.

Considering the unfortunate events of the past, as he has reconstructed them, and seeing in retrospect how character and coincidence have conspired toward inescapable tragedy,

Warren harshly describes the futility of after-knowledge, or second-guessing history: "And speculation rasps its idiot nails / Across the dry slate where you did the sum." The people of the past could not perceive their own destiny as we, looking back, can see it. That is why we must look on helplessly, as through a glass, while they shape their lives towards calamity:

> They will not turn their faces to you though you call,
> Who pace a logic merciless as light.   .   .   .

In this last line, there is a considerable strain of determinism, but not a determinism of character (like that evinced in Calvinism) so much as a determinism of event and circumstance ("their long shadow on the grass, / Sun at the back; pace, pass   .   .   ."). This determinism of event, which is also evident in *All the King's Men* (where Jack Burden delivers his two closest friends to their mutual death), is reminiscent of the determinism operating in *Oedipus Rex* in the form of the ancient prophecies. As in classical tragedy the issue of self-knowledge and the discovery of some personal deficiency is a major theme in Warren's work. And as in the tragic mode, again, this self-knowledge often comes too late in Warren's characters (like Willie Stark, Jeremiah Beaumont, and Percy Munn) to avert tragedy, and the insight into the true nature of the self is the only consolation amid personal chaos.

Warren presents in Stanza 9 some richly suggestive imagery evoking awareness of the immobility and unchangeableness of the past, describing people who once lived:

> Beyond your call or question now, they move   .   .   .
> .   .   .   .
> Sainted and sad and sage as the hairy ass, who bear
> History like bound faggots, with stiff knees.   .   .   .

These people, who shouldered history like asses bearing a burden of which they cannot know the significance, assume a permanence and immobility (hence, immortality) beyond the movement of time, much as the golden bird and tree in Yeats' "Sailing to Byzantium" and the figures on Keats' urn achieve timeless stature through the medium of art:

> .   .   .   [they] breathe the immaculate climate where
> The lucent leaf is lifted, lank beard fingered, by no breeze,
> Rapt in the fabulous complacency of fresco, vase, or frieze.

Unlike Yeats or Keats, however, Warren does not rest with these dead and passionless images of time past. Rather, he connects these images of immobile perfection by a startling image in the one-line Stanza 10: "And the testicles of the fathers hang down like old lace." The word "testicles" suggests the carnal transmission of life, and hence a connection between the "complacency of fresco, vase, or frieze," or the ancient, patterned perfection of "old lace," and the imperfect, incomplete present.

The dramatic narrative quickens in Stanzas 11 and 12 as once again Warren releases a profusion of "hard" consonants, including numerous "p's" ("piss," "sap," "maple," "lop-eared pup"), to vivify the action. The situation narrows down from a generalized perspective of the characters to a specific instance of impending crime, and characters take on a lifelike immediacy thereby:

> Big Billie called Little and said, "Saddle up,"
> And nodded toward the man was taking his sup
> With his belt unlatched and his feet to the fire.   .   .   .

Little Billie's character (rather than his father's) grows predominant in the poem from this point, when instead of riding to alert his father's henchman (Amos), as he was ordered, Little Billie decides to do this job himself. And so the narrator leaves Little Bille squatting "on his hams in the morning dew and damp" of the swamp, waiting for the traveler's appearance and grinning "to think / How his Pap would be proud and his Mammy glad / To know what a thriving boy they had."

In the interlude between Billie's decision and his attempted enactment of the crime, Warren interposes a parenthetical passage suggesting the philosophical significance of the deed. It means for one thing a change in identity, an awareness of exchanging an accustomed, familiar self for a new, as yet unknown, self:

> . . . who rode away from *goodbye, goodbye*,
> And toward *hello*, toward Time's unwinking eye;
> And like the cicada had left, at cross-roads or square,
> The old shell of self, thin, ghostly, translucent, light as air.

In depicting the transition from innocence to knowledge in Billie Potts, Warren places the onlooker (narrator and reader) in Billie's present indefinite position, showing past innocence (in a vegetable image, "leaf") and impending guilt (in a predatory image, "crouched"), and unable to determine, considering the wholeness of Time ("Time's unwinking eye"), whether the past or future identity is the real self ("Which are you?"):

> . . . land of the innocent bough, land of the leaf.
> Think of your face green in the submarine light of the leaf.
>
> Or think of yourself crouched at the swamp-edge,
>
> .   .   .   .
>
> Think of yourself at dawn: Which are you? What?

We see immediately that there is no external change in Little Billie, since he is recognized at once by the traveler

("Why, bless my heart, if it ain't Little Billie!"), and we see that his inner character is perceived as spontaneously:

> Just watching Little Billie and smiling and humming
>
> .   .   .   .
>
> But he must have had eyes in the side of his head
>
> .   .   .   .
>
> For when Billie said, "Mister, I've brung hit to you,"
> And reached his hand for it down in his britches,
> The stranger just reached his own hand, too.

Because of the farcical failure of his attempted murder, Billie has to leave town fast:

> So he turned and high-tailed up the trace,
> With blood on his shirt and snot in his nose
> And pee in his pants for he'd wet his clothes,
> And the stranger just sits and admires how he goes.

(Warren's use of extended rhyme and comically realistic narrative depiction is a parody of the convention of the Western ballad, such as "There was Ball-ud on the Saddle and Ball-ud on the Ground," and others. Warren's ballad has a much more serious purpose than such simple ditties, and yet Warren finds the convention useful for comic purposes.)

We have already seen how Warren used water imagery in his refrain ("the land between the rivers") and in the lines describing Billie's innocence ("the submarine light of the leaf"), both of which uses have much to do with Billie's identity. In Stanzas 19–25 Warren develops his theme of time and identity to a nearly mystical level through a complexity of water imagery. We first get the impression that water means the passage of time towards the end of Stanza 18, when Billie's exile from his Kentucky home takes him across the Missouri River:

> For it was Roll, Missouri,
> It was Roll, roll, Missouri.
> And he was gone nigh ten long year.   .   .   .

That the Missouri represents a separation from the past
and a seeming acquisition of a new identity is clear in the first
line of Stanza 19, which paraphrases a much-quoted line from
Marlowe's *The Jew of Malta:* "There is always another
country and always another place." But this acquisition of a
new identity is more apparent than real. The truth of the
matter is that Billie had never known his basic identity in the
first place, and underneath all the surface whorls and changes
rippling down the years there remained the unchanging self,
the enigmatic face within, that stared through Billie's growing
whiskers and hardening features, that disdained his changing
names and demanded deeper recognition:

> And the name and the face are you, and you
> The name and the face, and the stream you gaze into
> Will show the adoring face, show the lips that lift to you
> As you lean with the implacable thirst of self,
>
>   .   .   .   .
>
> To drink not of the stream but of your deep identity.

The Narcissistic image in this passage has been translated into
the terms of modern psychology; like his Greek prototype,
Billie feels a deep yearning after his own image, but unlike
Narcissus, Billie knows a way to achieve self-wholeness. Although he is presently divided, Billie Potts believes that he can
attain knowledge of his identity by confronting his past. And
so, after a decade of trying to hide his identity in the innocent
land out West, Billie returns to the place of his origin.

But Billie's problem is larger than confronting his remembered past. Although the passing time does contain the secret

of the identity of Billie Potts, Time itself is of inscrutable origin and destiny:

> But water is water and it flows,
> Under the image on the water the water coils and goes
> And its own beginning and its end only the water knows.

It is at this point that Warren becomes, of necessity, most explicitly religious. If Time itself has no meaning—if the water simply comes and disappears in some isolated cycle of its own—then obviously the image of Billie Potts contained in the water has no meaning either. The secret of Billie's identity is totally involved with Time; the meaning of Time controls and delimits whatever meaning may be attached to the life of Billie Potts. The definition of Time, then, is of supreme importance in determining any definition of man. But inasmuch as the ultimate meaning of Time is an inscrutable mystery to the inductive human mind, Warren can define Time only in terms of religious faith. By using imagery drawn from Christian mysticism, Warren can define Time as potentially redemptive, as offering a genuine new identity and new birth (in contrast to Billie's invalid new identity in the West) despite the guilt of the past, be it original sin or personal. The things of Time are not final, then; they are "only beginnings" of which the conclusions lie outside of Time:

> And Time is only beginnings
> Time is only and always beginnings
> And is the redemption of our crime
> And is our Saviour's priceless blood.

Although the passage above might be construed to mean quite the opposite of my interpretation—that is, the Christian Atonement might be ironically considered as no more effica-

cious than the mere passing of time itself as an absolver of guilt
(and is hence unnecessary)—nevertheless, all the implications
of Warren's other writings, besides the total import of this
poem, would deny such a hypothesis. In *All the King's Men,*
Jack Burden finds that nothing is ever lost, and Bolton
Lovehart in *Circus in the Attic* restores order to his life only by
returning into the world of the past after a dreamlike period of
living on the here-and-now plane of reality. Nearly every one of
Warren's fictional protagonists seeks psychological integrity by
the confrontation, exploration, and acceptance of the past. So
it is clear that Warren does not mean that the mere passing of
time will conceal or expurgate guilt. On the contrary, the
whole life of Billie Potts is a testimony to the inescapability of
the past. Thus, when the poet says, "For Time is motion / For
Time is innocence / For Time is West" (Stanza 25), he can
say so only in a sense deeply ironic or deeply religious, for
ultimate identity remains the same (like the image of a face on
running water) through Time.

So Billie Potts returns, perforce, to his father's country. He
looks different now from the sniveling boy who fled with "pee
in his pants" and "snot in his nose" into the wild country. He
is a man, now, "With a big black beard growing down to his
guts   .   .   .   And a look in his eyes like he owned the earth."
He has gained prudence and knowledge of the world, and he
has achieved that measure of success (portentously called
"luck") which identifies and distinguishes a man in the eyes of
the world:

> "Fer I bin out West and taken my share
> And I reckin my luck helt out fer fair."

We shall see at the end of the poem how Billie's "luck," or his
total identity, encompasses more than his success in compet-

ing with the world. But for now, his "luck" distinguishes him from his destitute parents, and Warren plays on that term to evoke some bland dramatic irony. Joe Drew, a childhood acquaintance, speaks to Billie Potts (Stanza 28):

> "Fer hit looked lak when you went away
> You taken West yore Pappy's luck
> And maybe now you kin bring hit back. . . ."

Stanza 28 makes the final preparations for the groundwork of tragedy. Billie's hidden identity is tragic on two levels; on the surface level, it is his changed appearance that leads his parents unwittingly to murder their son, and on the deeper level, it is his search for total identity that brings him home to die. Stanza 28 sets up the later visit of Joe Drew, through whom the Pottses learn who their victim was, and it also revives a dramatic hint of the fatalism we saw in Stanza 8 ("Who pace a logic merciless as light"). Billie Potts addresses Joe Drew:

> "But after yore supper why don't you come
>
> .   .   .   .
>
> But not too early fer hit's my aim
> To git me some fun 'fore they know my name,
> And tease 'em and fun 'em, fer you never guessed
> I was Little Billie what went out West."

Warren interrupts the dramatic narrative once again at this point—just before the tragic action reaches its climax—with another parenthetical passage that reconsiders Billie's quest from the perspective of time present. And now Warren describes the motives that brought Billie Potts home—that bring all men home in one way or another, whether to some

community like that yearned for in such primitive works as the
Old English "The Wanderer" and "The Seafarer," or to some
previous state of faith and innocence like that depicted in
Wordsworth's "Intimations Ode," or to a spiritual home, as
envisioned in nearly all the world's great religions. Although
all the external aspects of Billie's life would seem to preclude
any spiritual sensitivity, yet in the end it is a spiritual
compulsion that calls him home, and the theme of the poem
shows the inescapable spiritual values that even these relatively
bestial people live by (Stanzas 29, 31):

> (Over the plain, over mountain and river, drawn,
>   Wanderer with slit-eyes adjusted to distance,
>   Drawn out of distance .   .   .
>
> You came back.
> For there is no place like home.)

Home is, then, the place of our final identity. It is, as
Warren defines it (Stanza 30), the place to which one hastens
when he suddenly discovers that his real essence does not exist
in any of the daily activities by which the world defines him:

> Though your luck held and the market was always satisfactory,
> Though the letter always came and your lovers were always
>   true,
>
>   .   .   .   .
>
> Though your hand never failed of its cunning and your glands
>   always thoroughly knew their business,
> Though your conscience was easy and you were assured of
>   your innocence,
> You became gradually aware that something was missing from
>   the picture,
> And upon closer inspection exclaimed: "Why I'm not in it at
>   all!"

One begins to seek self-definition, a knowledge of what is man and his destiny, when one becomes aware of time flowing (compare the "and it was morning and it was morning" setting—Stanza 29—of Billie's westward journey to the evening setting of his return), and when one perceives the incompleteness of his knowledge in the shadow of death:

> For nothing is ever all and nothing is ever all,
> For all your experience and your expertness of human vices
>   and of valor
> At the hour when the ways are darkened.

Now, as the narrative reaches its climax, Warren produces a rapid fusion of images. We note, to begin with, that the three central figures have remained exactly true to character all these years: the son has maintained a false identity for so long that he cannot resist deceiving the folks a little longer; the father is still the treacherous rascal he was when we last saw him (although, probably because of Billie's mishap, not now so prosperous); and the mother is the Evelike instigator of the crime against her progeny (" 'I figgered he was a ripe 'un,' the old man said. / 'Yeah, but you wouldn't done nuthen hadn't bin fer me,' the old woman said."—Stanza 33). The water imagery, representing time and identity, reaches its apex here. Significantly, it is his request for fresh water that brings Billie down to the spring, to the waters of remembrance. Stanza 33 shifts into an ironically lyrical tone as Billie, followed by his Pap with the bucket, heads down to "the spring in the dark of the trees." The mood is deathsome, here; night birds are singing ("the owl" and "whippoorwill") and the water is still and "black as ink / And one star in it caught through a chink." This lone star, the only light showing in the inky black waters ("And the star is there but it does not wink") reminds us of the "Time's unwinking eye" under which Billie began his odyssey back in Stanza 12. Just before his death, the star winks out (Time transformed into eternity)—"And the star is gone but there is his face"—and Billie has one last glimpse of his identity before his father's arm cuts him off: " 'Just help yoreself,' Big Billie said; / Then set the hatchet in his head." (Notice how ironically the characterization has followed through; Big Billie has here typically followed his own advice of Stanza 18: "The next time you try and pull a trick / Fer God's sake don't talk but do hit quick.")

The tragic act completed, Warren next uses his parenthetical form (as always from the perspective of time present) to conjecture in flashback about Billie's final glimpse of his identity: ".   .   . under your straining face you can scarcely mark / The darkling gleam of your face little less than the water dark." And looking into the dusk and dimness of the water (time past), Billie realizes that his true identity was lost long ago ("When childlike you lost it   .   .   ."— Stanza 35), in some archetypal period representing the youth and innocence of man. And yet, Warren asserts—venturing again past the border of knowledge into religious speculation—our real identity and purpose and knowledge of self still exist from back there in primeval time, waiting only to be discovered by man yearning and seeking for wholeness, offering potentially a communion more fundamental than even that of family:

> And years it lies here and dreams in the depth and grieves,
> More faithful than mother or father in the light or dark of the
>   leaves.

But the communion is not realized. Billie Potts' situation suggests (Stanzas 36–37) the philosophy of Paul Tillich, who has often commented upon the lack of depth in modern life and the inability of our civilization to regain the lost dimension:

> After waters that never quench the thirst in the throat that
>   parches,
> After the sleep that sieves the long day's dubieties   .   .   .
>   .   .   .   .
> You come, weary of greetings and the new friend's
>   smile.   .   .   .

Again Warren evokes Biblical implications as he envisions Billie in the role of the Prodigal Son:

> You come   .   .   .
>   .   .   .   worn with your wanderer's wile,
> Weary of innocence and the husks of Time,
> Prodigal, back to the homeland of no-Time.   .   .   .

Billie has, indeed, returned to "the homeland of no-Time," or to the eternity which produced him; but Warren at this point significantly departs from the Prodigal's story as Jesus told it. Insofar as the natural father is concerned, Warren sees Billie's inheritance in terms of original sin ("the patrimony of your crime") and hence, death ("What gift—oh, father, father—from that dissevering hand?"), for in the natural world, death is as much the gift of our fathers as life is. And yet, Warren now sees this truth in a broadly humanistic, as opposed to naturalistic, context. He does not recriminate against the nature of the universe, as he had in "The Mango on the Mango Tree," nor does he see man as a victim unjustly bandied about by circumstance. Originally, man is somehow responsible for his plight. No external force, but a human arm of human volition murdered Billie Potts, and even in this incident, the responsibility is divided between the individual man (Billie's father) and man as a universal creature, whose inherent nature Big Billie was only representing. There are also moral implications in the victim's role, for it was Billie's final deception, after years of refusing to divulge his identity (for fear of retribution), that led to his death.

Warren would forsake modern psychology in favor of the orthodox Christian view on this point: he feels that man must accept his responsibility for the past, with whatever guilt it may brand him, before man can really know himself. To disown, or to rationalize out of the moral sphere, the ugly aspects of man's nature—as modern psychology tends to do—is to leave available only a partial definition of man.

And indeed, Warren makes it very clear that whether we recognize our darker nature or not, evil will ultimately force knowledge of its presence upon us. We are reminded of the happy optimism that dominated our civilization just before World War I, when thinkers proclaimed that man was too enlightened to go to war in the modern age, but hardly had the chaos of that struggle been completed ("The war to end all wars") when a still more appalling demonstration of human depravity shook the world. And so, we in the modern age can understand the horror and dismay arising from the sudden insight into the true nature of the self that gripped these uncouth parents when they realized they had slain their dearly beloved son:

> "Ain't Billie, ain't Billie," the old woman cries,
> "Oh, hit ain't my Billie, fer he wuz little
> And helt to my skirt while I stirred the kittle
> And called me Mammy and hugged me tight. . . ."

We see again some possible Christian symbolism in this scene: just as the death of Jesus pointed up human guilt as well as offered absolution, so Billie's death suddenly made his parents aware of their darkling nature, even while their love for Billie showed what is redemptive in man.

The final stanza restores the poem conclusively to the perspective of time present. Here again the poem attains a lyrical tone, sorrowful but not (this being the narrator's own eulogy) primarily ironic. From this final tragic perspective, Warren recapitulates his themes for their final resolution. First he considers the profound yearning for home, amounting ultimately to a religious quest, which extends in analogy even to the lower reaches of the animal kingdom. This poetry is very moving in its appeal to something subconscious and intuitive:

> The bee knows, and the eel's cold ganglia burn,
> And the sad head lifting to the long return,
> Through brumal deeps   .   .   .
> Carries its knowledge, navigator without star.   .   .   .

Like the birds in Bryant's "To a Waterfowl," these creatures demonstrate an instinctive purpose and assertion of identity without conscious knowledge of them ("navigator without star"). Similarly, mankind is stirred by the deepest urges for identity, for purpose, for home, for final destiny; but man, having reason, encounters the additional problem of knowledge. It is not sufficient for him to journey unconsciously to a place of origin. He, having the religious dimension, must know *why* his life has the pattern it has:

> The salmon heaves at the fall, and, wanderer, you
> Heave at the great fall of Time, and gorgeous, gleam
>
> .   .   .   .
>
> In your plunge, fling, and plunge to the thunderous stream:
> Back to the silence, back to the pool.   .   .   .

Here the water imagery takes on a new meaning; in the religious or intuitive sense it *is* possible, Warren implies, to plunge back through time to the beginning. Mankind here is no longer merely a helpless observer seeing his face manipulated on the surface of the water as the river flows to and from he knows not where. Mankind joins the whole of the animate creation, as it were ("Brother to pinion and the pious fin that cleave / Their innocence of air and the disinfectant flood"), in the mighty quest, conscious or unconscious, for the meaning of existence. That Warren regards this quest as a religious one is evident in his broad use of religious terminology ("pious fin," "innocence of air," "disinfectant flood," "hope," and "humble promise"), and the implication that he considers it efficacious is seen in the prevailing of the quest against time:

> And bear through that limitless and devouring fluidity
> The itch and humble promise which is home.

For mankind, this quest has tragic implications, as evidenced in the death of Billie Potts and in this final resolution of the poem ("And you, wanderer, back, / For the beginning is death . . ."). This tragic ending shows that in many ways the knowledge of death (spiritual or physical) is the beginning of our quest (much as in T. S. Eliot's *The Waste Land*, which begins with "The Burial of the Dead"). But "the end," Warren affirms, "may be life." For as "the beginning was definition" in a tragic sense, meaning the delimitation of man in terms of time and sin and death, so perhaps "the end may be definition" in a liberating sense, meaning the redemption of man from these evils upon the completion of the as yet inscrutable pattern of his destiny.

It is with this ultimate perspective of man, acknowledging, in the fable of Billie Potts, man's guilt but recognizing his religious quest and his redemptive qualities, that Warren declares: "And our innocence needs, perhaps, new definition." Warren explains this thought further in the lines that follow, making clear in explicit religious imagery that he is not speaking of a Freudian all-justifying innocence:

> And the wick needs the flame
> But the flame needs the wick.

This passage connotes a compromise between the ideal of perfection and the reality of human fallibility: the flame, an ancient religious symbol of purification, feeds upon the impure, transforming it gradually with time.

"And the father waits for the son." Again, the poet evokes—in restating the main theme of the poem—the idea of a pattern awaiting fulfillment in time. This pattern is the fundamental one in human experience; it is the relationship of father and son, the contact of time past and time future, the natural justification for the existence of the passing generations, and above all, the hope of some ultimate meaning in this visible perpetuation of the self—the one possibly permanent work of the self in all of the natural world.

This pattern extends beyond the natural world, moreover, as the poem makes clear in the last stanza, while reaching its greatest religious intensity. Here the mythical connotations merely hinted at in the first stanzas become powerfully explicit, and the Christian symbolism emerges tragically clear. For the pattern, as the Potts fable showed us, is broken; the son has been slain by the father, just as the Second Adam was slain for the sins of the First:

> And you, wanderer, back,
> After the striving and the wind's word,
> To kneel
>
> .   .   .   .   .
>
> At the feet of the old man
> Who is evil and ignorant and old.   .   .   .

Thus Warren presents the final picture of the poem: two archetypal figures representing in terrible simplicity and power the human situation—representing, in fact, the two prime aspects of human nature. There stands the old man ("who is evil and ignorant and old"), representing the inherent depravity in the nature of man—the patrimony of evil, or original sin, which means death. And beneath him kneels, in agonizing submission, the son—the religious nature of man, enduring ("in the sacramental silence of evening") with Christlike humility (the kneeling posture reminds us of the "humble promise" above) even the death which is his heritage.

Whether the old man, "evil and ignorant and old," represents a guilt-ridden God (like the God in "The Mango on the Mango Tree") as well as man, the fallen Adam, is a problem that has bothered some critics.[17] It seems unlikely to me that Big Billie Potts is to be construed as an image of God, even of the jealous tribal God of the Old Testament. He simply does not have the credentials of supernatural omnipotence which even a naturalistic God of hate must have in order to be a responsible God. Big Billie's one Godlike function, as giver of life and death, is too commonplace in human experience to elevate its owner to divine status. Rather than representing the malicious God of "The Mango Tree," Big Billie Potts instead embodies the dark inner self which awaited embracing in *Eleven Poems on the Same Theme*. He represents the unconscious self, "mankind's collective dark shadow," which was locked outdoors in "Original Sin" and was murdered in "Crime." The negative image of God in "The Mango Tree," we must remember, was accompanied by a corresponding assertion of innocence on the part of the naturalistic narrator. Here in "Billie Potts," where such innocence is disavowed, the image of God (if there were one) must correspondingly gain absolution as mankind accepts its share of responsibility for the universal guilt and isolation. But in such acceptance there is, paradoxically, a hope of redemption. In his submission, in his acknowledgment of inherent sin (the first condition of salvation in orthodox Christianity) and his acceptance of the death it entails, the son achieves the object of his lifelong quest. The final symbol of the poem is that of personal identity—the little black birthmark that was "his luck." Located significantly over the heart ("under his left tit"), this little mark, which had at birth distinguished Billie Potts from all the other men about him, had been carried indelibly with him through all his years of exile. It had accompanied him all the way, lying immutable beneath "the new name and new face" that were ever-changing on the surface, and composing, in its immutability and in its singularity, Billie's "luck": his final identity, his determinate distinction from the outer world in which all his surface features were blended and lost among those of other men. The black mark signified the past, which Billie Potts ran from and thought he had eluded, but to which he inevitably returned. Time had provided a disguise that fooled even Billie's parents, but even time had not altered the black spot. The ultimate identity of the individual was as immobile and secure and undeniable as the past itself, from which it had originated. And since in no wise did the individual create himself—the utmost extent of his powers lay in the province of self-discovery, not self-creation—his identity was basically his "luck."

In conclusion, the definition of man as Warren conceives it in "The Ballad of Billie Potts" involves a great range and depth of speculation, although the poem is superficially in the mode of local color. The poem ranges from the tragic perspective of archetypal myth to the comic representation of a here-and-now episode on the highway. It ranges in form from sorrowful lyric to blustering parody. The plot and theme rise directly out of the characters, and it is in the characters that the final resolution occurs.

With the rustic on the highway, the readers, and, finally, the narrator himself forming the complete spectrum of perceptive sensitivity, three symbolic characters of the past are scrutinized from the perspective of time present. The journey of Billie to his ancestral home is like the quest of many other Warren characters—some, like Jack Burden, fully conscious of their motivation, and others, like Billie, seeking unconsciously for clues to their identity. The thematic scheme in this respect is much like T. S. Eliot's return to his ancestral home in the "Burnt Norton" and "East Coker" sections of *Four Quartets*, and it bears an even closer resemblance to Charles Bon's fatalistic return to the Sutpen plantation in search of identity in Faulkner's *Absalom! Absalom!* The father's character, and even Sutpen's "luck," is quite similar in this novel to that of the father of Billie Potts, and in both cases the father's pattern of living brings both father and son to mutual ruin.

But in the final scene of son kneeling to father in evening dusk, there is, despite the ruin and despite the encroaching dark, a hint of redemption. And in this return home there is at last, positively and finally, the establishment of individual identity. A possible end may thus be anticipated for Warren's long, dark night of the soul. Perhaps a dawn is dimly foreseen as the son waits in darkness. Thus, the hatchet blow of the father—his gift of death—may yet have positive value after all, as Walt Whitman surmised in "Song of Myself" (Stanza 6): ". . . to die is different from what any one supposed, and luckier."

CHAPTER TWO

Brother to Dragons:
"Warren's Best Book"

WHEN *BROTHER TO DRAGONS* came out in 1953, its reviewers were inclined to show deep admiration. "An event, a great one," was Randall Jarrell's opinion, as he sought to substantiate his judgment that "this is Robert Penn Warren's best book." [1] Another of Warren's fellow poets, Delmore Schwartz, likewise evinced high enthusiasm, calling *Brother to Dragons* "a work which is most remarkable as a sustained whole," a work having "perfect proportion throughout." [2] Both these reviewers, furthermore, placed Warren in some very distinguished company on the basis of this work, Jarrell by finding echoes of Milton, Shakespeare, and Eliot, and Schwartz by observing "Warren's resemblance to Melville."

In the wake of high praise such as this, one might have expected serious, full-length studies to appear soon after. Curiously, such was not to happen. Only one really significant, comprehensive study of the poem has come forward, that being Frederick McDowell's "Psychology and Theme in *Brother to Dragons*." [3] This very perceptive article, by discussing the theme in terms of character analysis (or character psychoanalysis), helped us to understand *Brother to Dragons* as a drama, or play, and as such was indeed useful. But *Brother to Dragons* is not only a play. It is a poem—a "dramatic poem," its author tells us—and so it requires poetic as well as dramatic analysis.

In viewing *Brother to Dragons* as a dramatic poem, rather than a poetic drama, we find the structure of the work depending not so much on characterization as on a finely wrought pattern of images, images calculated to transmit Warren's theme to the reader in a subtle but convincing way. Unfortunately, this imagery appears to have been a bit too subtle for many readers: although it permits Warren to avoid mere didacticism, so distasteful to the modern temper, this framework of images carries a high risk of leakage of meaning in so long and complex a work. I propose to reduce that leakage by tracing out the poem's master metaphor—the beast image—and its two major subsidiary metaphors, the Lewis house (the house of the psyche) and the twice-recurring winter setting (the winter of philosophic naturalism). These dominant and interrelating image patterns bear the major burden of Warren's theme, and I should like to consider each in its turn.

Since Warren nowhere tells the source of his title allusion, it may at first surprise the reader to find that the title of his most celebrated poetic achievement comes from the most ancient book of the Bible, the Book of Job (30:29): "I am a brother to dragons and a companion to owls." As the poem develops, however, the reference becomes clear. The occasion of Job's complaint is his feeling of resentment towards his Maker for bringing intolerable humiliation upon him. The loss of wealth and family and even his physical torment he could possibly abide, but the humiliation is another matter: "But now they that are younger than I have me in derision, whose fathers I would have disdained to have set with the dogs of my flock" (Job 30:1).

It is most revealing to observe that Warren's attention is focused not on Job's suffering and loss and endurance but upon the one thing he could not endure, his loss of pride. Being a brother to dragons and a companion to owls, after all, is a fate singularly undeserved for a man who had always (like Thomas Jefferson) walked "upright and perfect . . . and eschewed evil." "Did I not"—Job puts the question bitterly—"Did I not weep for him that was in trouble? was not my soul grieved for the poor?" (30:25). And all Job gets for a lifetime of high-minded service, tendered in absolute innocence, is ridicule at the hands of "base men   .   .   .   viler than the earth" (30:8–9):

> They were children of fools, yea, children of base men:
>   they were viler than the earth.
> And now am I their song,
>   yea, I am their byword.

Job's bitterness at finding himself a "brother to dragons" (a condition he actually refuses to admit until the very end of the Book of Job) provides a most satisfactory analogy to the attitude of Warren's Thomas Jefferson. Both men lacked, in Warren's estimation, the sense of limitation which is essential to the religious attitude. Both thought themselves freed, by dint of an absolute virtue, from the common human contamination. Even Divinity must surely recognize their triumph, their disentanglement from the influence of the Fall, they would contend. Surely God, if He be just and true, could not fail to distinguish the righteous from "base men . . . viler than the earth."

But, of course, Warren does not grant such a distinction. Humanity's black collective shadow, the acknowledgment of which formed the crux of *Eleven Poems on the Same Theme*, belongs as much to a Job or a Thomas Jefferson, for all their innocence and virtue, as to all the rest of mankind. Warren's answer to Job's complaint of injustice, then, is to fling Job's own protest back at him shorn of its original sarcasm: You are indeed a brother to dragons, Brother Job (and Brother Jefferson). And so we have the poem's master metaphor, its dominant and most recurrent image.

The exact meaning of this master metaphor has not, I feel, been completely or properly understood. Critics have been inclined to lean too heavily on the significance of one particular use of the beast-image, ignoring its recurrence. Such an approach would be useful if the beast-image meant the same thing each time it appears, but it does not: like Melville's whale, Warren's beast has a different meaning for each of his characters. Thus I believe that George Palmer Garrett and Frederick McDowell err when they agree in viewing "the birth of the minotaur and the creation of the Labyrinth" as "a symbol which dominates the poem." [4] This is actually only Thomas Jefferson's view of the beast within the self, and it is a view badly distorted by an excess of outrage and revulsion.

For this reason, the minotaur image, though in itself a masterpiece of poetic brilliance and power, is only briefly handled. After the first few pages, it gives way to something more akin to the title image, "dragons." Here I refer to the serpent seen by R.P.W. with startled fright, but without outrage or revulsion.

Because R.P.W. lacks Jefferson's outrage and revulsion—because, that is, R.P.W. has (like Melville's Ishmael) the most comprehensive and objective perspective of anyone in the story—we must consider his vision of the beast-image to be the most accurate and crucial of them all. The actual dominant symbol of the poem, then—to which the minotaur image is related but subordinate—initially appears as R.P.W. describes his first visit, in the heat of summer, to the ruined home site on the hill:

> I went up close to view the ruin, and then
> It happened.   .   .   .
>
> .   .   .   .
>
> In some black aperture among the stones
> I saw the eyes, their glitter in that dark,
> And suddenly the head thrust forth, and the fat, black
> Body molten flowed, as though those stones
> Bled forth earth's inner darkness to the day.   .   .   .[5]

We have seen this fellow before somewhere. To be specific, he first appeared in *Eleven Poems on the Same Theme*, where in such poems as "Crime" and "Original Sin" he lay toadlike in the "hutch and hole" of the "cellar-dark," and was later repudiated altogether by the conscious mind and locked out of the mind's metaphorical house. He reappears here in *Brother to Dragons*, however, in truly awesome magnitude, for in this tale of subconscious depravity he can no longer be locked out by even so high-minded a consciousness as Jefferson's. His existence, as this tale (drawn from actual history) proves, is real; the "fat, black" serpent rising from "earth's inner darkness" represents the unconscious self, which "haunts beneath earth's primal, soldered sill, / And in its slow and merciless ease, sleepless, lolls / Below that threshold where the prime waters sleep" (p. 33).

Because of its central importance in the poem, Warren devotes several pages to this first encounter of R.P.W. and the serpent. The poet's highest powers of imagination go into this attempt to describe the emergence of the inner self from "earth's inner darkness to the day." Transmuted by the viewer's imagination, this perfectly natural serpent ("just a snake") attains a mythical superstature appropriate to its symbolizing of the unconscious self (p. 33):

> Thus it flowed forth, and the scaled belly of abomination
> Rustled on stone, rose, rose up. . . .
> I saw it rise, saw the soiled white of the belly bulge,
> And in that muscular distension I saw the black side scales
> Show their faint flange and tracery of white.
> And so it rose and climbed the paralyzed light.
> On those heaped stones it was taller than I, taller
> Than any man, and the swollen head hung
> Haloed and high in light. . . .

"Taller than any man," R.P.W. called it, as his "natural tremor of fatigue converted to the metaphysical chill" and his "soul sat in [his] hand and could not move." But being a representative of modern man, R.P.W. quickly assures himself that "after all, the manifestation was only natural." This was not, surely, the serpent whose archetype appears throughout the history of religion in various civilizations: "Not Apophis

that Egypt feared, / . . . Nor that Nidhogg whose cum-
brous coils and cold dung chill / The root of the world's tree,
nor even / Eve's interlocutor by Eden's bough." It was not
even a "Freudian principle": "Nor symbol of that black lust all
men fear and long for / Rising from earth to shake the
summer sky." (Warren specifically rejects the "Freudian
principle," I am sure, in an effort to discourage those critics
who insist on reading all literature as sexual allegory.)

But if the snake is neither a traditional religious image nor
a Freudian principle of sexuality, neither is he (despite
R.P.W.'s scientific classifications) "just a snake." His rising
"taller than any man" evokes too many parallels in other parts
of the poem for us to be able to dismiss his appearance so
easily. The first such parallel, the beast-image rising "taller
than any man," appears in connection with Jefferson's minotaur image at the poem's beginning. At that time, however, the
image of man's unconscious self seemed to Jefferson, rapt in
his folly of joy, not a beast but an angel (p. 9):

> . . . I was nothing, nothing but joy,
> And my heart cried out, "Oh, this is Man!"
>
> And thus my minotaur. There at the blind
> Blank labyrinthine turn of my personal time,
> I met the beast. . . .
> . . . .
> . . . But no beast then: the towering
> Definition, angelic, arrogant, abstract,
> Greaved in glory, thewed with light, the bright
> Brow tall as dawn.

As we shall see, Jefferson will have plenty of time to correct his
mistaken impression of the nature of man's innermost self.
This revision, in fact, will constitute the main substance of

Jefferson's commentary until his final speech of the poem, where he finally accepts the beast within the self as neither minotaur nor angel but deeply human.

The third major occurrence of this beast-image in *Brother to Dragons* arises in connection with the third major character, Lilburn. The first two occurrences, noted above, represent the beast-image as seen by the other two of the poem's three main characters, R.P.W. and Thomas Jefferson. What distinguishes Lilburn's version of the beast "taller than any man" is that Lilburn does not *see* the horrendous inner self; he *is* that darksome entity. I do not mean to oversimplify Lilburn's position in the poem, for Warren takes great pains to emphasize throughout the work that Lilburn is not *merely* the monster-self which Jefferson tries so hard to exorcise. Lilburn is, as R.P.W.'s consistent sympathy with him ("poor Lilburn") is intended to show, a real, recognizable, commonplace human being, motivated by an understandable though horribly perverted love for his mother. It is clear, however, that Lilburn does embody personally that dimension of unconscious evil which the serpent symbolizes and which is present, whether acknowledged or not, whether active or latent, in every man. Our authority for this identification of Lilburn with R.P.W.'s serpent and Jefferson's minotaur is the hapless Laetitia, seer and (aware or unaware) exponent of truth in the poem.

The occasion of Laetitia's vision is the scene where Lilburn persuades her to describe in words, and wickedly to relish such telling, the "awful thing"—something unspeakably carnal— he had done to her the previous night. ("Then he did it. And it was an awful thing / I didn't even know the name of, or heard tell"—p. 75.) After she finally "said the words," and Lilburn answered, "Now didn't you like it some, and even to tell me?" this is what she saw (p. 79):

And sudden rose up from my side,
And stood up tall like he would fill the room,
And fill the house maybe, and split the walls,
And nighttime would come pouring in like flood,
And he was big all sudden, and no man
Was ever big like that, and way up there
His face was terrible and in its dark,

.   .   .   .

His eyes were shining, but they shone so dark.

Like the serpent "taller than any man," Lilburn assumes a symbolic superstature ("no man / Was ever big like that") that identifies him with the monster-self in the subconscious and foreshadows the greater "awful thing" around which the story is woven, the incident in the meat house.

In addition to the above passages, the image of the beast within the self recurs at least a dozen separate times within the poem, the recurrence in each case being colored by the speaker's individual perspective. Jefferson always speaks of it in bitterness and sarcasm, his voice filled with loathing for both the conscious self, aspiring futilely for sainthood or heroism, and the monster-self within that thwarts such aspiration (p. 42):

And as for the heroes, every one,
.   .   .   .   .   .
The saints and angels, too, who tread, yes, every
And single one, but plays the sad child's play
And old charade where man puts down the bad and then feels
          good.
It is the sadistic farce by which the world is cleansed.
And is not cleansed, for in the deep
Hovel of the heart that Thing lies
That will never unkennel himself to the contemptible steel,
Nor needs to venture forth ever, for all sustenance

Comes in to him, the world comes in, and is his,
And supine yearns for the defilement of his slavering fang.

(Jefferson's description of the beast within as "that Thing," we
may note in passing, probably ties in with the "awful thing"—
again undefined—which Lilburn did to Laetitia and which
subsequently gave rise to her vision of Lilburn standing "tall
like he would fill the room, And   . . .   house, maybe, and
split the walls.") On one very important point, Jefferson is
wrong about the nature of "that Thing" within the "Hovel of
the heart." He claims it will "never unkennel himself" to the
"contemptible steel," but the truth is that the monster-
self continually unkennels itself (as its prototype did in
"Original Sin" and others of the *Eleven Poems*), even at the
risk of repudiation and destruction (and both befall Lilburn),
in the hope of attaining acknowledgment and definition. It is
only Jefferson's excess of revulsion which blinds him, until the
poem's resolution, to the more redemptive possibilities of the
deeper self.

This master metaphor recurs again with the appearance of
Meriwether Lewis, whose bitter accusations against his uncle
finally bring Jefferson to an awareness of his own part in the
universal complicity, and thus to an acceptance of Lilburn.
Meriwether's recollection of having slain a wolf and a bear,
both rather extraordinary creatures ("*This day a yellow wolf
was slain*," and "We slew the great bear, / The horrible one"),
seems to tie in with the theme of the beast within the self,
though the correlation is not explicitly indicated (pp. 179,
180). The connection, if there is one, would be ironic, since, as
Meriwether finds out upon his return to civilization, no
amount of dragon-slaying will avail against the dragon in the
human heart. It is interesting to note, in this connection, the

similarity between Bates and Jefferson's description of the
minotaur, who "hulked . . . hock-deep in ordure, its
beard / And shag foul-scabbed, and when the hoof-
heaves— / Listen!—the foulness sucks like mire" (p. 7).
Bates' heart, "ordure" and all, is a suitable home for this
creature: "And treachery gleamed like green slime in the
backwater.— / That Bates, whose hell-heart is a sink and a
bog / Of ordure—that Bates, he smiled. He stank in sunshine"
(p. 182).

By far the most frequent and most significant references to
the beast-image, the master metaphor, come from the tongue
of R.P.W., the spokesman for modern man and the chief
advocate of reconciliation in the poem. In his desire to effect a
reunification of the divided self, conscious self and unconscious (Jefferson and Lilburn), R.P.W. always speaks in a
temperate voice, urging understanding, acknowledgment, and
acceptance, even though he clearly identifies the inner self
with the monstrous collective guilt of mankind which theolo-
gians call "original sin" (p. 64):

> And there's always and forever
> Enough of guilt to rise and coil like miasma
> From the fat sump and cess of common consciousness
> To make any particular hour seem most appropriate
> For Gabriel's big tootle.

Probably the most obscure and complex, though a very
significant, version of the "beast within" metaphor is that of
the catfish with "the face of the last torturer" underneath the
Mississippi ice (p. 94):

> The ice is a foot thick, and beneath, the water slides black like
>   a dream,

And in the interior of that unpulsing blackness and thrilled
zero
The big channel-cat sleeps with eye lidless, and the brute face
Is the face of the last torturer, and the white belly
Brushes the delicious and icy blackness of mud.

Warren has frequently used water imagery—as in "The Ballad of Billie Potts," for example—as an archetype for time flowing into the sea of eternity, but here the meaning of the river is, I think, quite different. Although the movement of time may be related to this usage, the primary meaning of the river is that which the metaphysical poets were so fond of exploring in their comparisons of macrocosm to microcosm. John Donne comments in "Meditation Four" that "the whole world hath nothing, to which something in man doth not answer," and in filling out the details of this comparison Donne makes, in passing, the exact analogy which Warren is driving at above: "If all the Veines in our bodies, were extended to Rivers."

In the "catfish" passage, Warren does extend the collective "Veines" of mankind into a river (and the Father of Waters at that), at the bottom of which is the familiar face of our collective unconscious, the bestial, never-sleeping ("with eye lidless") inner man wantonly delighting in the "delicious" muck and ooze of the channel-bottom. The "unpulsing blackness" where he makes his home, far beneath the star-lit world of the conscious mind above the ice (the "pulsing" world of time), should remind us of the "blind dark" wherein dwelt Jefferson's minotaur and of the "earth's inner darkness" out of which R.P.W.'s serpent appeared.

The distinctive feature of the catfish image, that which elevates its significance above most recurrences of the master metaphor, is its extension from the psychological realm into the theological. In its perfect adjustment to its environs,

primeval as they are, the unconscious self has attained absolute
identity and, thereby, oneness with God (p. 94):

> . . . there is no sensation. How can there be
> Sensation when there is perfect adjustment? The blood
> Of the creature is but the temperature of the sustaining flow:
> The catfish is in the Mississippi and
> The Mississippi is in the catfish and
> Under the ice both are at one with God.
> Would that we were!

Repugnant as it appears, the inner self has something which
the conscious self has not, and wants desperately. Its being "at
one with God" ("Would that we were!") pretty well obviates
its lack of respectability, in the end. In this synthesis of
psychology and theism we are reminded of C. G. Jung's
contention that the unconscious is the only accessible source
of religious experience.[6] The way to God is not onward and
upward, but the way back and the way down, until the
conscious self besmirches its sanctity in the primeval slime,
"the delicious and icy blackness of mud" where our catfish
brother awaits "with lidless eye" our brotherly embrace.
There, incredibly, unreasonably, may be found oneness with
God, that state in which the unified self finds at last its
absolute identity, which is all the surface self has ever longed
for.

The major point that needs to be clarified about the master
metaphor concerns the relationship between the conscious and
the unconscious self, a relationship that was the central subject
of *Eleven Poems on the Same Theme* and which continues to
be the central theme in *Brother to Dragons*, where the drift of
events centers on the efforts of Lucy Lewis and R.P.W. to
reconcile Jefferson to Lilburn.[7] Up until the very end, Jefferson

stoutly maintains his individual sanctity, for after all, *he* had
not wielded any meat-axe (p. 188):

> JEFFERSON: But I know this, I'll have no part, no matter
> What responsibility you yourself wish.
>   LUCY: I do not wish it. But how can I flee what is nearer
> Than hands or feet, and more inward than my breath?

Even up to three pages before his exit from the poem,
Jefferson can recoil in indignation at the suggestion that he
take Lilburn's hand ("take it, and the blood slick on it?"—p.
191), but he breaks down at last and begins to see the truth as
Lucy and R.P.W. see it. This final vision of universal complicity, a vision espousing Warren's characteristic tragic view of
the human condition, sees all human good not as "given," in
the manner presumed by the Romantic utopians, but as
earned out of the general human "wrath" and "guilt" and
suffering "in the midst of our coiling darkness" (p. 195):

> We must strike the steel of wrath on the stone of guilt,
> And hope to provoke, thus, in the midst of our coiling
>   darkness
> The incandescence of the heart's great flare.
> And in that illumination I should hope to see
> How all creation validates itself.   .   .   .

"Nothing   .   .   . / Is lost," Jefferson goes on to say, and
follows that fundamental Warren premise with another: "All
is redeemed, / In knowledge." That such knowledge includes
acknowledgment of the monster-self within, the catfish in the
general human bloodstream, is clear enough, for Jefferson goes
on to say that "knowledge   .   .   .   is the bitter bread." But
bitter or not, Jefferson partakes at last of that communion
symbol—"I have eaten the bitter bread"—and so earns, in his
last speech of the poem, access to lasting joy: "In joy, I would

end" (pp. 195, 196). This joy, which stands in contrast to the delusory jubilation when Jefferson thought man an angel, comes from his two-part reconciliation, involving, on one hand, an acceptance by the conscious self of the darker self, the beast in the labyrinth (Lilburn), and on the other hand, a return of the awakened, self-knowing individual to the group.

This reconciliation of Jefferson to his darker self within paves the way for R.P.W.'s lengthy synthesis which ends the poem. Here the serpent-self, his recognition accomplished at last, sinks back into "earth's dark inwardness" again, imperturbable (like the catfish) in his timeless dark (p. 208):

> Down in the rocks . . .   looped and snug
> And dark as dark: in dark the white belly glows,
> And deep behind the hog-snout, in that blunt head,
> The ganglia glow with what cold dream is congenial
> To fat old *obsoleta*, winter-long.

(The serpent's scientific name, we may note in passing, is particularly useful to Warren's purpose in an ironic way, for the whole scheme of the poem is calculated to show that "old *obsoleta*," as a symbol of something innate in human nature, is not really "obsolete" after all, even in an age which has repudiated the notion of original sin, the alleged brotherhood with mythical dragons.) Here, too, in his concluding synthesis, R.P.W. specifically identifies himself and his age with Lilburn's crime ("We have lifted the meat-axe in the elation of love and justice"—p. 213), and he later apprehends, as did Jefferson, something redemptive in such painful awareness of guilt: "The recognition of complicity is the beginning of innocence" (p. 214). "And our innocence needs, perhaps, new definition," Warren had said at the end of "The Ballad of

Billie Potts"; here, at the end of *Brother to Dragons,* our innocence has achieved that "new definition," and has achieved it, paradoxically, through a descent to the ooze at the river's bottom, through an acceptance of guilt and complicity, through reconnecting the lines of communication between the conscious self, aspiring toward sanctity, and the unconscious self, polluted, bestial dweller in darkness.

This matter of communication between the conscious self and the unconscious is, as I have said, the crucial issue in *Brother to Dragons* as in much of Warren's earlier verse. As in Warren's earlier verse, also, and with particular reference to *Eleven Poems on the Same Theme,* the initial overtures are made by the deeper self, the beast in the labyrinth, the serpent-self which the conscious mind tries so hard to repudiate. In contrast to the surface self, aloof in its pride and sanctity, the deeper self appears not so monstrous after all. Instead, it comes forward in shy, sad humility, begging and giving forgiveness simultaneously, asking only to be reunited with its brother self, the conscious identity. Unlike Jefferson, R.P.W. had seen this redemptive aspect of the deeper self in his first encounter with the serpent (p. 35):

> .   .   .   he reared
> Up high, and scared me, for a fact. But then
> The bloat head sagged an inch, the tongue withdrew,
> And on the top of that strong stalk the head
> Wagged slow, benevolent and sad and sage,
> As though it understood our human pitifulness
> And forgave all, and asked forgiveness, too.

This remarkable passage may well be the most important key to the poem, for it anticipates the moral and thematic resolution of the tale. All that remains after this vision, this "moment of possibility" (as Warren calls it in "Gull's Cry," in *Promises*), is to get Jefferson and all he stands for in the modern world to see it too, and thus to restore the broken lines of communication. The deeper self, "benevolent and sad and sage" under its brute countenance, patiently awaits the necessary, redeeming embrace throughout the remainder of the poem. Because of this redemptive humility and need, the monster-self transcends its loathsomeness in the end. The "sad and sage" head sagging in the above passage thereby takes its place alongside the similar brute faces we have seen in Warren's earlier verse, the "sad head lifting to the long return, / Through brumal deeps" at the end of "The Ballad of Billie Potts," and the even sadder face in "Original Sin: A Short Story" (in *Eleven Poems*), the face that "whimpers and is gone" in the fashion of "the old hound that used to snuffle your door and moan."

Of the remaining recurrences of the master metaphor, two in particular deserve mention. The first of these shows that Jefferson's darker self, Lilburn, has his own inner self as well, and that both Jefferson and Lilburn are guilty of the same butchery in the end, though Jefferson's act of mutilation is spiritual, Lilburn's physical. It is Lucy Lewis who calls her brother's attention to the damaging analogy (p. 189):

> He saw poor George as but his darkest self
> And all the possibility of the dark that he feared,
> And so he struck, and struck down that darkest self,
>
> .   .   .   .
> And   .   .   .   in your rejection you repeat the crime.
> Over and over, and more monstrous still,
> For what poor Lilburn did in exaltation of madness
> You do in vanity.   .   .   .

The other reference to the monster-self, and the last I shall
consider, is the face whose "red eye" glares in spontaneous
hatred at R.P.W. on the highway (p. 15). The occasion of this
apparition, it is worth noting, is the ironic contrast Warren
sets up between Jefferson's idyllic vision of the Promised Land,
his West, and the actual waste land on which, amid flies,
R.P.W. urinates (making appropriate answer to Eliot's prayer,
"If there were only water"). Jefferson's vision of the West,
"great Canaan's grander counterfeit," was originally paradisia-
cal (p. 11):

>   . . . like the Israelite,
> From some high pass or crazy crag of mind . . .
> I saw all,
> Swale and savannah and the tulip-tree
> Immortally blossoming to May,
> Hawthorn and haw,
> Valleys extended and prairies idle and the land's
> Long westward languour lifting toward the flaming
>   escarpment at the end of day.

Through the handiwork of Jefferson's protege, the Common
Man, the Promised Land has devolved into a waste land by the
time R.P.W. comes ripping over the highway a century and a
half later, there to encounter the unforgiving red eye of New
Canaan's present inhabitant (p. 15):

> We ripped the July dazzle on the slab—
> July of '46—ripped through the sun-bit land:
> Blunt hills eroded red, stunt-oak, scrag-plum,
> The ruined coal-tipple and the blistered town,
> And farther on, from the shade of a shack flung down
> Amid the sage-grass by the blasted field,
> A face fixed at us and the red eye glared
> Without forgiveness, and will not forgive.

The ferocity of hatred in this red glare, casual, anonymous, and impersonal as the hatred is, carries forward the beast-image into the realm of time present, I should say, and into a permanent time present, moreover—into the "any time" Warren speaks of in his headnote. And though R.P.W. says, "But touch the accelerator and quick you're gone / Beyond forgiveness, pity, hope, hate, love," he knows very well that he cannot really escape the red eye's pitiful malediction. As a matter of fact, R.P.W. himself helps to perpetuate the general cursedness of things when, the accelerator being abandoned by reason of a natural compulsion, he spatters the parched earth with hot urine, while the sunlight screams and a million July-flies voice their "simultaneous outrage" at what he has done (p. 15):

> So we ripped on, but later when the road
> Was empty, stopped just once to void the bladder,
> And in that stunning silence after the tire's song
> The July-fly screamed like a nerve gone wild,
> Screamed like a dentist's drill, and then a million
> Took up the job, and in that simultaneous outrage
> The sunlight screamed, while urine spattered the parched soil.

There are those who take exception to passages such as the one above, which are not unusual in Warren's poetry, on the grounds that such coarseness and crudity is offensive and unnecessary. With respect to such responses, I would like to conclude this part of my discussion by rendering a personal opinion. Most of the time Warren's humor, whether coarse or delicate, is absolutely functional; the passage above, as I have read it, is a case in point. But even aside from its technical function in any particular context, Warren's humor and irony deserve nothing but our deepest gratitude, it seems to me. In an age of carefully self-protective and self-conscious poets, Robert Penn Warren has written poetry with a broad, generous, manly irony that gives his work a refreshing, almost unique quality, by comparison with which even the work of so great an ironist as T. S. Eliot seems frequently lacking. Warren's irony, unlike Eliot's, is never petty, cruel, or superior. More than that, it is never (except in his very early poems) self-pitying. For all his involvement with the Puritan Mind, which is especially evident in his concern with "original sin," it is clear that Warren does not commit the fundamental Puritan error of taking himself (so far as his conscious identity is concerned) too seriously. His poetry is enriched, surely, by such unstinting, straightforward giving of himself to his art.

Up to now, I have considered the master metaphor, the motif of the beast within the self, pretty much on its own terms, exploring its inner meanings and implications in this and earlier poems. I think this has been the proper approach to the poem, for it is a work that deals primarily with the inner darkness of man, that sense of debasement which led Job to complain about being a "brother to dragons." The title allusion clearly indicates that Warren's central concern is what we might describe as the inner dimension of the dark night of the soul: a sense of moral anxiety. Here as in previous poems, the search for identity begins with a journey inward and downward through fearsome pollution and darkness.

It is important to note, however, that Warren places this central theme within a larger perspective—within, ultimately, the largest possible perspective. That largest perspective would relate to the external dimension of darkness, that part of the dark night of the soul which relates the individual man to final reality—an immensity of time and cosmos that leads finite, transient man to despair of his own significance. This perspective is the main substance of R.P.W.'s lengthy concluding statement, which takes place after the poem's main issue has been satisfactorily resolved, Jefferson having acknowledged his darker self and the serpent having withdrawn into his primal, subterranean drowse.

Warren begins to develop this larger perspective quite early in the poem. R.P.W.'s first long speech, in fact, places the events of the story in the vast, minimizing perspective of time. Speaking of the long-vanished Ohio boatmen, who represent the generations of man on the river of time, Warren recapitulates the time perspective we saw in "The Ballad of Billie Potts." The narrator is particularly moved here by the hearty strength with which those vanished forefathers of ours undertook their one-way river journey (p. 17):

> Haired hand on the sweep, and the haired lip lifts for song,
> And the leathery heart foreknows the end and knows it will
>   not be long,
> For a journey is only a journey and only Time is long,
> And a river is only water. Time only will always flow.   .   .   .
>   .   .   .   .
> The last keel passes, it is drawing night.

We shall see this river image several times again in the poem. One instance, which I have already touched upon, is the passage about the catfish in the Mississippi mud. Another is R.P.W.'s vision of "All men, a flood upon the flood," as the poem ends (p. 210). Still a different variation of this motif is the glimpse R.P.W. has, near the end of his first long speech, of a "lost clan feasting" at nightfall by the sea of eternity. This image parallels T. S. Eliot's vision of his ancestors' merriment in "East Coker." Whereas Eliot saw "Feet rising and falling. Eating and drinking. Dung and death," Warren sees "a lost clan feasting while their single fire / Flared red and green with sea-salt, and the night fell— / Shellfish and artifact, blacked bone and shard, / Left on the sea-lapped shore, and the sea was Time" (p. 21).

In addition to these images suggesting the immensity of time, there are also a number of passages in *Brother to Dragons* bespeaking the vastness of space, the purpose here also being to place "the human project," as Warren later calls it, in its proper perspective. Jefferson begins this motif when he says, "I was born in the shadow of the great forest" (p. 37). Although this dark forest may have Biblical allusions, most likely to the myth of Adam and Eve being cast out of Eden because of Original Sin, it is likely also that this "great forest" has naturalistic connotations suggesting, in a manner reminiscent of Faulkner's "The Bear," the vast unconquerable wilderness of nature against which the encroachments of human civilization seem negligible. R.P.W. takes up this motif a few pages later when, commenting on "the massive dark of forest," he observes that "the forest reaches / A thousand miles in darkness beyond the frail human project" (p. 45).

This sense of nature's all-encompassing vastness reaches its consummation towards the middle of the poem when R.P.W. describes the coming of winter in the *annus mirabilis*. The lyric power of this passage and its breadth of imagination make it one of the most moving reading experiences in the book. Even the great forest, whose vastness swallows up the "human project," appears small and submissive under the onslaught of "the unleashed and unhoused force of Nature, / Mindless, irreconcilable, absolute: / The swing of the year, the thrust of Time, the wind." Primal forces of nature move in over the planet as "far north the great conifers darkly bend." Whereas the summer journey to the site of the Lewis house (the summer bespeaking the high noon of human life and energy) had afforded R.P.W. a glimpse into man's inner darkness (the serpent metaphor), the winter setting here and at the end of the poem serves to dramatize man's relationship to the outer darkness, the black abyss of nature. In the "glittering infinitude of night" the arctic stars' "gleam comes earthward down uncounted light-years of disdain" as the wide empty land lies waste and frigid in a scene deathsome and static as eternity: "in radius of more than a thousand miles the continent / Glitters whitely in starlight like a great dead eye of ice" (p. 95).

The fullest expression of this mood, this sense of time-space immensity, comes significantly at the end of the poem, when R.P.W. makes his winter visit (December 1951) to the Lewis home site. Here, as R.P.W. stands near "the shrunken ruin," watching the "last light of December's, and the day's, declension" and thinking "of the many dead and the places where they lay," he sees how "winter makes things small. All things draw in" (p. 215). Underscoring this feeling of diminishment, as R.P.W. looks at the pathetic decay and rubble of what was once a "human project," are the vast "emptiness of light," or "cold indifferency of light," and the great, vacant hush of afternoon in which the sounds of living creatures ("Some far voice speaking, or a dog's bark") are thin and faint, waning into nothingness. Even the river of time has a "cold gleam" in this perspective. Thinking how "the grave of my father's father is lost in the woods" and "how our hither-coming never knows the hence-going," R.P.W. sees that river for the last time as "that broad flood" on which men move, and are moved, together: "The good, the bad, the strong, the weak, all men . . . All men, a flood upon the flood" (pp. 204, 209).

Taken together, these images suggesting the immensity of time and space, images that seem to dwarf the "frail human project," effectively culminate the "naturalistic considerations" that R.P.W. mentioned early in the poem (p. 29). When first mentioned, these "naturalistic considerations" applied to the inner darkness of man, the psychological theory of determinism which, if accepted, would render virtue meaningless and nonexistent, and which, consequently, R.P.W. rejects, though he has seen man's inner darkness: "But still, despite all naturalistic considerations, / Or in the end because of naturalistic considerations, / We must believe in virtue" (p. 29).

This qualification of the "naturalistic considerations" applying to man's inner darkness has, as we might expect, a counterpart with respect to the naturalistic darkness exterior to man. Though he has seen both the inner and outer darkness, Warren does not accept the premises of naturalism as the final truth of existence. Just as "we must believe in virtue," despite naturalistic considerations ("considerations" implies something less than dogmatic acceptance), so, too, Warren would say, we must believe in an ultimate meaning to our existence despite the all-enveloping oppressiveness of external darkness.

Warren's answer to the problem of cosmic darkness is, in the end, theological. Since the inner darkness is his main concern in this poem, these theological implications are not very profuse in number or obvious in meaning, but clearly they do exist. There is, first of all, the concept of being "at one with God," which I have already discussed in connection with the catfish image. More important than this, I think, is the motif of natural calamity as an index of "God's Wrath"—a motif notably anticipating such poems in *Promises* as "Summer

Storm (Circa 1916), and God's Grace" and "Dragon Country: To Jacob Boehme." Warren uses the term "God's Wrath" in such a way as to direct sarcasm at modern religious skepticism in the passage where R.P.W. discusses the perpetual propriety, by reason of the world's moral corruption, of an immediate Apocalypse, the End of Time (p. 64):

> . . . that hour seem[ed] perfectly made to order
> For the world's end, as this present hour would seem
> To any of us if the earth shook now and the sun darkened—
> To any of us, that is, if we weren't so advanced
> Beyond the superstitious fear of God's Wrath.

Although Warren makes it clear that he is not speaking literally when he uses nature to dramatize God's wrath, he does draw boldly upon natural calamity as an image of some spiritual reality. In describing the *annus mirabilis*, Warren shows how nature is out of joint in the Shakespearean manner, piling up myriad eerie details of natural disorder—a comet shedding "a twilight of shuddering green / Over the immensity of forest" and the beasts of the forest participating in the "peculiar dislocation," having "lust / Out of season, and lust for strange foods, as when / Rome shook with civil discord, and therefore the beasts, / Augustine says, kept not their order" (p. 101).

The use of nature to imply a supernatural reality, or at least a reality beyond visible appearances, becomes yet more explicit when Warren describes the hour of Lilburn's butchery as "that last hour indefensible, / When the stars sweat and the dear toad weeps in the hole" (p. 111). After the act is committed, likewise, Warren describes the subsequent earthquake in terms suggesting the supernatural: "the earth shook and oak trees moaned like men, / And the river sloshed like dish-suds and spilled out," and "God shook the country like a rug, / And sloshed the Mississippi, for a kind of warning" (pp. 144–45). Warren immediately qualifies these supernatural implications by stating the secular view of things ("No, what great moral order we may posit / For old Kentucky, or the world at large, / Will scarcely account for geodetic shifts"), but his effect—and his intention, I think—is rather like that of the lawyer who makes an improper appeal to the jury and smiles blandly as the judge orders it stricken from the record.

The most significant theological content of the poem, and that which most closely approximates religious orthodoxy, is the series of Christian paradoxes that form the thematic resolution of the work. Both the style and the content of these lines resemble the resolution of *Four Quartets*, but the ideas are much older than Eliot or anything in the modern period. These paradoxes were a favorite theme of the metaphysical poets and preachers, such as John Donne and Lancelot Andrewes, and their ultimate source goes all the way back to the sayings of Jesus. The inner and outer darkness come together here, as Warren considers virtue and a permanent identity ("the beginning of selfhood") ultimately interrelated (p. 214):

Fulfillment is only in the degree of recognition
Of the common lot of our kind. And that is the death of
vanity,
And that is the beginning of virtue.

The recognition of complicity is the beginning of innocence.
The recognition of necessity is the beginning of freedom.
The recognition of the direction of fulfillment is the death of
the self.
And the death of the self is the beginning of selfhood.

We may note in passing, by way of explaining the abstract, prosaic style of this passage (poetry of statement, one might call it), that all these ideas were implicit in "The Ballad of Billie Potts"—there was the "recognition of complicity" and of "necessity" and the "fulfillment" through the "death of the self"—but critical understanding of that poem was very scant. For this reason, I believe, Warren undertook in *Brother to Dragons* to restate these fundamental premises of his art in explicit, prosaic terms, since subtler modes of communication had apparently failed in his earlier poetry.

Having now discussed both the inner and the outer darkness in *Brother to Dragons*, I would like to make a comment on the relationship between those dual dimensions of the dark night of the soul. The relationship between the inner and outer darkness, or between the beast-metaphor and the "naturalistic considerations" of the great forest and the "glittering infinitude of night," is rendered, as I see it, by means of an intermediary image—the "house" of the human psyche. We saw this image elaborately worked out in "Crime," one of the *Eleven Poems*, where the conscious self sat in the attic amid rubbish suggesting temporal identity ("the letter / Names over your name") while the deeper self lay buried (only to be humiliatingly resurrected) in the "hutch and hole" of the "cellar-dark." It may be fanciful to attach similar connotations to Lilburn's house, but there is some evidence that Warren intended such a meaning.

Jefferson first broaches this use of the "house" image when he speaks of "that sweet quarter of the heart where once . . . faith / Her fairest mansion held" (p. 24). The lines following this one, where Jefferson tells Lucy, "Sister, we are betrayed, and always in the house!" would strongly imply the concept of the house of the psyche, I would think.

R.P.W.'s subsequent comment, "If you refer to the house
Charles Lewis built . . . [it's] nothing but rubble,"
could be taken both literally and metaphorically. If taken both
ways, it ties together the motifs of inner and outer darkness,
for Lilburn and Nature between them have indeed reduced a
nation's proudest household to "rubble," morally and physi-
cally.

If we assume that the Lewis house is indeed the house of
the psyche—and every such house does in fact have its own
meat house, Warren would insist—then R.P.W.'s first look at
the ruins, in his July visit, has some very interesting, though
not immediately apparent, overtones. First of all, there is the
contrast between the "huddled stones of ruin," which is all
that remains of the surface self, and the underground burrow
where the serpent-self still endures (p. 32). This contrast is
repeated in R.P.W.'s second visit—his December trip at the
end of the poem—where we picture the serpent "looped and
snug" underground, safely beyond the reach of naturalism's
winter (p. 208). The image of the catfish, perfectly adjusted to
its utterly dark, frigid surroundings under the ice, also reinforces this contrast between the conscious self and the unconscious. What these images add up to, we may surmise, is
Warren's concept of individual immortality: the conscious
self, that part of the psyche represented by the "huddled
stones of ruin," dies away in time, leaving the human hope for
survival to reside in the collective human unconscious, the
inscrutable bedrock identity which renders us "all one Flesh,
at last" in *Promises* (see Lyric 3 of "Ballad of a Sweet Dream
of Peace").

A number of obscurities come clear, I think, as a result of
this reading. It explains, for example, the urgent, repetitious
insistence on accepting the inner self that we have seen as the

central theme in much of Warren's poetry. Only the deeper, unknown self can hope to transcend time's decay; the conscious, temporal self is doomed to naturalistic oblivion. And such oblivion is hardly hope-inspiring, if we may rightly infer that Warren's description of the ruined house extends to the house of the psyche (p. 32):

> And there it was: the huddled stones of ruin,
> Just the foundation and the tumbled chimneys,
> To say the human had been here and gone,
> And never would come back, though the bright stars
> Shall weary not in their appointed watch.   .   .   .

The concept of the house as an extension of human identity appears elsewhere in the poem with similar implications of ruin. R.P.W. evokes his lyrical depiction of winter in the middle of the poem for the specific purpose, he says, of escaping the human house, dominated now by the dark psyche of Lilburn (p. 95):

> .   .   .   we also feel a need to leave that house
> On the dark headland, and lift up our eyes
> To whatever liberating perspective,
> Icy and pure, the wild heart may command,
> To escape the house, escape the tightening coil.   .   .   .

The perishable self is again identified with the house in the scene, late in the poem, where R.P.W. thinks of his vanished ancestors of only one or two generations ago. Riding with his father under the "lemon light" of December, R.P.W. looks out over "the land where once stood the house of his [father's] first light," and observes, "No remnant remains. The plowpoint has passed where the sill lay" (p. 204). The conscious, temporal identity has disappeared into nothingness—"I do not know what hope or haplessness there / Inhabited once"—and so R.P.W. concludes that "the house is a fiction of human possibility past." Warren's feeling that "nothing is ever lost," an idea that Jefferson affirmed after his conversion ("It would be terrible to think that truth is lost"—p. 194) is tenable, I think, only because of the potentiality of the deeper, undiscovered self, the serpent serenely "looped and snug" under the ruins of the house above ground. This mysterious, undefinable self, our collective unconscious, is the sole repository of all experience, and our sole hope, against "naturalistic considerations," of transcending temporal limitations. This is the final significance of the beast-metaphor: there is not only shame but hope in acknowledging oneself a brother to dragons.

What *Brother to Dragons* does in relation to Warren's total body of poetry is to restate, with admirable power and eloquence, the main themes of Warren's earlier poetry. The black abyss without—the dark night of naturalism as seen in *Thirty-six Poems*—and the black abyss within—man's dark, innermost self as sought in *Eleven Poems:* both of these themes recur in *Brother to Dragons,* embodied in this poem's beast-metaphor and in its winter setting. Moreover, the ideal of a united self, predicated on the hope of reestablishing the lines of communication between conscious and unconscious, is the recurrence of a theme (not widely understood) from "The Ballad of Billie Potts." In witnessing the reconciliation of conscious and unconscious, of Jefferson and Lilburn, the reader may well feel a sense of *déjà vu,* recalling a similar reunion between Billie (the conscious self, made desperate by emptiness and lack of identity) and his father (like Lilburn, a hatchet-wielder, "evil and ignorant and old"). In a way, then, *Brother to Dragons* consummates several decades of writing, recapitulating in unified form its author's previous themes and images and offering that synthesis of psychology and religion which Warren had earlier evolved as a solution to the central problem of our age, the question whether man can live on the purely naturalistic level.

Much more, of course, might be said about *Brother to Dragons*. Warren's metrics, for example, will support a full-length study. The power and flexibility of Warren's blank verse in this work have excited an almost unanimous feeling of admiration in critics and reviewers, fellow poets included. Passages of sustained lyrical power, of brilliant imagery and diction, alternate successfully with suspenseful, fast-moving representation of dramatic action. In fixing levels of speech for his characters, ranging from Jefferson to Isham or Aunt Cat, Warren has approximated the excellence of Mark Twain or Shakespeare, I would venture to say. As for suiting the sound to the sense, Warren has rendered a performance worthy of Pope or Tennyson in such scenes as the rape of Pasiphaë or the coming of the *annus mirabilis*. *Brother to Dragons* must be acknowledged, in short, a remarkable technical achievement.

Whether *Brother to Dragons* is Warren's greatest achievement in verse (or in fiction, either) is hard to say. I believe, and in the next chapter shall attempt to validate this judgment, that *Promises* is a misunderstood and underrated volume, but its character is so different from *Brother to Dragons* that a comparison between the two is hardly feasible or profitable. *Brother to Dragons* has been widely hailed as the greatest narrative poem of the twentieth century, and whether or not we agree with Randall Jarrell's unqualified assertion, we do, I think, have to agree with his feeling that the appearance of *Brother to Dragons* was "an event, a great one."

CHAPTER THREE

Promises: A Legacy

PROMISES, THE 1957 collection which made Robert Penn Warren the first man ever to win the Pulitzer prize in both fiction and poetry, called forth high praise from nearly all the reviewers. Anthony Hecht, for example, wrote in the *Hudson Review* that "the overwhelming majority of poems included in the book are absolute and unqualified triumphs." [1] And James Dickey, writing about Warren and other poets (such as Richard Wilbur and Richard Eberhart) in the *Sewanee Review*, paid Warren the kind of tribute normally accorded only to the great poets of the ages: "When he is good, and often even when he is bad, you had as soon read

Warren as live. . . . Of all these poets, Warren is the only one to give you the sense of poetry as a thing of final importance to life." [2]

To judge from comments like this, appearing in some of America's most highly respected forums of critical opinion, one might suppose *Promises* to be a well-criticized volume. As with *Brother to Dragons*, however, such is not the case. Except for brief reviews shortly following its appearance, hardly anything of real significance has been written on *Promises*. For this reason, I shall undertake to explicate the main themes and image-patterns in *Promises*, and particularly to explain the obscure, almost surrealistic poems that bear the crucial burden of Warren's meaning—poems, that is, like "Ballad of a Sweet Dream of Peace," where there are presences that can be sensed but never encompassed by the conscious mind. Only after such analysis may *Promises* be properly considered with respect to Warren's body of poetry as a whole.

Before proceeding with this analysis, however, a curious quirk in modern sensibility—only incidentally unfavorable towards Warren—needs to be considered. Most critics, as I have indicated, have been enthusiastic about Warren's achievement in *Promises*, yet we know that a strong dissenting opinion exists—even more widely outside of print, we may assume, than would be implied from what has been printed, for Warren has never achieved much recognition as a poet (perhaps *Brother to Dragons* excepted) from any intellectual audience in the country. A leading reason for this state of affairs appears in the September 1961 issue of *Horizon*, where Donald Hall cites a passage from Kenneth Koch in reporting on the latest skirmishes between Palefaces and Redskins.[3] Although Warren's verse shows both Paleface and Redskin characteristics, the Redskins, probably because of Warren's

well-known academic status, classify him in the enemy camp,
and accordingly, Redskin Koch makes Warren an explicit
object of his contempt in his seven-page satire called "Fresh
Air":

> Where are young poets in America, they are trembling in
>   publishing houses and universities,
> Above all they are trembling in universities, they are
>   bathing the library steps with their spit,
> They are gargling out innocuous (to whom?) poems about
>   maple trees and their children   .   .   .
> Oh what worms they are! they wish to perfect their form.

Any reader of *Promises* will probably recognize the allusion in
Line 3 of the above excerpt to the poem that introduces
Gabriel's section of the volume: "What Was the Promise
That Smiled from the Maples at Evening?"

The reasons for Koch's disgust are not difficult to fathom.
As representatives of a growing New Romanticism, Koch and
the beatnik poets at large evince a ferocious hatred of anything
they might construe as "domestic" subject matter—"domestic" appertains to any of the established forms of civilization,
we might suppose—and a feeling of revulsion towards the strictures of traditional poetic disciplines. What this all adds up to
is a latter-day primitivism: an insistence on all emotion and
sensation and no intellect or ethic in poetry. All that matters is
that one pours out what one feels. Koch is engagingly demon-
strative of this attitude:

> You make me sick with all your talk about restraint and
>   mature talent   .   .   .
> I am afraid you have never smiled at the hibernation
> Of bear cubs except that you saw in it some deep relation
> To human suffering and wishes, oh what a bunch of crackpots!

Although Koch's displeasure may be explained as an understandable reaction against the excessive formalism of the
poetry of the previous two decades, nevertheless it is surprising
and a bit dismaying to see in his attitude a recurrence of the
division of sensibility which emasculated so much of the verse
of the eighteenth and nineteenth century, with a resulting lack
of emotional intensity in one age (magnificent exceptions are
at once admitted) and a lack of intellectual substance in the
other. The finest poetry of the ages has been produced by men
or by periods of a unified sensibility, such as the metaphysical
or the modern period, for the simple reason that such poetry
satisfies the whole man, both intellect and emotion. Warren's
is a unified sensibility; and the reason why Koch's comment
about the bear cubs is a false judgment is precisely that
Warren does share (and, with his Kentucky heritage, probably
exceeds) Koch's sensitivity and joy towards the world of
animals—the ending of "The Ballad of Billie Potts," for
example, shows a reverence and empathy for the animal world
that compares with Hemingway's or with the Book of Job. But
reverence and joy, however sweet a champagne, cannot feed
the entire man; we are so designed that we need the meat and
potatoes of intellectual sustenance. Warren encompasses and
transcends the Kenneth Kochs of modern literature; he knows
and uses the manner of poetry of sensation, but he knows its
limitations and counters these with poetry of intellect and
form. His is a comprehensive art, a poetry too mature merely
to transmit the details of raw experience. He consciously tries,
as Koch and the beatniks unconsciously and against their own
pious denials likewise try, to meet the artist's innermost urge to
perceive some kind of order—and even primitivism or nihilism
imply an order—within the chaos of experience, for only
within the context of a self-transcending order can the self

attain a real, that is to say, a permanent, meaning. Aspiring to
perceive such a meaning, and so to bequeath it to his children,
Warren devotes this book of lyrics to a scrutiny of his experience, his own and his generation's, in order to derive a vision of
the total meaning of experience, encompassing its past, present, and future, its heritage and its promises.

The Rosanna Poems

THE GOVERNING theme of the five poems which comprise
the section of *Promises* dedicated to Warren's little daughter, Rosanna, may be inferred from the heading of that
section, which reads: "To a Little Girl, One Year Old, in a
Ruined Fortress." The innocence, faith, and merriment of this
little girl—qualities of spirit which are maintained and even
justified within the limited scope of her experience—are set off
in stark and shocking contrast to the background, which from
the larger perspective of the poems' narrator (obviously Warren himself) appears grim and menacing: the Ruined Fortress
of the World; the fallen, decayed, and corrupted Eden; the
place of sin and loss and moral disorder. Both the girl's and the
narrator's perspectives turn out to have some validity. They
begin in sharp conflict, but in the end they come to modify one
another: the girl's innocence will have to undergo the stress of
experience, will have to acknowledge the curse over the ruined
fortress and submit to its limitations; but for his part, the
narrator must give ground a little, so as to submit his initial
despair to the "moment of possibility," the chance to "redeem,

redeem!" offered by the girl's laughter in "Gull's Cry."

The development of the governing theme may likewise be inferred from the titles of the individual poems, taken in their order of appearance. "Sirocco" elaborates upon the setting, the ruined fortress of the world, into which the narrator and his wife have brought this lovely, innocent butterfly—apparently experiencing anxiety over whether they have wronged her thereby: "To a place of ruined stone we brought you. . . ." "Gull's Cry," the second poem, constitutes a lyric outcry of anguish and hope about this setting, about its limitations and possibilities, wherein man and his fellow creatures find themselves imprisoned. The third poem, "The Child Next Door," creates a foil to Rosanna. The child is an infant whose "defective" body bears tragic testimony of original sin and whose proximity ("next door") to Rosanna—indeed they become almost twin halves of the same total human Self—brings her perfection under such a pall as nearly to annihilate the narrator's tentative hope ("redeem, redeem!") of the previous poem: "I smile stiff . . . and think: this is the world." Against this central slough of despair in the third poem Warren counterposes an opposite image of hope in the following poem, "The Flower," which reasserts the girl's perspective and brings an uplift to the narrator's. Just as "The Child Next Door" elaborates upon the narrator's cry of anguish in "Gull's Cry," so "The Flower" explores in depth the "moment of possibility," the laughter of hope, which the girl had proffered in the second poem. As we might expect, the last poem, "Colder Fire," transmits a retrospective final synthesis, a summation of images and perspectives, a comprehensive last word and promise, or interpretation of experience, from the narrator to his daughter.

Aside from their part in the general structure of this poetic sequence, the individual poems themselves require and deserve detailed analysis, with particular regard for the connotations and interrelationships of images, for shifts and development of perspective (involving tone, mood, interaction of characters, and the like), and for technical devices, influencing the sound and shape of the verse (rhyme and rhythm, stanza patterns, special effects). But Warren's technique will receive in this study less attention than it deserves, for Warren's synthesis of original and traditional elements of form might warrant a full-length study in its own right. I shall, however, occasionally note the most effective of these devices, particularly when they function to reinforce the sense.[4]

As I have said, Poem I, "Sirocco," establishes the setting of the whole sequence, the ruined fortress of the world, a place whose very military posture bespeaks at worst man's greed and cruelty and selfishness and at best some fundamental failure, old as history, of human communion. It is a place where man's highest gifts, his "most fastidious mathematic and skill," have been appropriated for the predatory purpose implicit in Warren's description of the *rocca*: "fortress, hawk-heel, lion-paw." A vain and ironic splendor, a hint of thwarted possibilities, lingers over these stones, which attest a perversion of the human genius for creating order, much as the Great Pyramids are a monument to man's genius and to his soulless rapacity. To indict the soullessness of the fortress world, Warren describes its grievous splendor in arid mathematical terms; this is a place "where geometry of a military rigor survives its own ruined world."

Ruinous as the fortress is in suggesting the deficiencies of human nature, the worst ruin of all in the narrator's eyes is not within man, but outside him. Stanza 2 shows not only that man is ethically defective, but that the whole universe is morally disordered. Even the morally upright man, the pious, the faithful, the well-intentioned, meets only frustration and abuse, for Philip of Spain, the builder of the fortress, was just such a man, and yet he was one "for whom nothing prospered, though he loved God." Warren's description of Philip as "the anguished" identifies Philip to quite an extent with the narrator, whose anguish provides most of the substance of the next two poems. The present status of this God-loving ruler may be inferred from the place the symbol of his rule occupies in Warren's final reference to Philip: his coat of arms lies "under garbage," imbedded in the filth of the moat forever. God's own Time, we observe, has compounded the moral injustice of the world, has not rectified or even softened it.

At this point, immediately after the bitterest words in the poem, "under garbage," a sudden, unexpected shift in tone takes place; our eyes subtly shift their focus from the garbage at the moat's bottom to the "moat-brink," where we see "rosemary with blue, thistle with gold bloom, nod." This is the girl's perspective; this—not the garbage—is what she would have noticed; and this intrusion of the girl's perspective into the narrator's bitter despair is what forms the dramatic structure of this poem.

As though to reinforce this sudden perception of natural beauty—Warren frequently makes deliberate use of the pathetic fallacy—the air is suddenly glorified by the sun-glitter of a sirocco, which Webster defines as "a hot, dust-laden wind from the Libyan desert, experienced chiefly in Italy, Malta, and Sicily. A moist, oppressive southeast wind   .   .   ." Although we might normally give heavier weight to the negative connotations of this definition, to the "hot," "dust-laden," "oppressive" qualities, it seems clear here that the sirocco in this poem serves a beatific function:

> Sun blaze and cloud tatter, it is the sirocco, the dust swirl
>   is swirled
> Over the bay face, mounts air like gold gauze whirled; it
>   traverses the blaze-blue of water.
> .   .   .   .
> And sun regilds your gilt hair, in the midst of your laughter.

The motif here seems to be that nature's benediction is nearest at hand when and where we would least expect it: it is near the garbage at the moat's edge, or it arrives with delicate loveliness, "like gold gauze whirled," on the back of a "hot, dust-laden, oppressive" wind from Libya.

The concluding couplet of this sonnet begins by synthesizing the major conflicting images: "Rosemary, thistle, clutch stone." The rosemary and thistle blooms, we remember, are what supplanted the garbage in the poem's central shift of focus, but the "clutch stone," which refers to the "great scutcheon of stone" that still lies in the pollution of the moat, serves to remind us that the tension of the poem has by no means been conclusively resolved. To be sure, there are now two alternative perspectives instead of the one overriding despair, but on the other hand, no amount of natural loveliness, and no intensity of perceiving the same, can elevate the scutcheon of a noble prince out of the garbage and up to its rightful eminence. What is obviously needed, in order to resolve this impasse of perspectives, is some kind of transcendence, a greater vision that can comprehend the two lesser ones. Such transcendence is precisely what is yearned after as the final couplet continues: "Far hangs Giannutri in blue air. Far to that blueness the heart aches."

This, then, is the need and the promise of "Sirocco"; both are comprehended in the blue farness towards which the heart yearns in its efforts to transcend the limitations, to resolve the dilemma, of the ruined fortress. The last word in this sonnet is one of faint promise: "the last gold of gorse bloom, in the sirocco, shakes." The gorse, which the dictionary describes as "an evergreen shrub with yellow flowers, common in Europe," may indicate a final emphasis on the girl's perspective, particularly because the evergreen has often been used to typify eternal life, but it is at best a faint emphasis. This is, after all, the *last* gold of gorse bloom, and the dramatic tension which we have noted is far from satisfactorily resolved at the poem's end.

As we enter the second poem, the most immediate fact to strike our awareness is that the glory of the sirocco has departed. Instead of the "air like gold gauze whirled," we have here a heavy, stagnant atmosphere of total stasis: "I do not think that anything in the world will move, not goat, not gander   .   .   . ; the sun beats. . . ." And with the departure of the sirocco, the narrator's original perspective of the first poem has apparently returned; the same focus of vision which picked out the garbage of the moat in "Sirocco" is similarly at work noting the refuse of the animal kingdom in "Gull's Cry": "Goat droppings are fresh in the hot dust. . . ." Just to make sure that we do not misconstrue his tone—to a Whitman or a Kenneth Koch, after all, fresh dung could be grounds for rejoicing—Warren adds a particularly offensive detail, "not yet the beetle," to reinforce an air of stagnation so pervasive that even the maggots are not to be observed at their customary lunch.

Against these images of monotony, of uneventful waiting in hot sun-glare ("And the she-goat,   .   .   .   under pink oleander, waits"), Warren again counterposes an image of transcendence of perspective, an image connoting emancipation from the drab, constricting, monotony of the here-and-

now world of Stanza 1. It is an image which obviously carries
forward the "Far hangs Giannutri in blue air" motif of the
previous poem:

> . . . over blue-braiding sea-shadow,
> The gull hangs white; whiter than white against mountain-
> mass,
> The gull extends motionless on shelf of air, on substance of
> shadow.

Normally we might expect such a bird to represent something
enviable—a suprahuman perspective and a consequent sense
of liberation like that of the hawk that soared high over the
watershed in "Kentucky Mountain Farm," an early poem of
Warren's. But in "Gull's Cry" something is wrong with the
picture—the bird's large perspective yields no such sense of
freedom and exultation. As anyone who has lived near the
ocean knows, the sea gull's cry is not, like that of most birds, a
happy one. It is a high, piercing, shrill sound, with a falling
cadence, rather than a rising one or a warble, and with a
mournful tone in a minor key. That Warren considers the
sound unhappy in tone is indicated later in the poem, when
the beetle, the dung-eater of Stanza 1, and the gull, whose
transcendent perspective in Stanza 2 seems the opposite of the
beetle's, both conjoin to represent the height and depth of
human anguish and futility: "Let the beetle work, the gull
comment the irrelevant anguish of air." From the narrowest
perspective of the dung-dropping, then, to the widest perspective of the gull's straddling of shore and eternity, we see only
reason for despair, the alternatives presented ranging from the
loathsome carnality of the beetle, through the futile and
meaningless waiting of the goat, up to the sorrow-giving
overview of the gull. The use of the word "anguish" in

connection with the gull ties in with the adjective, "the anguished," which describes Philip of Spain in "Sirocco"; this repetition points up a continuation of the narrator's own anguish although suggesting a different reason for it.

What that reason is—and the reason for the gull's anguish as well—is indicated at the end of Stanza 2: "The gull, at an eye-blink, will, into the astonishing statement of sun, pass." "The astonishing statement of sun" could be interpreted in a number of ways, but in view of the tragic pessimism of the following stanza, I think the sun's statement must be construed as a negative one. This seems to be a naturalistic sun, which carelessly brought forth life—such as the beetle, the goat, the hunchback, and the defective child—and which presides with mechanical indifference over the dissolution under its reign. It is the sun whose face Yeats described as "blank and pitiless" in "The Second Coming"—a sun whose presence reminds us of the cause-and-effect relationship that ties together all things in the universe, from the gigantic powers that in cosmic antiquity produced the sun itself, to subsequent "astonishing" production by the sun of our own pitiful bodies; a sun whose impersonal creative powers may be appreciated—or even worshiped, as in primitive religions—but not supplicated. Hence, the gull's and the narrator's anguish are "irrelevant," are an "anguish of air."

The details of that anguish eloquently appear in Stanza 3, where Warren paints with a few deft brush-strokes a typical scene of domestic suffering in the ruined fortress. Chief among the sufferers is the most innocent of them, the "defective child" next door who, having cried all night, "now squats in the dust where the lizard goes." This last reference, when we consider the secularized mode of original sin implicit in the boy's infant body, suggests certain Biblical echoes. If we take the lizard as a latter-day serpent of Eden, his sharing the dust with the deformed child shows their common bondage to a nature under the curse. The use of the word "dust" carries an especially humbling connotation about man's origin in the light of this possible Genesis reference. T. S. Eliot used the same device—referring to the Genesis myth shorn of its promise of redemption—in his definition of man at the beginning of *The Waste Land:* "I will show you fear in a handful of dust."

The next sufferer we encounter—the narrator himself we may take for granted—is the hunchback's wife, who tries in vain to get away from the sun: "The wife of the *gobbo* sits under vine leaves, she suffers, her eyes glare." Whether this woman is the mother of the defective child is not clear, but either way, the child and the *gobbo's* wife taken together represent the realities of love and marriage, the basic reality being that of the crippled self helpless and isolated and uncommunicating, and together they form a dreadful contrast to the sweet delusions being fostered in a typical manner amidst all this misery: "The engaged ones sit in the privacy of bemusement, heads bent: the classic pose."

This ironic contrast between what sexual love promises and what it delivers, both visible side by side in a harrowing proximity, is what prompts the narrator's deepest despair and his bitterest sarcasm. It is at this point, after seeing the lovers, that the narrator brings together the two perspectives which had hitherto been developed separately as seeming opposites: "Let the beetle work, the gull comment the irrelevant anguish of air." At this juncture, the beetle in the goat dung and the gull hanging high above it all are no longer opposites; they are simply complementary aspects of the same meaninglessness, and the breadth of vision is not a means of emancipation for the gull or the narrator, but only a source of additional suffering, of "irrelevant" anguish.

At this lowest point in the poem, as at the lowest point of the previous poem, when the focus shifted from the garbage to the moat-brink, the girl's completely contradictory perspective intrudes upon the narrator's gloom and forces an affirmative modification.

What the girl displays is nothing more than laughter, the spontaneous joy of a one-year-old who is not defective, who has not cried all night; but it is enough to impart new possibilities of outlook, neither tragically wide of scope like the gull's nor selfishly narrow like the lovers', whose "privacy" of bemusement had so galled the narrator earlier. The girl's joy is sufficient cause for the narrator to regard both man and nature in a different way. Rather than seeing nature in terms of a grim and "astonishing statement of sun," he now sees it as a "molecular dance" that glimmers "like joy." Nature has taken on human values here; it can "dance" and evince "joy" in the same way that the little girl, who is part of nature, can dance and laugh: "But at your laughter let the molecular dance of the stone-dark glimmer like joy in the stone's dream. . . ." The choice of the stone to represent a fallen but redeemable nature is particularly effective here not only because it ties in with the "ruined stone" that composes the "ruined fortress" of the world in "Sirocco," but also because of a Biblical parallel which the girl's joy seems to evoke. The setting of this parallel is the Triumphal Entry, and the occasion is the Pharisees' demand that Jesus silence the disciples, who had begun "to rejoice and praise God with a loud voice": "And he answered and said unto them, I tell you that, if these should hold their peace, the stones would immediately cry out."

As the girl's laughter imparts a glimpse of the redeemability of even inanimate nature, so too it affords a "moment of possibility" in which all the broken human communications appear reconnectable: "And in that moment of possibility, let *gobbo, gobbo's* wife, and us, and all, take hands and sing: redeem, redeem!" In a sense, this scene of human communion in the ruined fortress is almost as bizarre as Eliot's similar image in *The Hollow Men,* "Here we go round the prickly pear / prickly pear   prickly pear," for here we have a strange commixture of opposites, hunchback and narrator, the defective child and angelic Rosanna, perhaps even—within the context of the major images in the poem—the gull and the beetle, all participating in an incongruous and ostensibly absurd ritual of brotherhood in a surrealistic atmosphere. The difference between Eliot's and Warren's imagery, however, is that Eliot's is sarcastic and despairing, whereas Warren's is genuinely indicative of hope.

Warren's compression of so profound a change of perspective into the final couplet is itself a considerable artistic achievement, comparable to the abrupt, last-minute resolution of ideas in a Donne sonnet or in one of Herbert's religious poems, but the brevity of this vision—we must remember that it lasts for only a *moment* of possibility—does something more: it sets the stage for the third and most critical phase of the conflict between hope and despair. This is the phase in which Warren pursues the darker implications of the ritual of brotherhood he has just now, rather hopefully, envisioned.

As we enter Poem III, then, it should not greatly surprise us to see the narrator once again deep in the abyss of despair, for by virtue of his newly affirmed brotherhood he is confronted yet again with the substance of tragedy. By his identification with the sufferers of "Gull's Cry," he must now focus his attention and sympathy upon the chief and most

innocent of those sufferers, the defective child next door:
hence the title of this poem, "The Child Next Door." The
perspective of uplift which had concluded "Gull's Cry" is not
totally vanquished here, for at least the moral chaos in this
poem is within the arena of human sin and responsibility,
whereas earlier the whole universe had seemed implicated in
the design of purposeless suffering. But the moral crisis here is
none the less tragic for all that, because the mother who
transmits original sin here is herself victimized by undeserved
evils of circumstance and may indeed have been motivated to
the tragic deed more by compassion than by any thought of
self:

> The child next door is defective because the mother,
> Seven brats already in that purlieu of dirt,
> Took a pill, or did something to herself she thought would not
>   hurt. .   .   .

We see now that the same wretched perversity of the world
which had kept Prince Philip's scutcheon imbedded in garbage
and which had brought the gull and the beetle together in the
narrator's vision is still as strongly as ever at work: the woman
with seven brats who had wanted only to forestall certain
misery has by her efforts compounded the same, "for there
came this monstrous other." As previously, moreover, there is
presented an affirmative alternative to the narrator's anguish,
but it is an affirmation to which, for the first time in this
sequence, the narrator offers sharp rebuttal:

> The sister is twelve. Is beautiful like a saint.
> Sits with the monster all day, with pure love, calm eyes.
> Has taught it a trick, to make *ciao*, Italian-wise.
> It crooks hand in that greeting. She smiles her smile without
>   taint.

> I come, and her triptych beauty and joy stir hate
> —Is it hate?—in my heart.   .   .   .

The start-and-stop rhythm of the stanza describing the sister, a staccato effect produced by the use of periods where we would expect commas, indicates, I think, the disharmony or even hostility the girl's appearance produces in the narrator; he observes her presence in a remote, mechanical, piecemeal fashion.

The cause of the narrator's hostility is the girl's innocence, a quality he could accept in his year-old daughter but believes objectionable in a twelve-year-old as intimate with the evils of the ruined fortress as this one:

> .   .   .   Fool, doesn't she know that the process
> Is not that joyous or simple, to bless, or unbless,
> The malfeasance of nature or the filth of fate?

At this juncture, with the narrator's sour dismissal of the sister's perspective, it seems evident that his original pessimism has prevailed, and conclusively so. It would seem that now and for always his deep awareness of an amoral world, of a fate which perpetrates and augments unwarranted suffering, shall overrule any perspective which is less aware than his, or which appears oblivious of such a world and fate. But it is not so. The same compelling honesty which obligated the narrator to confront the darkest implications of the child's deformity likewise compels him to admit the possibility of a happier outlook:

> Can it bind or loose, that beauty in that kind,
> Beauty of benediction?

The answer to this question leads to the major promise of this poem, as the narrator admits once again the existence of

alternatives of outlook and chooses by dint of that admission
to modify his initial despair:

> . . . I trust our hope to prevail
> That heart-joy in beauty be wisdom, before beauty fail
> And be gathered like air in the ruck of the world's wind!

The last half of the above excerpt shows a very serious
qualification of the "promise" in the first half: although joy in
beauty is justified, is "wisdom," the beauty itself is seen as
temporary and eminently perishable when subjected to the
inevitable "world's wind." The narrator's attitude here is
much like Hemingway's typical stance; he will make the most
of a messy world by permitting "heart-joy in beauty," despite
his profound awareness of all-embracing tragedy, while such
beauty is available—before it succumbs to the "world's
wind."

As we might expect, the final couplet of this sonnet is more
stoical than exuberant in tone. Once again, the narrator draws
together the major conflicting images of the poem, thinking of
"your goldness, of joy, how empires grind, stars are hurled,"
but the effort at synthesis seems more painful and soul-rifting
than ever before: "I smile stiff, saying *ciao*, saying *ciao*, and
think: this is the world." Warren's subtlety of technique is
very effective indeed in this last line of the poem, for here we
find the main import carried not by the main statement but by
the subordinate modifier, "saying *ciao*, saying *ciao*." This
repetition by the narrator of the defective child's only mode of
communication shows that he, the narrator, is defective, too.
He, too, carries the stamp of original sin, of congenital inadequacy, within his person, not credentialed by an obvious
deformity of flesh, perhaps, but evident just as certainly and as
tragically and cripplingly within the province of spirit and

psyche. It is a brilliant touch on Warren's part to indicate by the simple repetition of the child's greeting a major shift in the narrator's perspective, from an external attitude of pity to an internalized identification of the narrator with the defective child. This is the culmination of the ritual of brotherhood. In the ultimate view of things, considered from a spiritual perspective, the child and the narrator are one: both are tragically defective through an inadequate inheritance, both communicate only very imperfectly, both are bounded by insuperable limitations and subject to the caprices of the "world's wind." But there are more positive aspects of this human communion, too; through the "beauty of benediction" both the narrator and the defective child find available the sister's love and joy, which can provide some sustenance, if not a foolproof inner defense, against the world where "empires grind, stars are hurled." Taken together, then, the defective child and his angelic sister round out the full range, both negative and positive, of the ritual of brotherhood that ended "Gull's Cry." The family relationship of this monster-baby and his saintlike sister, both derived of the same parentage, bespeaks a larger relationship of the whole human family, and it is the perception by the narrator of this larger relationship, embracing him and all the rest, which forms the major thematic contribution of the poem to the sequence as a whole, and which furthermore emancipates the narrator spiritually for the movement of uplift to follow.

Only after dealing with the painful problem of the defective child next door, it would seem, can the speaker return with the requisite honesty of intellect to his little model of perfection, Rosanna. But when he does return to Rosanna, in "The Flower," he appears so gratified at the alternative she presents that even the form of the poem seems to participate in the celebration. Its lovely falling rhythms ("Above the beach the vineyard / Terrace breaks to seaward"), its simple rhyme scheme, and its sensuous descriptive passages make this the most lyrical of the five poems. Rosanna represents the beginning of the "way up" after the worst is over on the "way down"; she betokens the tilt of the earth's axis towards the spring after the deepest winter dark. Even the setting and the perspective are different here. For the first time in this sequence, we are looking at things from outside the ruined fortress of mankind, and as a result, we are able to view the fortress and all from a calmer, less anguished perspective: "The path lifts up ahead / To the *rocca*, supper, bed."

It is not that the narrator has simply cast off what he had learned on the "way down," as he would hurl a pack from his back. Quite the contrary, what he has seen of the family next door—and what he has thereby seen of himself—qualifies the joy in this poem quite strictly. What the narrator has done is to go back to the first poem of the series, "Sirocco," where the central conflict between joy and despair was first imaged in the discrepancy between the garbage in the moat and the "rosemary with blue, thistle with gold bloom" at the moat's edge, and resume his unfinished work. Up to "The Flower," the sequence has dealt almost entirely with the "garbage" of life, with the "beetle work" in "Gull's Cry," or the "filth of fate" in "The Child Next Door." But in "The Flower" Warren shifts the emphasis back to that other set of images, the rosemary and thistle, whose affirmative power had seemed ineffectual in the darker sonnets. Considered in this perspective external to the ruined fortress, however, those images of natural loveliness, as opposed to man-made, "ruined fortress" garbage, take on more power.

The source of that power, it becomes clear, is natue herself. The ritual in this poem is not the ritual of brotherhood, "let *gobbo, gobbo's* wife, and us, and all, take hands and sing," which pertains to the world within the ruined fortress. Rather, this is a ritual pertaining to the relationship between man and nature:

> So here you always demand
> Your flower to hold in your hand,
> And the flower must be white,
> For you have your own ways to compel
> Observance of this ritual.
> You hold it and sing with delight.

Whereas man's world within the ruined fortress was, except for Rosanna and the saintlike sister, overwhelmingly tragic, the wider world of nature with its inscrutable ambiguities does not yield up a ready interpretation. Rather, the theme of this poem submits, it is for us to yield; we must yield ourselves over to the powers larger than ourselves which circumscribe our existence, powers such as nature, time, and death. So the image of the flower itself bears an obvious moral: in return for what nature gives us (the flower itself signifying, I would imagine, the gift of life), we must accept the limitations which an imperfect nature imposes, particularly the limitation of time.

In an effort to emphasize the beneficent aspects of nature as the giver and sustainer of life, and thereby to counteract the negative emphasis in the "astonishing statement of sun" passage in "Gull's Cry," Warren puts his finest esthetic talent to work creating passages of lush sensuousness. First of all, we note in Stanza 1 how nature provides our bulwark against the sea of eternity, even if only temporarily:

> The lava will withstand
> The sea's beat, or insinuant hand,
> And protect our patch of sand.

In Stanza 2, Warren makes nature so attractive to us through an irresistible appeal to the senses that we almost entirely forget the hideousness of the ruined fortress. Warren's verse texture here—his richness of rhyme, both internal and terminal—and his imagery of opulence have a Spenserian luxuriance:

> Bee-drowsy and blowsy with white bloom,
> Scarcely giving the passer-by room.
> We know that that blossomy mass
> Will brush our heads as we pass,
> And at knee there's gold gorse and blue clover,
> And at ankle, blue *malva* all over.   .   .   .
>
> .   .   .   .
> If no breeze stirs that green lair,
> The scent and sun-honey of air
> Is too sweet comfortably to bear.

After what he had seen in "The Child Next Door," we remember, the narrator gritted his teeth, saying *"ciao,"* and thinking, "this is the world." Here in "The Flower," as a result of Rosanna's influence, he has adopted enough of the child's perspective to be able to see all the highest beauty in the world and now he says of this, too, that "this is the world." The total range of human experience, then, offers us two extremes: a world too horrible to bear, or a world "too sweet comfortably to bear."

The basic flaw of this loveliest world is its transitoriness. Fundamentally, "The Flower" is a poem about time, about the possibilities and the limitations wherein time defines man and nature. Even though this loveliest of worlds is protected for the time from the sea of eternity ("the black lava-chunks stand off / The sea's grind, or indolent chuff"), it is susceptible even within this limited area of safety ("our patch of

sand") to the internal erosions of time, erosions which are
doubly imaged, both by the setting of evening, as we watch the
loveliness of scene rapidly fading into darker and darker
shadow, and by the setting of season, whereby Warren contrasts a past perfection of beauty in June with the present
sparseness of bloom much later in the year.

The contrast of a time present with a time past is, as even
the most casual reader must observe, nothing new in Warren.
This contrast is an initial prerequisite to his eventual effort to
conceive of time as an entirety, much as his efforts to scrutinize
the world of horror and the world which is "too sweet comfortably to bear" are dual prerequisites for a final synthesis of all
human experience. What triggers off this particular contrast
between time present and time past is Rosanna's insistence on
a ritual whose meaning is disintegrating with the advance of
the season: "Yes, I'm well aware / That this is the spot, and
hour, / For you to demand your flower." When this ritual had
first come into being, it had a rich and moving significance for
both the narrator and the little girl; it was a moment of almost
mystical, almost timeless immersion of the self in nature, very
similar to the central experience in Wordsworth's finest poetry:

> When first we came this way
> Up from the beach, that day
> That seems now so long ago,
> We moved bemused and slow
> In the season's pulse and flow.
> Bemused with sea, and slow
> With June heat and perfume,
> We paused here, and plucked you a bloom.

It is clear that both the narrator and the little girl shared
the original moment of rapture, but since then, only the girl

seems able, through the repetition of this ritual, to relive the full enchantment of that hour. For the narrator, the glory has departed, just as the glory of the sirocco had disappeared. When, in Stanza 5, the narrator returns his focus from the insubstantiality of memory to the palpable here-and-now, he finds that even nature, like the fortress, is ruined by an inner process of decay: "But the season has thinned out." So it is that he must supply the girl's ritual with less and less satisfactory emblems of the original experience:

> . . . we have found
> No bloom worthily white,
>
> .   .   .   .   .
> We give the best one to you.
> It is ruined, but will have to do.

The girl's response to the ruined flower is such indiscriminate joy ("And you sing as though human need / Were not for perfection") as to suggest a comparison between Rosanna and the saintly sister who, "with pure love, calm eyes," blessed the defective child and the defective narrator in "The Child Next Door." Both of these girls, one at an age of reason and the other not, seem to transcend the ruins, whether ruins of man or of nature—within or without the fortress—through an attitude of total acceptance of things as they are. While the narrator grimly contrasts the ideal with the real, the past with the present, these girls cheerfully work with whatever is available, content with whatever the ruins offer, however imperfect a defective brother or a ruined flower might be.

Because of his greater intellectual awareness, the narrator cannot evince so spontaneous an acceptance of imperfection as the girls can, yet an acceptance of some kind is implicitly necessary. The condition of the girls' acceptance is innocence;

they lack the intellect which makes distinctions, which can see the defects in the child next door, or which can distinguish between time past and time present (Rosanna lives in an eternal present). The narrator, lacking innocence, sees distinctions and sees in the distinctions the substance of injustice and tragedy. The only way he can surmount such injustice and tragedy, once he has seen them, is once again to remove the distinctions, not by disregarding them, which would be dishonest, but by reconstructing them into a new conception of unity. Such a vision of total reality was the poet's great need as early as "Kentucky Mountain Farm" in *Thirty-six Poems* (1935). It here continues to be the great need, as the poet's imagination answers the need with increasing power of sight.

In this poem, the conception of unity which is needed involves a view of time. It is the distinction between past and present, between the perfect flower and the ruined one, which provides the basis of tragic awareness in "The Flower," and it is the reunification of past and present into an integrated and meaningful whole which alone can release the narrator from the tragic predicament occasioned by his fragmentary perceptions:

> Let the future reassess
> All past joy, and pass distress,
> Till we know Time's deep intent.   .   .   .

In terms of the imagery in this poem, the above conception of unity gives the original moment of rapture "in the June heat and perfume" a permanence of meaning. That experience of communion with nature was not, in this perspective of wholeness, a happy but unavailing accident; it was, instead, the culmination of a cause-and-effect sequence that embraces all human experience:

> And the last integument
> Of the past shall be rent
> To show how all things bent
> Their energies to that hour
> When you first demanded your flower.

This, then, is the promise of experience in Poem IV: through observing the unifying relationships among all things as well as the distinctions between them one can breach the limitations of self, such as time and identity, and can assume a self-transcending importance. The image whereby Warren pictures this all-unifying totality of time suggests, in the last two lines of the passage below, a resemblance to Plato's image of the original self-division of man into two sexes, each yearning above all else to be reunited into the half of man represented by the opposite sex. This passage follows directly after the one quoted last:

> And in that image let
> Both past and future forget,
> In clasped communal ease,
> Their brute identities.

As a result of the reconciliation envisioned in the above passage, which is the thematic crux of the poem, the remaining three stanzas of "The Flower" reconceptualize the earlier images of anguish and horror—the *rocca*, the gull, the sea, and the night—in a mood of calm and deliberate acceptance:

> The *rocca* clasps its height.
> It accepts the incipient night.
> . . . . .
> On sunset, a white gull is black.

It hangs over the mountain crest.
.   .   .   .   .   .
It makes its outcry.
It slides down the sky.

Symbolizing the theme of acceptance is the posture of absolute submission, the sinking "on unruffled wing," with which
the gull executes its plunge into the darkness over the sea. It is
a submission which seems justified by the description of the
sea which concludes the poem. Unlike the sea from which
"our patch of sand" required protection at the poem's beginning, this is a benign, "rustling" sea, a sea which sustains the
confidence of the two sleepers, the narrator and his daughter,
who are in their own way about to emulate the gull and plunge
"on unruffled wing" into the darkness, the nightly darkness of
lapse of consciousness, which prefigures death:

It sank on unruffled wing.
We hear the sea rustling.

It will rustle all night, darling.

The narrator's acceptance of time, his submission to night and
the sea, even as the girl cheerfully accepted the ruined flower,
or as the gull sank on unruffled wing, comprises the major
"promise" of this poem, then, and perhaps the most significant
promise of the whole sequence. To the totality of time the
narrator consigns his self, his own and his daughter's identity,
and from that entirety of time he draws into his self whatever
significance the totality of time may possess. Such achievement of self-transcending significance is almost invariably the
aim of the Warren protagonist, and the degree to which this
aim is fulfilled in "The Flower" is surely one of the high-water
marks of his career as a writer.

"Colder Fire," the fifth and last poem of the "Rosanna" sequence, takes as its central theme a final appraisal of the development of perspective which has occurred in the total sequence, and it makes this appraisal in the deliberate, meditative manner prescribed in Wordsworth's notion of "emotion recollected in tranquillity." This poem gathers together the fragments of experience we have observed and imposes a last, magnificent, mountain-top perspective over the whole. Here the promises of transcendence are realized to the fullest extent that human experience allows. Here we are transported to the regions we vainly yearned after in "Sirocco": "Far hangs Giannutri in blue air. Far to that blueness the heart aches."

The setting as well as the method of this poem suggests Wordsworth, the beginning of "Resolution and Independence" offering a particularly noteworthy comparison:

WORDSWORTH:
>There was a roaring in the wind all night;
>The rain came heavily and fell in floods. . . .

WARREN:
>It rained toward day. The morning came sad and white
>With silver of sea-sadness and defection of season.

>. . . . .

>We moved . . . in muteness of spirit past logical reason.

The similarity between these two poems continues in the identical tone of gratitude with which each speaker welcomes the clearing after the storm:

WORDSWORTH:
>But now the sun is rising calm and bright;
>The birds are singing in the distant woods;

>. . . . .

>And all the air is filled with pleasant noise of waters.

WARREN:
> Now sun, afternoon, and again summer-glitter on sea.
> As you to a bright toy, the heart leaps.

Even the response of the lesser creatures to the sun after the storm is observed by the two poets in a like manner. Much as Wordsworth marvels how "The hare is running races in her mirth," Warren exults in watching "White butterflies over gold thistle conduct their ritual carouse."

Beyond these specific comparisons, it is interesting to observe how each poet voices similar misgivings over the capricious unsteadfastness of the sensitive spirit:

WORDSWORTH:
> As high as we have mounted in delight
> In our dejection do we sink as low;
> To me that morning did it happen so;
> And fears and fancies thick upon me came;
> Dim sadness—and blind thoughts, I knew not, nor could
> name.

WARREN:
> We moved—your mother and I—in muteness of spirit past
> logical reason.
>
> .   .   .   .
>   .   .   . though we know, shamefaced, the heart's weather
> should not be
> Merely a reflex to solstice, or sport of some aggrieved equinox.

From this point on, the two poems proceed in different directions, but even in their basic variation, they maintain a roughly analogous structure: Wordsworth's narrator is seeking wisdom and sustenance from an older man, and Warren's narrator seeks to impart the same to his infant daughter.

The wisdom and sustenance which the speaker offers his

daughter begins on a somewhat negative note: the same butterflies which a moment ago had given joy now begin, at the end of Stanza 4, to circumscribe that joy: ". . . they mount light, pair by pair, / As though that tall light were eternal indeed, not merely the summer's reprieve." What we see here, of course, is a recapitulation of the narrator's misgivings when his daughter accepted the ruined flower: "And you sing as though human need / Were not for perfection." Unlike the girl or the butterflies, the narrator knows the transitoriness of light, in the case of the butterflies, and of beauty, in the case of the girl who loves flowers. He knows the ruinous working of time.

What this poem becomes, in the light of this knowledge, is a search for a permanent beauty, a beauty beyond the corrosive reach of time and above the havoc of everyday experience. It is an intellectual beauty; a beauty of perspective so magnificent as to be almost incommunicable; a beauty of vision such as might lastingly enrapture the soul, regardless of what might later ensue within the narrower limits of the valley or the ruined fortress. Such beauty, perpetuated in memory, is what comprises the "colder fire" of the poem's title.

The extent both of human limitations and of their concomitant possibilities is represented towards the middle of the poem by the mountain peak, which thrusts its head far, far above, into the vastness of "the sky's dream":

> The sky's dream is enormous, I lift up my eyes.
> In sunlight a tatter of mist clings high on the mountain-mass.
> The mountain is under the sky.   .   .   .

What must lie ahead, then, is some sort of ascent of the soul, some striving to attain the best perspective that the mountain offers, the vision that sustains. But the ascent is not easy. The

place is very high, and getting there requires an effort that will
carry the climber past every other landmark of human ascent,
past the markings of every other human activity:

> . . . there the gray scarps rise
> Past paths where on their appointed occasions men climb,
>   and pass.

> Past grain-patch, last apron of vineyard, last terrace of olive,
> Past chestnut, past cork grove, where the last carts can go,
> Past camp of the charcoal maker, where coals glow in the
>   black hive,
> The scarps, gray, rise up. Above them is that place I know.

Higher yet we must go; the secret place apparently challenges
not only the efforts but the faith of the seeker. The glade
appears unexpectedly almost at the uppermost limits of the
tree-line:

> Shelf above scarp, enclave of rock, a glade
> Benched and withdrawn in the mountain-mass, under the
>   peak's duress.
> We came there—your mother and I—and rested in that severe
>   shade.

Arduous as it is, the climb once achieved pays the richest of
dividends. Here a "hawk-hung delight" of perspective not
normally available to human beings is offered. Here from a
place of beauty the seeker can peer over "the empty threshold
of air" at the glade's edge so as to comprehend in a single
perception all that is humanly visible of the "sky's
dream"—"distance unspooled" and "bright space spilled" and
sea and land merging "in the far light":

Pine-blackness mist-tangled, the peak black above: the glade
    gives
On the empty threshold of air, the hawk-hung delight
Of distance unspooled and bright space spilled—ah, the heart
    thrives!
We stood in that shade and saw sea and land lift in the far
    light.

"The heart thrives!" So effectual was this imbibing of beauty that in the very next stanza the image that formerly meant perishing beauty, the "time-tattered" butterflies, now is seen as contributing by its very mutability to the permanent beauty of natural fulfillment and change. The image by which Warren renders this idea is an exceptionally lovely one. The beauty which comes through fulfillment and change is depicted in miniature by the manner in which the mist in the upper glade condenses at the ends of the pine needles, to glitter there for a moment and then fall:

Now the butterflies dance, time-tattered and disarrayed.
I watch them. I think how above that far scarp's sunlit wall
Mist threads in silence the darkness of boughs, and in that
    shade
Condensed moisture gathers at needle-tip. It glitters, will fall.

Having achieved in the above two stanzas everything that poetry can do, Warren goes on in the fashion of Eliot's *Four Quartets* to comment on the limitations of poetry. Much in the same spirit that Eliot calls art "a raid on the inarticulate / With shabby equipment always deteriorating," Warren observes the essential incommunicability of experience:

I cannot interpret for you this collocation
Of memories. You will live your own life, and contrive
The language of your own heart.   .   .   .

Because one's deepest experience is always too personal to allow its total transmission to another, even through such marvelous imagery as that offered by the secret mountain glade, the important thing is to be internally honest: to let "the language of your own heart" correspond as closely as possible to the realities that such a language is intended to identify, which is to say, to "whatever truth you would live."

Promises as a whole is Warren's attempt to impart to his children the truth *he* would live, and now as he concludes the section "To Rosanna," he devotes the last stanza of the whole sequence to a final synthesis of that truth as he has lived it in these five poems. This stanza is one of the most difficult to understand in the whole volume, but it is also one of the most important to our understanding of Warren's total artistry.

> For fire flames but in the heart of a colder fire.
> All voice is but echo caught from a soundless voice.
> Height is not deprivation of valley, nor defect of desire,
> But defines, for the fortunate, that joy in which all joys
>   should rejoice.

The conjunction "for" at the beginning of this passage indicates a cause-and-effect relationship with the previous stanza, the stanza which, as we have just noted, suggests the difficulty of communication confronting the poet as a result of the uniquely private language of every heart. The "for" which begins the final stanza, then, must continue the theme of the efficacy of art.

It is difficult to paraphrase Warren's final statement about the efficacy of art, but there can be no mistaking his general tone: it is strongly affirmative. The "fire" and the "colder fire" of Line 1 attain clarity of meaning in terms of their counterparts, the "voice" and the "soundless voice," in the second line. The "fire" and the "voice," it seems to me, refer to the poet's motive and to what that motive produces—what through his art he says. The "colder fire" and the "soundless voice" tie in with the exhortation to recognize honestly "whatever truth you would live" in the previous stanza; these images imply that that private truth of the next-last stanza is, if it is honestly acknowledged, not so private after all. The vision of truth which each heart claims as distinctly its own partakes in fact of a larger vision, a generalized truth, embracing in composite all the lesser ones: "For fire flames but in the heart of a colder fire." Consequently, the body of art (the "voice") whereby the individual seer renders his particular vision of truth may appear distinct from all others, but actually every artist is only adding his strength to a composite voice—the voice, which is ultimately inarticulate, of all men seeking truth: "All voice is but echo caught from a soundless voice."

The efficacy of art being thus confirmed, Warren gives a final summary and justification of what his art has done in the five "Rosanna" poems, and he does this essentially in a half-line: "Height is not deprivation of valley." This image explains and defends the ascent of the soul which occurred in this poem. It explains the ascent as a genuine attainment of perspective through supreme effort, not to be confused with the ideal of life as a smooth, distinctionless plain or plateau without suffering or struggle, and it defends the ascent from the appearance of callousness: the moment of culmination does not project the climber into a haven of self that is forevermore secure from all the anguish he had known in the valleys; does not rescind the ritual of brotherhood that had connected him with the hunchback and the defective child in the ruined fortress; does not make him a superhuman creature unmindful or scornful of the limitations of life in the valley, where he had himself so lately agonized over the "filth of fate" and the imperfections inherent in even the highest beauty, as represented by the flower. Nor is the height a "defect of desire"; the grand perspective is not an all-satisfying opiate of the soul, guaranteeing so pervasive a tranquillity as to obviate the "human need for perfection" that at lower ground seemed crucial.

What the height, or the sublime breadth of vision, does provide—and this is Warren's last word and promise to Rosanna—is a sound basis for the joy of life, a joy of life which Rosanna assumes without question now but which will later require solid intellectual undergirding. And the view from the height is the only such undergirding available; without such a vision, the joy of life must surely be extinguished in a world which is largely tragic, a world which seems everywhere polluted by the "filth of fate," a world where whatever beauty does exist in consigned shortly to "the ruck of the world's wind." But to "the fortunate" who attain this perspective, it not only gives joy in its own right but provides true justification for all other joys of life. It is "that joy in which all joys should rejoice."

Warren's legacy of experience, then, as pertaining to Rosanna at least, is a composite of horror and joy, and through a masterful exploitation of the best resources that poetry offers, he makes both the horror and the joy movingly convincing. His resolution of the conflict is not simple or easy, since throughout the sequence his poetry reflects the painful ambiguities of actual experience, but in ending the sequence on a note of joy, he shows that his resolution is ultimately affirmative, providing only that one's perspective be broad enough, and sufficiently self-transcending.

The Promise to Gabriel: Oneness of Time and Flesh

THE SECTION of *Promises* dedicated to Gabriel is roughly analogous to the Rosanna sequence in its probing of experience to find the limits of human horror and joy, but there are notable differences of approach, subject matter, and resolution. The approach has little of the dramatic conflict which we observed between the narrator and child in the Rosanna sequence, ostensibly because this child is too young to permit any such interchange. The few times when Gabriel does appear, he is seen sleeping in his cradle, receiving the benediction of the "Lullaby" poems and representing a promise in return to the narrator who sings them, much in the fashion of Coleridge and his baby in "Frost at Midnight." In place of dramatic tension we see in the Gabriel sequence at large a bequest to the infant involving the narrator's exploration of self, an old Warren quest refurbished anew by the seeker's desire to provide not only himself but his successor with a meaningful identity.

Warren's subject consequently runs through all the primary sources of identity in his own life, including personal, family, and even national history, considered from the varied perspectives of his or his nation's boyhood and maturity. He includes also such sources of identity as the psychological and theological probings of self can afford, probings which Warren frequently dramatizes by use of dream imagery set against a surrealistic background. The emergence of an explicit religious position particularly distinguishes the Gabriel sequence from its counterpart. Although the ritual of brotherhood and the

ascent up the mountain give the Rosanna poems a recognizable Christian ethic and metaphysic, neither the ethic nor the
metaphysic gets as full or as emphatically Christian a treatment here as they get throughout the Gabriel poems. Moreover, the setting of the Gabriel poems is more characteristically
Warren's than the Rosanna poems could ever be. Although
the old world (or ruined fortress) setting occasionally obtrudes
into the longer sequence, the typical setting here is the familiar
one of Warren's heritage, the western "Pennyroyal" region of
Kentucky, a landscape which has proven so congenial to
Warren's art through the years as to invite comparison with
Faulkner's Yoknapatawpha mythology. Whatever one may
think of Warren's literary uses of the "homing" psychology,
there can be little doubt that this very instinct has operated
throughout Warren's career, perhaps most strongly during his
"expatriate" years, in so powerful a fashion as to have released
his best creativity in poetry and fiction.

Psychologically, Warren seems always to have been himself a Billie Potts, riding east instead of west but repeatedly
feeling within himself "the itch and humble promise which is
home," and repeatedly returning to that early landscape in his
imagination so as to peer once more into the crow-black waters
of identity, or to start with fright at the hilltop serpent's hiss,
or to probe anew and all alone the deepest, darkest caverns of
the self. Here in *Promises* the search for identity is carried on
with a more personal intensity than ever before, for here the
esthetic distance is reduced to nothing: across that Kentuckian
landscape pass the actual people of Warren's reminiscence—
his father and mother, his Confederate cavalryman grandfather, various acquaintances of school and neighborhood, a
tragically rootless wandering bum, fellow workers getting hay
—and all appear in the person of the original, with neither

name, appearance, nor credentials altered for the sake of artistic discretion. Here, too, Warren bares his own self to his audience with unprecedented candor, for here Warren himself is narrator, not as in *Brother to Dragons* by means of a fictional construct distinct from and less than the author of the whole work, but in the total unfathomed fullness of his whole self. Here, in sum, Warren offers himself more frankly than ever as the material of his art. In such directness and nakedness of self lies the basic power of lyric poetry. In this respect, Warren falls in with the New Romanticism that has recently gained vogue with such writers as Robert Lowell and Karl Shapiro.

Although the nineteen poems (not counting subdivisions) of the Gabriel sequence do not exhibit the interlocking continuity of the shorter Rosanna sequence, they do have a thematic integrity in their own right. Sometimes this development takes place through subgroupings within the entirety of the sequence. Poems III and IV, "Gold Glade" and "Dark Woods," constitute one such grouping in their use of a common image—the moment of vision in the forest—to show the bright and the dark of mystic perception; and taken together, these two poems form the enchanted-forest backdrop for Poem XVI, "Ballad of a Sweet Dream of Peace." Poems V, VI, and VII, entitled "Country Burying (1919)," "School Lesson Based on Word of Tragic Death of Entire Gillum Family," and "Summer Storm (Circa 1916), and God's Grace," are likewise a subgrouping set off in contrast to the mystical "Dark Woods" and "Gold Glade." These poems have a common mood, realism; a common theme, the awakening of young Robert Penn Warren to tragedy (much like the initiation of Hemingway's Nick Adams); and a common subject, the actual experiences of Warren's adolescence. Other groupings do not occur in consecutive sequence, but rather appear in recurrent fashion at strategic locations. Poems XII and XVIII, for example, are the two "Lullaby" poems, "Smile in Sleep" and "A Motion like Sleep." The first of these, which affirms the efficacy of the will ("Dream the power coming on"), follows a group of poems describing failure and disillusion in midcentury America, whereas the other "Lullaby," the next to last lyric in the book, qualifies the "Boy's Will" of the preceding poems by anticipating the self's return to its darksome origins: "all that flows finds end but in its own source."

Other subgroupings in recurrent rather than consecutive order of appearance include Poems II and VIII, "Court-martial" and "Founding Fathers, Nineteenth-Century Style, Southeast U.S.A.," a pair of excursions into the world of Warren's ancestors, and Poems IX, XIII (1), and XIV, three poems treating the knowledge of death in a foreign setting ("Foreign Shore, Old Woman, Slaughter of Octopus," "Moonlight Observed from Ruined Fortress," and "Mad Young Aristocrat on Beach"). By means of the Italian setting, these poems not only tie in the Gabriel sequence with the poems to Rosanna but also serve to clarify and reinforce some the central images of the earlier sequence. The meaning of the gull image, for instance, so crucially important in the Rosanna poems, is clearly articulated in "Foreign Shore, Old Woman, Slaughter of Octopus": "And agleam in imperial ease, at sky-height, / One gull hangs white in contempt of our human heart, and the night."

Another method of maintaining continuity of theme is the use and development of recurrent images, even in poems of ostensibly different subject matter. The motif of the callously mutilated snake, for example, appears in "The Hazel Leaf" (part of Poem IV, "Dark Woods"), where the creature's "jeweled head" is crushed and observed by emotionally

detached passers-by. The same motif takes on larger implications when it reappears in Poem XVII, in the sections entitled
"The Snake" and "Hands Are Paid," for here the snake is
raised on a "propped pitchfork" almost as though in a religious
parody.

Variations of this motif include the slaughter of other
unfortunate creatures, ranging from the shooting of the bullbat in Poem I and the frenzied knifing of a chance octopus
(Poem IX) to the murder, sometimes insane (Poem VI, on
the death of the Gillum family), sometimes methodical
(Poem II, "Court-martial"), of human beings. Sometimes,
too, this slaughter is the result of natural agency, rather than
human, as in "Country Burying (1919)" and "Summer Storm
(Circa 1916), and God's Grace," whereas in other poems,
such as "Dragon Country: To Jacob Boehme," the agency of
destruction is neither human nor natural, but supernatural.

Taken together, these images of wanton slaughter and
destruction add up to a judgment at once grim and tender.
The grimness lies in the breadth of depravity here chronicled,
where man, nature, and supernature are engaged in heartless
carnage, not just to satisfy inherent predatory needs, but more
often than not simply to divert or amuse. Yet, for all the
depravity and grimness of judgment, there is a tenderness in
Warren's vision as well. It is the tenderness of the tragedian
who sees suffering and guilt and even cruelty in partly deter-
ministic terms; it is the extraordinary sympathy amounting to
identity with the villain, be he even so gross a butcher as Big
Billie Potts or Lilburn Lewis, based on a logic of total human
complicity.

In the framework of these poems, that complicity is illumi-
nated as never before by the presence of the nonhuman
agencies, natural and supernatural. The moral agonies of the
human condition receive a sobering reappraisal when sub-

jected to this external standard of judgment: what right have human beings to decry God's "sadistic idiocies," it is implied (in "Summer Storm"), when human beings themselves are seen throughout this sequence perpetrating equally sadistic idiocies on bullbat, snake, octopus, and fellow human beings? In this particular phase of his vision, Warren's tenderness is very much akin to certain Romantic precepts: where Blake says, "For everything that lives is holy," and Coleridge affirms, "He prayeth well, who loveth well / Both man and bird and beast," Warren asserts in a similar vein, "we're all one Flesh, at last" (in "Go It, Granny—Go It, Hog!").

That Warren considers this "one Flesh" to encompass more than human flesh is clear in many poems, in *Promises* and elsewhere, but perhaps the most convincing evidence may be found in a comparison of two scenes of slaughter. In one instance, "Court-martial" (Poem II), the victims are human, whereas in the other, "Boy's Will, Joyful Labor without Pay, and Harvest Home (1918)," the victim is a black snake. The behavior of the self while confronting extinction is so similar in both instances, whether that self be embodied in human or reptile, as to suggest that in the ultimate showdown the distinctions are secondary. We are one Flesh indeed:

> They took shape, enormous in air.
>   . . . enormous, they hung there.
>
> Each face outraged, agape,
> Not yet believing it true.
> Each hairy jaw is askew,
> Tongue out, out-staring eye,
> And the spittle not yet dry
> That was uttered with the last cry.
>
>   ("Court-martial")

But a black snake rears in his ruined room.

Defiant, tall in that blast of day,
Now eye for eye, he swaps his stare.
His outrage glitters on the air.
Men shout, ring around. He can't get away.

("Boy's Will")

Their "outrage" is none the less because the victims are themselves killers and predators. This is where Warren departs from the Romantic precepts—he sees the tragedy and complicity of the world in such a way that both guilt and innocence, when claimed by the self in isolation, are delusory. This is a world where all are innocent and all are guilty alike. The one unforgivable sin in Warren's ethic is to deny that complicity, that oneness of Flesh; and consequently, the one unredeemable character in Warren's art is the person, such as Ikey Sumpter in *The Cave*, who sets himself apart from his fellow creatures by insisting upon his absolute innocence, his absolute independence of self.

In *Promises*, the character who fails to see the oneness of Flesh is an insensitive old man, though not a particularly callous or selfish one, who brings up the ending of the poem "The Snake" after the killing and raising of the snake on a pitchfork has taken place:

Against the wounded evening matched,
Snagged high on a pitchfork tine, he will make
Slow arabesque till the bullbats wake.
An old man, standing stooped, detached,
Spits once, says, "Hell, just another snake."

The word "detached" here signifies that all Flesh is not one at this point, and it correlates with the similarly cold and objective word "observed" in "The Hazel Leaf":

Who passed, struck; now goes on.
    The snake waits, head crushed, to be observed by the next
        to pass.
    He will observe it, and then pass.

Warren's own attitude, unlike the old man's or the casual
"observer's," is one of continued contemplation of the incident, with the result that this subject is not only extended into
the poem, "Hands Are Paid," which follows "The Snake," but
there assumes an increased importance through religious connotations:

The little blood that smeared the stone
Dropped in the stubble, has long since dried.

.   .   .   .

In the star-pale field, the propped pitchfork lifts
Its burden, hung black, to the white star.

I apply the term "religious connotations" to this passage only
in a broad sense—in the sense that these images counsel
humility. The blood-smeared stone and the propped pitchfork
starkly point up human limitations and human depravity.
Without being too hard on the "detached" old man, too
exhausted by work even to remove his clothes (he is one of us,
as the snake is), the narrator appears to be calling for a
recognition of something here, for a sense of complicity. This
dying snake (like its fellow creatures in the other poems of
slaughter) might be part of man's self, momentarily external-
ized and gruesomely offering to the aware observer an image
of his own condition whereby he might have true knowledge of
self and knowledge of death.
    This total participation, this sharing alike of innocence and
guilt by the "one Flesh" of all creatures, past, present, and

future, is what Warren is getting at when he says, in various contexts, "And our innocence needs, perhaps, new definition." This complicity is what is implied in the minotaur image of *Brother to Dragons*, where the half-man, half-bull represents the "one Flesh" of all creatures. The serpent, too, is our brother; the blood of dragons flows through the veins of the image of God. The oneness of Flesh, the interrelationship of all creatures throughout the entirety of the time continuum, is perceived by Warren with much the same mystical intensity as Robert Frost evinces in his memorable couplet describing evolution in "Sitting by a Bush in Broad Sunlight": "And from that one intake of fire / All creatures still warmly suspire."

More could be said about the slaughter imagery in *Promises*, but I shall limit my attention to two further instances. The first, the slaughter of the octopus, reinforces—that is to say, it clarifies and is clarified by—the mutilated serpent. One way in which the octopus poem ("Foreign Shore, Old Woman, Slaughter of Octopus") restates the serpent image is through the setting. Both "The Snake" and "Slaughter of Octopus" preface a vision of horror with scenes of joy, in the former instance a scene of "Joyful Labor" and in the latter a scene of play: "All day there was picnic and laughter." The resemblance of theme grows more obvious with the appearance of the unexpected intruder. Just as the snake had interrupted the "joyful labor" by rearing "big in his ruined room," so now the octopus breaks up the picnic and laughter by rising "up from some . . . dark lair of water" so as to "spread out on stone."

The most important correlation between octopus and snake is the principle of self which each embodies, a principle of self which their human slaughterers share unawares. Ugly monstrosity that he is, "Ectoplasmic, snot-gray, the obscene of the life-wish," the octopus nevertheless participates in the oneness of Flesh with all his identity, like every other creature, and no impulsive act of destruction can obliterate this ugliness and obscenity from the universal selfhood. Like the serpent propped on a tine, it is perpetually there, risen from the darksome depths to confront mankind with a ghastly image of self that outlasts the creature's destruction. The major difference between these two poems is in the point of view. Whereas the boy in "Hands Are Paid" perceived all alone "The little blood that smeared the stone / Dropped in the stubble," the narrator of the octopus poem sees the "pearl-slime of the slaughter, on black stone" together with another observer, the old woman in black, who, herself near death, sees in the slaughter of octopus a portent of her own extinction: "She knows, as the sea, that what came will recur."

The second and more important slaughter image is that of the hogs in Lyrics 3 and 6 of "Ballad of a Sweet Dream of Peace," where the effect is not one of reinforcement so much as of apotheosis. Here is the ultimate outcome and climax of the universal guilt that is implied throughout these specific instances of slaughter. Here in the mystical borderland between life and death, where the issue hangs between damnation and redemption, the relationship between slaughterer and victim is seen in a horrifying and truth-revealing reverse order: here the hogs, who in this world are raised for the very purpose of being slaughtered, wait to devour their former devourers.

In this other-worldly context, the appeal to innocence is so much chaff in the breeze, so many words for the wind, in the face of the hogs' hunger. The mysteriously omniscient narrator of the poems that comprise the "Ballad of a Sweet Dream of Peace"—he guides his visitor around and answers the wide-

eyed questions much as the guide does in Dante's or Virgil's
classic journeys to the underworld—quickly demolishes the
innocence of the newly arrived initiate, a youth who had
helped raise these hogs for slaughter (the initiate's speech is in
italics; the narrator's, in regular print):

> *Out there in the dark, what's that horrible chomping?*
> Oh, nothing, just hogs that forage for mast,
> And if you call, "Hoo-pig!" they'll squeal and come romping,
> For they'll know from your voice you're the boy who slopped
>   them in dear, dead days long past.
>
> *Any hogs that I slopped are long years dead,*
> *And eaten by somebody and evacuated,*
> *So it's simply absurd, what you said.*

The initiate's protestation of innocence, couched in the
logic of the much-quoted Jew of Malta ("But that was in
another country, and besides, the wench is dead"), clarifies yet
once again a basic motif in all Warren's art: "Oh, nothing is
lost, ever lost!" ("Original Sin: A Short Story" and elsewhere). Since nothing is ever lost, or since the initiate's
supposition that he is rid of the hogs once they are killed and
digested is belied by the "horrible chomping" "out there in the
dark," he must find another mode of justification than innocence. Eternity has uprooted evidence which he had thought
safely buried under Time's alluvium, with the eaten and
evacuated hogs, and now those hogs, resurrected and ravenous,
chomp frightfully, close by.

Stripped thus of his innocence, the initiate's only appeal,
the narrator makes clear, is to the oneness of Flesh, a concept
which here, as in the incident of the mutilated snake, offers
salvation in return for depth and accuracy of vision, and in
return for the humility that such vision generates: "You fool,

poor fool, all Time is a dream, and we're all one Flesh, at last."
And just in case the humility is not forthcoming, the hogs
graphically provide metaphysical instruction by devouring old
granny, the distracted old skeleton in search of identity in the
two previous poems—she whom the initiate had at that time
called "old fool" and "old bitch":

> .   .   .   all Time is a dream, and we're all one Flesh, at last,
> And the hogs know that, and that's why they wait,
> Though tonight the old thing is a little bit late,
> But they're mannered, these hogs, as they wait for her creaky
>   old tread.   .   .   .
>
> .   .   .   .
> Then old bones get knocked down with a clatter to wake up
>   the dead,
> And it's simply absurd how loud she can scream with no shred
>   of a tongue in her head.

By dint of this grisly meal, hogs and granny and observer
too—since he can hardly resist the force of this
instruction—are rendered "one Flesh" indeed, all protestations of innocence being to no avail. For granny, the implication is that her identity has been found at last—her skeleton
form ("with eyeballs gone," "with no shred of a tongue," etc.)
has been assimilated into the "one Flesh" represented by those
traditional emblems of fleshliness, the all-devouring hogs. In
any event, this is the last we see of grandma: naturally enough,
she disappears from view following her transubstantiation into
hogflesh. For the initiate, this lesson smarts home with a
special sting because the narrator seizes upon the initiate's
logical affirmation of innocence ("So *it's simply absurd*, what
you said") so as to hurl the phrasing of that logic back in
his teeth: "A*nd it's simply absurd* how loud she can
scream.   .   .   ."

Abundant as they are, the images of slaughter in the Gabriel sequence are further corroborated by a somewhat different pattern of recurrent images. These are the images of bodily decay and dissolution, differing from the images of slaughter in that the agent of destruction here—most often it is nature—is of secondary importance to the actuality of death as a *fait accompli*. This strand of imagery begins with Poem I, where the narrator's parents are seen "in a phosphorus of glory, bones bathed" under the ground, and proceeds through a number of other poems until reaching its apotheosis, like the imagery of slaughter, in the "granny–Hog" imagery of "Ballad of a Sweet Dream of Peace."

Sometimes this imagery of dissolution is shockingly gruesome, as in the poem "The Dogwood" (in "Dark Woods"), where a cow's skull provides a "cathedral for ants," and at other times it can be movingly delicate and subtle. "The Hazel Leaf" centers upon an image of this kind whereby death is pictured as a gentle letting-go from the Tree of Life, followed by a delicious floating-back to the origin of all, the earth: "The hazel leaf falls in autumn. / It slants athwart the gold air." A group of boys kick and trample the gold leaves—their focus being on the value of the nuts they can find—as carelessly as the passer-by crushes the head of "The little green snake by the path-side" and as exuberantly as other boys had knifed the octopus, but in the deepening dusk only the tranquil solitude of eternity seems of any moment:

> Now at dusk-hour. The foot
>   Of only the squirrel stirs leaf of this solitude.
>   Otherwise, only shadow may intrude.

The imagery of dissolution is transmuted into an ironically abstract generalization, "the arithmetic of losses," in Poem VI,

"School Lesson Based on Word of Tragic Death of Entire Gillum Family." The word "arithmetic" is of course calculated to reinforce the title image, "School Lesson," but the cool abstractness of this term quickly evaporates under the touch of the specific details behind those losses. The "arithmetic of losses" further assumes an exceedingly personal impact with the "getting on to sun" of the final couplet:

> Studying the arithmetic of losses,
> > To be prepared when the next one,
> By fire, flood, foe, cancer, thrombosis,
> > Or Time's slow malediction, came to be undone.
>
> *We studied all afternoon, till getting on to sun.*
> *There was another lesson, but we were too young to take up*
> > *that one.*

By phrasing the central tragedy of this poem in the mathematical terminology of "arithmetic of losses," with its implication that every individual unit is exactly equal in value to every other such unit, Warren subtly anticipates his major theme in "Ballad of a Sweet Dream of Peace" and in *Promises* as a whole: "we're all one Flesh, at last."

Of clearly climactic importance in the tissue of dissolution images is the marvelous figure of granny in the first three lyrics of "Ballad of a Sweet Dream of Peace." In her obsessive hankering after the past, imaged in her polishing of the old-fashioned bureau, she is a typical Warren heroine. She knows that her identity, "that poor self she'd mislaid," must at all costs be rediscovered, and she knows, too, that it can be found only through exploring the past, on the premise that nothing is ever lost. Disregarding the cynical young initiate, who calls her "old fool" and "old bitch" and obviously thinks her insane, wishing she were not his grandma, old granny goes right ahead polishing up that old bureau and all the heritage of the past it represents.

What is important in light of the imagery of dissolution is the fact that granny is a skeleton; her "bones let the wind blow through." The title of Lyric 1 assumes a double irony with this understanding. "And Don't Forget Your Corset Cover, Either" is ironic because she needs the corset cover, to conceal her bones, but not the corset, for she has no flesh—until the supernatural hogs provide it—to need conforming into shape. It is doubly ironic because both clothes and flesh have been stripped from grandma in the interest of casting away identities which in this world are oh-so-important but which are ultimately false:

> *But why, in God's name, all this privacy for a simple*
> *household chore?*
> In God's name, sir! would you simply let
> Folks see how naked old ladies can get?
> *Then let the old bitch buy some clothes like other folks do.*
> She once had some clothes, I am told,
> But they're long since ruined by the damp and mold.   .   .   .

A complete nakedness of self, stripped of all its deceptive auxiliaries, then, is prerequisite to finding true identity. The transient superficialities of flesh and clothing do not contain our ultimate identity, except as the flesh partakes of the mystical oneness of Flesh, and that Flesh is of supernatural origin, obtained only after the natural has been laid aside. Knowing all this, granny isn't really concerned with her corset cover; it is the unawakened initiate who appears to be handing out the futile advice in the title.

Important as they are, images of slaughter and their companion images of dissolution are not the only recurrent motifs

in the Gabriel sequence, nor, for that matter, are they finally
the most important. Set off against the slaughter and dissolution are a series of images involving, like their opposite counterparts, man and nature and supernature, but having a distinctly beatific function.

Warren's has always been an art involving opposite polarities. In the Rosanna sequence the basic structure, as we
remember, was the conflict and eventual resolution of polarities between garbage and thistle bloom, beetle and gull, the
defective child next door and Rosanna. In other works too,
there is always a central conflict of opposites: the idealism of
Adam Stanton against the realism of Willie Stark, the higher
innocence of the Greek against the delusion of innocence in
the "Jew" (Ikey Sumpter) in *The Cave*; the Band of Angels
against the Brotherhood of Dragons. In *Promises* to Gabriel,
Warren's approach is no less comprehensive. Against the
imagery of slaughter and dissolution he erects all-
encompassing imagery of benediction; offsetting the slaughterers are those who "died for love"; against nature the destroyer,
of "Summer Storm," is nature the uplifting and sublime, in
"Gold Glade"; counteracting the ravaging Beast of "Dragon
Country" is the redemptive supernatural, the "purchaser of
the woods," in "Ballad of a Sweet Dream of Peace."

As was the case with the imagery of destruction, the
imagery of benediction gets underway in Poem I of the Gabriel
sequence, "What Was the Promise That Smiled from the
Maples at Evening?" The ultimate "promise" which the title
refers to brings up the rear of the poem, thereby shedding
peace upon a context which up to that point had grown
increasingly darker, colder, lonelier, more sinister. It is the
promise entailing a willing sacrifice of self, ultimately meaning
death, by which every generation paves the way for its succes-

sor. The narrator here is both receiving this ultimate benediction (from his parents) and bestowing it, by means of this poem, upon his own offspring:

> . . . in a cold and coagulate evening, I've stood
> Where they slept, the long dead, and the farms and far woods
>   fled away,
> And a gray light prevailed and both landscape and heart
>   were subdued.
> Then sudden, the ground at my feet was like glass, and I say
> What I saw, saw deep down, and the fleshly habiliments
>   rent—
> But agleam in a phosphorus of glory, bones bathed, there
>   they lay,
> Side by side, Ruth and Robert: the illumination then spent.
>
> Earth was earth, and in earth-dark no glow now. . . .
>   .   .   .   .
> Then her voice, long forgotten, calm in silence, said:
>   "Child."
> Then his, with the calm of a night field, or far star:
> "We died only that every promise might be fulfilled."

There is much here deserving of comment. The depiction of the parents in skeletal terms, for example,—"bones bathed," "and the fleshly habiliments rent"—anticipates the appearance of old granny in the "Ballad of a Sweet Dream of Peace." Old granny's whisper, "I died for love," constitutes in fact a restating of the above assertion: "We died only that every promise might be fulfilled." The circumstances of this vision likewise require some cross references. The subdued atmosphere ("both landscape and heart were subdued") and "gray light" of this scene call to mind the "wan light" and "muteness of spirit past logical reason" preceding the ascent of the soul in "Colder Fire."

Perhaps more important than either the circumstances of this epiphany or its content is the tone: "her voice, *calm* in silence" and "his, with the *calm* of a night field, or far star." (The transcendence of this "far star," by the way, ties in with other images of "far-ness" in both the Gabriel and the Rosanna sequences.) This calmness is what is chiefly of value: it is the ultimate recompense to those of the phosphorescent bones for their having endured and having given all. It is a calmness which, emanating out of total darkness ("in earth-dark no glow now"), alleviates the relative darkness of the previous stanzas, whose settings had increasingly implied death ("at evening," "sunset," "after the last light had died," "after the dying was done"). This calmness had been the particular need of the fourth stanza, where the knowledge of death had been crushing: "All the long years before, like burnt paper, flared into black, / And the house shrunk to silence." It is a calmness which is finally apotheosized and bestowed by the author upon his children and his audience in the final poem of the book, "The Necessity for Belief": "The sun is red, and the sky does not scream. . . . The moon is in the sky, and there is no weeping." It is only through understanding the significance of calmness in Poem I that we can appreciate the meaning of the final poem and so determine why Warren did not end the *Promises* sequence with "Ballad of a Sweet Dream of Peace." Beyond the vision, the oneness of Flesh, and the redemption, he had one further blessing to give. The "sweet dream of peace" becomes actual peace only with the recipience of that blessing, the state of perfect calm and absolute accept-ance which pervades "The Necessity for Belief."

The benediction of Poem I, which we have just discussed, has supernatural overtones, but it is essentially a human benediction, given to assuage the pain of a world where both time and flesh are as yet fragmented into seemingly isolated units. Although the anticipation "that every promise might be fulfilled" offers hope of some ultimate synthesis, such promise is not fulfilled as of now, with the result that mankind is still sectioned into two opposite categories: the dead generations of the past as against the living generation of the present. The "far star" to which the narrator's dead father is compared suggests the essential isolation and inaccessibility of the living from the dead, despite their ultimate oneness. Although it is valuable enough to warrant transmission to the next generation, then—both in this poem and in "Lullaby: Moonlight Lingers" (below)—the human benediction requires strengthening from external sources, without which strengthening it remains, however sacred and uplifting, essentially insubstantial:

> Moonlight falls on sleeping faces.
> It fell in far times and other places.
>
> .   .   .   .   .   .
> And now in memory's stasis
> I see moonlight mend an old man's Time-crossed brow.
> My son, sleep deep.   .   .   .
>
> .   .   .   .   .
> Those who died, died long ago,
> Faces you will never know,
> Voices you will never hear—
> Though your father heard them in the night,
> And yet, sometimes, I can hear
> That utterance as if tongue-rustle of pale tide in moonlight:
> *Sleep, son. Good night.*

To supplement the human benediction, in view of its essential insubstantiality, Warren draws strength from two other sources, natural and supernatural. The benediction of

nature is best seen in the poem "Gold Glade," where the
narrator unexpectedly receives an esthetic perception of permanent value:

>   . . .   and so I
> Went on, in quiet, through the beech wood:
> There, in gold light, where the glade gave, it stood.
>
> The glade was geometric, circular, gold,
> No brush or weed breaking that bright gold of leaf-fall.
> In the center it stood, absolute and bold
> Beyond any heart-hurt, or eye's grief-fall.
> Gold-massy in air, it stood in gold light-fall,
>
> No breathing of air, no leaf now gold-falling,
> No tooth-stitch of squirrel, or any far fox bark,
> No woodpecker coding, or late jay calling.
> Silence: gray-shagged, the great shagbark
> Gave forth gold light. There could be no dark.[5]

Like Yeats' "Lake Isle of Innisfree" and "Land of Heart's
Desire," this poem furnishes a private sanctuary of the soul, a
retreat where the facts of nature are so selected as to wholly
sustain the fragile heart of man. Those facts of nature which in
ordinary life prove so ruinous to human welfare are here walled
out, with the result that here there can be no suffering, no
"heart-hurt" or "eye's grief-fall." The major source of suffering, the movement of time, here ceases to exist: "There could
be no dark."

We have seen this place before. In Poem IV of the
Rosanna sequence we came to a place "Bemused with sea, and
slow / With June heat and perfume," where a "blossomy
mass" would "brush our heads as we pass." Just as here in
"Gold Glade" there is an utter stasis suggesting timelessness

("No breathing of air . . ."), so too the vision of nature's perfection in "The Flower" involved absolute stasis:

> If no breeze stirs that green lair,
> The scent and sun-honey of air
> Is too sweet comfortably to bear.

Unfortunately, in both "Gold Glade" and "The Flower," the stasis is illusory. Although the experience of seeing perfection in nature imparts a permanent psychological sustenance, it cannot permanently fend off the grimmer realities: time and death and limitation. Hence, the feeling that "there could be no dark" proves illusory: "But of course dark came."

Like the human benediction, then, the benediction of nature is real and valuable but has built-in limitations. Much as the parents' benediction looks ahead to some completion of reality as yet unrealized—"We died only that every promise might be fulfilled"—so, too, the benediction of nature borrows its final efficacy from the grace of future possibility: "It stands, wherever it is, but somewhere. / I shall set my foot, and go there." The fulfillment of this promise—the actual setting foot to go there—will occur, it is implied, only after another "setting foot" takes place, which is to say, only after the "purchaser of the woods" comes to "set / White foot-arch familiar to violet" on His redeemed property, whereby He "subdues to sweetness" the entirety of nature at the conclusion of "Ballad of a Sweet Dream of Peace."

Before we take up the benediction of supernature, however, two aspects of Warren's attitude towards nature need further scrutiny while the material of "Gold Glade" is still within our focus of attention. These two aspects are the opposite polarities of mysticism and "realism" (for lack of a better word) in Warren's view of nature. The mysticism is evident in the fact that Warren will not, like the naturalists, take nature for granted; he will not presume that nature's essence and substance are identical, that nature is wholly self-contained and self-explaining. In such images as the "molecular dance of the stone-dark glimmer like joy in the stone's dream" ("Gull's Cry"), an image repeated in Lyric 4 of "Ballad of a Sweet Dream of Peace" ("dark stone-glimmering place"), Warren makes it apparent that even inanimate nature is dependent upon the completion of "Time's dream" for its meaning, just as animate nature is dependent upon the unity of Time and the oneness of Flesh for its identity. It is not surprising, then, to find that Warren's handling of mystical perceptions is essentially similar for both natural and supernatural phenomena. In either instance the vision comes suddenly upon an unprepared and unexpecting observer. Thus, in "What Was the Promise That Smiled from the Maples at Evening?" the recipient of "the illumination" stood in a "cold and coagulate evening," where "a gray light prevailed and both landscape and heart were subdued," whereas in "Gold Glade" the blessing befell a boy "Wandering, . . . Heart aimless as rifle, boy-blankness of mood." The latter description suggests once again a comparison to the nature mysticism of Wordsworth.

Together with this mysticism concerning the source and destiny of nature, its final meaning, there is also an insistence on realism in Warren's treatment of nature. This is not a realism of technique only—although Warren's observations of natural phenomena, whether used as a source of imagery or not, are uncommonly acute—but is more significantly a realism of conception. Warren does not share the Transcendentalist doctrine that nature is only a symbol of ultimate reality, which is Spirit. Rather, he insists that nature is real in its own right, and not only real, but important. Thus, although he shares the nature esthetic of William Butler Yeats to some extent, as I have noted, he does not end up as Yeats does, in "Sailing to Byzantium," using nature mainly as a source of imagery for the heavenly city of art. Perfect or imperfect, nature retains its absolute and permanent reality in Warren's work, and if the "Gold Glade" will prove to be of ultimate value it will be so by reason of its own reality and not because it undergirds an ivory tower of art:

> Perhaps just an image that keeps haunting me.
>
> No, no! in no mansion under earth,
> Nor imagination's domain of bright air,
> But solid in soil that gave it its birth,
> It stands, wherever it is, but somewhere.

Both the human benediction and the blessing of nature, with their opposite polarities, were equally significant in the Rosanna sequence as in *Promises* to Gabriel. Contrasted to the curse of original sin in "The Child Next Door" was the saintlike sister, who with "beauty of benediction" would "bless . . . the filth of fate." Consummating such human benediction was the ritual of brotherhood in "Gull's Cry": "let *gobbo, gobbo's* wife, and us, and all, take hands and sing: redeem, redeem!" The benediction of nature was similarly evident: as against the "astonishing statement of sun," "the ruck of the world's wind," and the "malfeasance of nature" in "Gull's Cry" and "The Child Next Door," there was the "green lair . . . too sweet comfortably to bear" and the "hawk-hung delight" of the mountain glade in "The Flower" and "Colder Fire." What particularly distinguishes the Gabriel sequence, then, aside from its greater depth of detail, is the element of the supernatural here predominant. Although the Rosanna sequence had some metaphysical implications, particularly evident in the ascent of the soul in "Colder Fire," those implications were by no means so elaborate or emphatic as the supernatural motif in the sequence to Gabriel. Other differences, such as the imagery of slaughter, do of course exist, but the most important difference between the two sequences lies in the handling of religious content.

As we might expect in a work of Warren's, that religious content has both divine and demonic dimensions. As we might further expect, those divine and demonic dimensions usually appear together, intertwined like a Gordian knot of good and evil. In all three major poems of supernatural import, "Summer Storm (Circa 1916), and God's Grace," "Dragon Country: To Jacob Boehme," and "Ballad of a Sweet Dream of Peace," this conjoining of divine and demonic dimensions forms the thematic center of attention.

Both "Summer Storm" and "Dragon Country" are poems which espouse the orthodox Christian point of view concerning the uses of natural evil. In both poems the raw material of evil—that is to say, the source of suffering—is natural disaster (what the insurance companies might call "an act of God"), but the point of view taken by the narrator imparts supernatural significance to the events he describes. So considered, a summer storm becomes indeed "an act of God" of more than economic consequence, and the "natural daylight" of "Dragon Country" somehow fails to suffice any longer for revealing truths a man has to know. The effect of natural disaster—which becomes increasingly unnatural in "Dragon Country"—is to inculcate in the victims an awareness of human limitations, limitations which are otherwise too readily forgotten by those made in the image of God. The religious

dimension in man inevitably depends upon such an awareness
of inherent limitations.

The thunderstorm described in "Summer Storm" is indeed
of such a caliber as to inspire an awareness of human limitations. All nature is cowed by its approaching fury:

> The green of woods was doused to black.
> The cattle bellowed by the haystack .   .   .
> .   .   .   .
> Up the lane the plowhands came pelting back.
>
> .   .   .   .
> The mole, in his sod, can no more hide,
> And weeps beneath the naked sky.
>
> .   .   .   .   .   .
> The toad's asthmatic breath is pain,
> The cutworm's tooth grinds and grates,
> And the root, in earth, screams, screams again. .   .   .

Although the narrator may be taking liberties in having the
mole, the cutworm, and the "root, in earth" share his anxieties,
his description of what's going on above ground is not only
believable but compellingly precise and vivid:

> .   .   .   [you] spy
> The crow that, laboring zenith-high,
> Is suddenly, with wings askew,
> Snatched, and tumbled down the sky.
>
> .   .   .   .
> And darkness rode in on the wind.
> The pitchfork lightning tossed the trees. .   .   .

The next to the last stanza shows that the origin of this
poem is the same experience that Warren describes in his short

story, "Blackberry Winter." The aftermath of this storm, like that in the short story, leaves a scene where "the bridge had washed out," where a "drowned cow bobbled down the creek," and where by reason of financial ruin, "raw-eyed, men watched." The measure of disaster is seen by the attitude of the one onlooker who was not badly affected by it: "one shrugged, said he thought he'd make out. / Then turned, took the woods-path up the creek." The indifference of this charac-ter to the plight of his unluckier friends underscores the religious function of the disaster: it smashed the illusion of self-containment, to Warren the deadliest sin.

The big difference between this poem and "Blackberry Winter" comes clear in the poem's conclusion. Whereas the short story reflects an outlook of naturalism, the drowned cow and hens being described with the morbid accuracy sometimes characteristic of Hemingway, the poem ends with a prayer. The narrator himself assumes a posture of benediction at this point, perhaps by virtue of his having received a blessing in Poem I:

> Oh, send them summer, one summer just right,
> With rain well spaced, no wind or hail.
>
> .   .   .   .
>
> And if a man wake at roof-roar at night,
> Let that roar be the roar of God's awful Grace, and not
> of His flail.

The "sadistic idiocies" attributed to God in Stanza 7 turn out to be, we now see, adjuncts of "His flail," and the awful power of the storm is actually God's rod of correction, which, how-ever unpleasant it may be, is still far preferable to the storm which in "Blackberry Winter" wiped out life and property with the blank indifference of a mechanistic universe. The closing prayer quoted above has an ethic and a metaphysic

which are both Christian at base. In saying "Oh, send them
summer" the narrator is showing a sense of brotherhood in
suffering not seen in the man who "shrugged, said he thought
he'd make out," and in anticipating "the roar of God's awful
Grace" the narrator appears to be thinking of the Christian
Day of Judgment.

The motif of the supernatural deepens considerably when
we get to "Dragon Country: To Jacob Boehme," a poem
which shows the operation of a mysterious evil not explainable
through reference to the familiar laws of nature. The allusion
to Jacob Boehme indicates the narrator's intention to impose
upon a modern setting the medieval-Renaissance world-view,
whereby happenings in this world were regarded as having
other-worldly significance. It obviously challenges modern cre-
dulity to consider human events according to such an "outmoded" world-view, but it is part of Warren's intention
deliberately to construct such a challenge. That aspect of his
search for identity which insists that "Nothing is ever lost"
demands constant inquiry into every corner of the past, with
all reverence, honesty, and humility. It is the prevailing fallacy
of the modern mind, with all its pride of intellect in its
political and scientific achievements, to consider itself so self-
sufficient as to find no value in the perspectives of the past,
whether the perspective be that of medieval Christendom, as
in "Dragon Country," or that of the classical world, as in *You,
Emperors, and Others*. Warren does not share this pride or
this fallacy, knowing well that the unanswerable questions are
no better answered by today's technology than they were by
Jacob Boehme's theology or Tiberius' stoic nihilism ("All is
nothing, nothing all").

In the poem "Dragon Country" the unanswerable question involves the mysterious disappearance, due to the activity
of a supernatural Beast, of various people and animals. As long

as the losses involved merely hogs and mules, the people were able to fight off the "constrictive pain" in the chest and go on believing their own lies concerning "what, standing in natural daylight, they agreed couldn't be true." But when the mysterious marauder made off with a teamster and a meat salesman, leaving no trace of the victims' bodies, and when, moreover, the same marauder displayed an ability to fly, leaving "weed unbent, leaf calm" at the end of his "track of disrepair," a response based on self-deception would no longer do. Instead of telling themselves lies, people began to fall silent: "No one talks. They think it unlucky."

Clearly, this story must be taken allegorically. In the context of the whole sequence, the main function of this poem is to provide concrete specification for the abstract "arithmetic of losses" that ended "School Lesson Based on Word of Tragic Death of Entire Gillum Family," and to place that "arithmetic of losses" in a properly religious perspective. By attributing these losses to a supernatural Beast, Warren seeks to restore a medieval sense of mystery to a fact of life which modern man wants to deprive of mystery, that fact of life being the disappearance of real, familiar people into the realm of death. Such a sense of mystery, by reminding men once again of their inherent limitations, activates the most essential of all religious virtues: humility.

The humility which ensues in "Dragon Country" is not terribly deep, human nature being what it is, but at least it is a beginning:

> The Catholics have sent in a mission, Baptists report new
> attendance.
> But that's not the point. We are human, and the human heart
> Demands language for reality that has no slightest dependence
> On desire, or need.   .   .   .

The Beast has done its job effectively. Men urgently aware of evil can no longer deceive themselves, no longer tell lies while "standing in natural daylight," or rationalize away evils they would prefer to ignore. We saw this theme at the end of the Rosanna sequence, where Warren urged his infant daughter to let "the language of your own heart . . . be always of whatever truth you would live," but here that theme is intensified by the overriding presence of Evil. Whereas Rosanna was urged to seek truth so as to gain "that joy in which all joys should rejoice," Warren here shows the opposite side of the coin, the dire consequences of not seeking truth: "Necessity of truth had trodden the land, and heart, to pain. . . ."

The need for the Dragon of truth in this poem, like the need for "God's flail" in "Summer Storm," is due to the perversity of human nature. Just as the least of the sufferers in "Summer Storm" shrugged and left his fellows, so here the people are moved to a religious awareness almost in exact proportion as they have suffered, and only through continued suffering is even this limited awareness maintained: "Now in church they pray only that evil depart." What would happen if the evil did depart is indicated in the last stanza, where the Dragon's function as reminder of ultimate values is clearly explicit:

> But if the Beast were withdrawn now, life might dwindle
>> again
> To the ennui, the pleasure, and night sweat, known in the
>> time before
> Necessity of truth had trodden the land. . . .

Just as "Height" was "not deprivation of valley" in "Colder Fire," so here in "Dragon Country" the opposite polarities of good and evil are mutually necessary. Without the valley, height becomes meaningless, and without the Dragon, "life might dwindle again." Fearful as it is, the Dragon's visit opens possibilities of real joy, as opposed to the "ennui, the pleasure, and night sweat" of life on the natural plane: "Necessity of truth had trodden the land   .   .   .   And left, in darkness, the fearful glimmer of joy, like a spoor." In this image, as in the image of "God's flail," Warren indicates that the path to a permanent joy, because of the perversity of human nature, has to be the traditional Christian way of submission and suffering. But ultimately the suffering and deprivation do not matter; what matters is that the supernatural joy, like its supernatural contrary, the Dragon, is there. The benediction of a supernature is real.

The third poem of supernatural significance, "Ballad of a Sweet Dream of Peace," is the grand climax of the sequence in respect to both resolution of theme and technical achievement. I have already shown how the images of slaughter and dissolution come to a head here with the transmutation of granny into the "one Flesh" represented by the supernatural hogs. Here, too, the benedictions of man and nature, acting against the imagery of slaughter and dissolution, achieve their ultimate meaning with granny's whisper, "I died for love," and with the redemption of nature by the purchaser of the woods. Here the search for identity comes to a truly cathartic conclusion. In these seven lyrics is released all the visionary power that poetry is capable of. Even the amazed and incredulous young initiate, whose brashness and skepticism so accurately represents the modern temper, finds his identity before the sequence is over. In "I Guess You Ought to Know Who You Are" he finds that the same hogs who devoured granny are waiting with similar patience and courtesy and ravenousness for him:

> . . . *But look, in God's name, I am me!*
> If you are, there's the letter a hog has in charge,
> With a gold coronet and your own name writ large,
> And in French, most politely, "Répondez s'il vous plaît."

This is richly ironic poetry. There seems to be no limit to Warren's resources, once his imagination has warmed to the possibilities inherent in his image patterns. The passage quoted above, for example, would provide a perfectly satisfactory ending for a lesser poet, but Warren has more. The dramatic irony of this situation is too rich to cut it short here, and so the narrator furnishes additional reassurance of a sort that is certain to produce anxiety: "Now don't be alarmed we are late. / What's time to a hog? We'll just let them wait." The upshot of the dialogue comes with the concluding couplet, where it appears that even the modernist initiate is converted at last. Our parting view of this neophyte shows him about to assume the traditional posture of religious humility:

> What's time to a hog? We'll just let them wait.
> But for when you are ready, our clients usually say
> That to shut the eyes tight and get down on the knees is the
> quickest and easiest way.

From this point on, the initiate says not another word, and his silence, I think, is most eloquent.

The ending of "I Guess You Ought to Know Who You Are" (above) leads directly into the last and most momentous lyric of the "Ballad," "Rumor Unverified Stop Can You Confirm Stop." This title alone, in view of the supernatural content of the poem, is itself a wonderful piece of artistic handiwork. To encompass the whole breadth of man's hope and fear concerning the unanswerable questions within a phrase in a telegram—"Rumor Unverified"—is surely the apex of poetic compression. Yeats and Eliot were never so succinct as this. Subsequently to denote man's yearning for ultimate truth in a three-word question—"Can You Confirm"—must compound the interest on this achievement. The word "Stop" at the end of each phrase adds yet more to the opulence of meaning by denoting the limitations of the human quest for ultimate knowledge.

The image of God that Warren offers in this culminating sonnet is, for all the originality of tone and setting, the traditional one of orthodox Christianity. He is a transcendent, supernatural God, one whose "heel, . . . smiting the stone, is not what is bruised," and He is coming to redeem His fallen nature:

>   . . .   speaking of change, there's a rumor astir
> That the woods are sold, and the purchaser
> Soon comes, and if credulity's not now abused,
> Will, on this property, set
> White foot-arch familiar to violet,
> And heel that, smiting the stone, is not what is bruised,
> And subdues to sweetness the pathside garbage, or thing body
>   had refused.

This premonition of the redemptive supernatural is, obviously enough, the highest promise in the book. Upon it, all else depends. The repeated use of the phrase, "in God's name," throughout the earlier lyrics in "Ballad of a Sweet Dream of Peace" takes on literal meaning as a consequence of God's imminent appearance in the final poem. Everything is indeed in God's name, as it turns out, by virtue of which fact the world can be redeemed.

The power of this vision of God appears to extend even

over the otherwise self-contained Rosanna sequence. The reference to "pathside garbage" being sweetened should logically relate to the only other mention of garbage in either sequence: the garbage which in Poem I of *Promises*, "Sirocco," covered with filth the scutcheon of Philip of Spain, the "anguished" lover of God. Even "the thing body had refused," which appears to be bodily death and its commitment of self to the ultimate oneness of Flesh, is "subdued to sweetness" by the supernatural heel of God. Indeed, death becomes welcome by reason of that final sweetness: "For Reality's all, and to seek it, some welcome, at whatever cost, any change." The search for identity ultimately coincides, then, with the search for God.

Much more might be said about the poems in *Promises*. That excellent image of nature's secrecy in "Dark Woods," the dogwood tree ("White-floating in darkness, . . . white bloom in dark air"), is an example of the need for careful and sensitive analysis. In passing, I can only submit that it furnishes an opposite polarity for the nature imagery in "Gold Glade." Whereas the beauty of "Gold Glade" fed the observer's hunger, providing him with a feeling of oneness with nature, the dogwood bloom withholds its mysterious beauty, aloof from human imperfection:

> . . . white bloom in dark air.
> Like an ice-break, broke joy; then you felt a strange wrath
>   burn
> To strike it, and strike, had a stick been handy in the dark
>   there.

But the frustration cannot be vented; no stick is handy, and tree retains its humiliating perfection of beauty, triumphant, self-contained, uncommunicating:

   . . .   you stood there, and oh, could the poor heart's
        absurd
Cry for wisdom, for wisdom, ever be answered? Triumphant,
All night, the tree glimmered in darkness, and uttered no
    word.

The two "Lullaby" lyrics are also particularly deserving of
attention. The first, "Lullaby: Smile in Sleep," brings together
some of the major motifs of the sequence with marvelous
delicacy. The imagery of slaughter, for example, appears in this
poem as follows: "You will see the nestling fall. / Blood flecks
grass of the rabbit form." The benediction of nature similarly
holds enchantment: "Dream that sleep is a sunlit
meadow / Drowsy with a dream of bees / Threading
sun. . . ." The other "Lullaby," subtitled "A Motion like
Sleep," uses water imagery, such as we saw in "The Ballad of
Billie Potts," to describe that aspect of the search for identity
which involves the subconscious self:

Past hush of oak-dark and stone's star-glinted upbraiding,
Water moves, in a motion like sleep,
Along the dark edge of the woods.
So, son, now sleep.

Sleep, and feel how now, at woods-edge,
The water, wan, moves under starlight,
Before it finds the dark of its own deepest knowledge,
And will murmur, in motion like sleep. . . .

Both "Lullaby" lyrics are notably shaped for melody, with
short lines of varying length, with a great deal of assonance and
consonance, with a simple rhyme scheme, and with variations
of a refrain to end each stanza. Taken together, the two
"Lullaby" lyrics constitute the loveliest bestowing of the hu-

man benediction in *Promises:* "Dream perfection. . . .
Dream grace, son. / Sleep on. . . . Dream the sweetness
coming on. / Dream, sweet son. / Sleep on."

Perhaps I should qualify that judgment a bit. The "Lullaby" poems are the loveliest of the human benedictions in a
technical sense, but in a different way the most poignant
benediction upon Gabriel comes not from the baby's father
but from a total stranger, an "old man, toothless and through,"
who blesses the child while under "the lattice of personal
disaster," himself doomed in the shadow of death. The scene is
in "Brightness of Distance," the last of three sections in
"Infant Boy at Midcentury":

> And once, on a strange shore, an old man, toothless and
> through,
>   Groped hand from the lattice of personal disaster to touch
>   you.
> He sat on the sand for an hour; said *ciao, bello,* as evening fell.

Like the scene of the defective child saying *ciao* in "The Child
Next Door," this scene shows that the human benediction is a
two-way relationship. In view of the ultimate oneness of Flesh,
it is not for saints and seers alone to impart benedictions.
Rather, the fact of total interdependence makes the human
benediction of equal efficacy whether coming from father or
saintlike sister or from a defective child and a ruined old man
saying *ciao* from "the lattice of personal disaster."

Another poem in need of careful analysis is "Man in
Moonlight," with its three lyrics developing the central image
of moonlight: "Moonlight Observed from Ruined Fortress,"
"Walk by Moonlight in Small Town," and "Lullaby: Moonlight Lingers." Leonard Casper observes in *Robert Penn Warren: The Dark and Bloody Ground* that "Those lines tendered

to Rosanna are deluged with sunlight, those to Gabriel with the moon." Upon this observation he bases his whole interpretation of *Promises:* "Counterforces in the dialectic upheaval have become counterparts. The day of creation is shared by, rather than divided between, the newest generation, girl:sun and boy:moon whose prophetic radiance replaces those torrents of blinding guilt that drench the conscience in *Eleven Poems on the Same Theme.*" [6] By thus equating the girl with the sun and the boy with the moon, Casper is able to derive through logical deduction a meaning for the concluding poem of *Promises,* "The Necessity for Belief": "Children then become their own promises, standing straight as two promises, which *could* be named Rosanna and Gabriel:

> "The sun is red, and the sky does not scream.
>
> .   .   .   .
>
> The moon is in the sky, and there is no weeping." [7]

This interpretation raises so many more questions than it answers that I believe we must adjudge Casper guilty of misreading here. The resemblance of sun and moon to Rosanna and Gabriel, if it exists at all, is hardly extensive enough to justify an exact correlation in the concluding poem of *Promises,* and even if the alleged resemblance had been extensive, it would not explain Warren's pair of assertions, relating to sun and moon, that "the sky does not scream" and "there is no weeping." Surely, Warren does not mean to suggest, as a parting assurance to his reader, that all manner of things will be well simply because his infant son and daughter are as yet too young to know enough to "weep" and "scream."

Rather, what Warren seems to be doing in "The Necessity for Belief" is offering an analogy by which human faith might be strengthened. The perfect calm and assurance of nature, as

seen in the sun and the moon, observers of all worldly suffering
and evil, might be instructive to less enduring human observers. The sun in "Gull's Cry" and the moon in "Man in
Moonlight" represent the same secret knowledge not given to
man that we saw in the dogwood bloom of "Dark Woods,"
but here ("Moonlight Observed from Ruined Fortress") the
frustration of not knowing is more constrained:

> . . . caught in that strict protocol of plenilune
> And that werewolf thirst to drink the blood of glory.
>
> We stare, we stare, but will not stare for long.
> You will not tell us what we need to know.
> Our feet soon go the way that they must go,
> In diurnal dust and heat, and right and wrong.

It is by reason of this secret knowledge withheld from man
that "the sky does not scream" and "there is no weeping."

In view of this secrecy on the part of the all-observing sun
and moon, their "prophetic radiance," as Casper describes it,
becomes ironic and ineffectual to the human supplicant for
knowledge. What the sun and moon do offer is not prophetic
vision, but the calmness and assurance accompanying greater
than human knowledge. By relying on belief in the absence of
higher knowledge, human beings can transcend their limitation of vision and so attain for themselves the imperturbable
calmness evident in the evening sky, which "does not scream"
although "the sun is red" and darkness is fast falling. This state
of approaching darkness is to the sky what death is to the
human being: a threat of annihilation. Only the thin hope
proffered by "much that is scarcely to be believed" stands
between the darkening of the sky, whether human or natural,
and absolute final darkness. But the sky relies with absolute
confidence on that thin hope, and lo! magic ensues: "The

moon is in the sky.   .   .   ." Replacing the vanished light of
the day is another, more enchanting light, whose radiance
transfigures all it illuminates. And so the faith which the sky
showed at the setting of the sun ("and the sky does not
scream") is here rewarded: "And there is no weeping."

Lest we find this too simple, too innocent an analogy
between nature and human life, we should remember that
Promises is a volume of poems in which there is a good deal of
screaming and weeping, from the narrator's anguish in
"Sirocco" to the imagery of slaughter in "The Snake" and
"Hands Are Paid." So it is not innocence, but a graphic
knowledge of evil that underlies "The Necessity for Belief,"
and the purpose of this concluding parable is to offset horror
with a positive perspective. The effect of this little parable is to
justify the reliance of sky or human on "much that is scarcely
to be believed," and that confirmation, infallibly attested by
the presence of the moon in the sky, constitutes Warren's last
word to Gabriel and to the reader: "Much is told that is
scarcely to be believed." Fantastic, tenuous though it is
("scarcely to be believed"), such belief, whose only alternative
is "screaming" and "weeping," is ultimately verified.

Before I conclude this discussion of *Promises*, one further
feature of Warren's art needs comment, and that is his strikingly effective and functional use of humor. Almost always,
Warren's humor is in the nature of irony, but it is neither the
bitter, self-corroding irony of T. S. Eliot or Stephen Crane nor
the smug and condescending irony of, say, Sinclair Lewis and
H. L. Mencken. On the contrary, Warren's irony is gentled by
a sense of identity with the object of ridicule. A real and
profound humility proceeding from his vision of the oneness
of Flesh has rendered the artist's eye anything but cold and
ironically scornful.

Coarse and robust as it often is, Warren's humor is calculated to impart grace to a body of art full of violence and horror. In such a context, ironic humor frequently offers the only means of controlling the tone. The most violent of the *Promises* poems, "School Lesson Based on Word of Tragic Death of Entire Gillum Family," modifies the horror of mass slaughter by just such discipline of humor. The second line of this poem, which describes the Gillum children, sets the tone: "And their noses were sometimes imperfectly blown." Good country diction carries this comic beginning forward in Stanza 2: "And the whang-doodle whooped and the dang-whoodle snorted." By the time we get to the more sinister foreshadowings of the poem, such as the following description of old Slat Gillum's homespun philosophy (his humanistic fatalism makes him a rough backcountry equivalent of Faulkner's Mr. Compson), we are somewhat cushioned by the padding of humor against the shock of tragedy:

> .   .   .   he'd stop and say: "Say, mister,
> .   .   .   .
> Human-man ain't much more'n a big blood blister,
>   All red and proud-swole, but one good squeeze and he's
>   gone.
>
> .   .   .   .
> But a man's got his chaps to love and to cherish,
>   And raise up and larn 'em so they kin git they chance."

As well as mitigating the effect of violence and horror, Warren's humor can serve other important functions. In the poems of the supernatural, humor counteracts the reader's tendency towards incredulity. In "Dragon Country," our first glimpse of humor—in Line 3 of the first stanza—is indeed disarming: "This is the dragon's country.   .   .   .   On a

frosty morning, that field mist is where his great turd steams."
In describing the aftermath of the Dragon's visits, the time
when "The Catholics have sent in a mission, Baptists report
new attendance" and "the local birth rate goes low" because of
the inactivity in lovers' lanes, Warren likewise employs the
power to convince in humor, and quite successfully.

The most important use of humor in *Promises* occurs in
"Ballad of a Sweet Dream of Peace," where the humor of irony
helps to dramatize a supernatural motif that might be
disparaged—as T. S. Eliot's religious poetry sometimes is—if
presented straightforwardly. The basic irony, of course, is built
into the very structure of the so-called "ballad," which consists
of a dialogue between a stupid, insensitive fellow and the
knowledgeable, sophisticated guide who initiates him into
ultimate reality with a commentary of devastating wit and
perception. But aside from this basic structural irony, which
culminates in the initiate's conversion to a posture of humility,
each lyric has an ironic flavoring in its own right. Lyric 2,
"Keepsakes," for example, weaves some incisive thrusts at
modern mores into granny's search for identity through the
bureau:

> *Well, what is the old fool hunting for?*
> Oh, nothing, oh, nothing that's in the top drawer,
> For that's left by late owners who had their own grief to
>   withstand,
> And she tries to squinch and frown
> As she peers at the Prayer Book upside down,
> And the contraceptives are something she can't
>   understand.   .   .   .

Although this passage does not readily yield up its meaning, I
would venture a guess that the "Prayer Book upside down"
represents formal religion, with its somewhat ossified mode of
worship, and the contraceptives might well suggest something

about sterility in contemporary culture. Granny's search for her mislaid identity is hardly assisted by such trifles.

The humor of irony becomes even more suggestive in Lyric 4, "Friends of the Family, or Bowling a Sticky Cricket." Underneath the surface absurdity in this poem seems to be a very serious theme indeed, for the "cranky old coot" who comes bearing "a placard proclaiming, 'I am the Law!'" appears to be some kind of modernized Christ-figure, not only because of his sign—which is later validated as true—but for other reasons as well: he has been "expelled from his club" because he has insisted on truth, "drowning crickets in claret," while his fellows have gone the apostate (and I suppose more pleasant or convenient) way of using cologne. Even the initiate knows the error of such practice—*"But they drown them in claret at Buckingham Palace!"*—but the King's standards mean nothing to His unfaithful followers, even as God's standards meant nothing to the Pharisees who rejected and ignored the man-God. Although this comparison may seem farfetched, some analogies seem reasonable. Certainly, Buckingham Palace seems as remote from these Kentucky hills as God's Kingdom is from organized religion. The "old coot," moreover, has been "expelled from the club" for Christlike reasons: he calls himself "the Law," he rejects the club's ways in favor of the King's, and he is "cranky" enough to bear isolation and ridicule rather than compromise his principles. The final picture of the "old coot" corroborates quite definitely his supernatural status. Though barefoot and rejected, he abides by his truth until he is recognized at the last:

> . . . law is inscrutable, so
> Barefoot in dusk and dew he must go,
> And at last each cries out in a dark stone-glimmering place,
> "I have heard the voice in the dark, seeing not who utters.
> Show me Thy face!"

I have talked about these poems perhaps too much, but one further mention of irony might be excused. Lyric 5, which carries the search for identity into the province of sexual love, is particularly discomfiting to the slowly awakening initiate. Here a former mistress of his, "the afternoon one who came to your bed, lip damp, the breath like myrrh," finds the meaning of love not in his (the initiate's) ministrations, but from observing "two toads in coitu on the bare black ground." What such a spectacle states about his—the initiate's—sexual relationships is eloquently clear, even to the initiate himself, and so the title might serve equally well as an epilogue: "You Never Knew Her Either, Though You Thought You Did, Inside Out." With one illusion after another falling away in this fashion, the initiate has by this time become well enough inducted into ultimate reality to undertake his own search for identity, which promptly ensues with the letter from a hog ("Répondez s'il vous plaît") in Lyric 6.

This brings to a conclusion my discussion of *Promises*. The excursion through these poems is a rich and wonderful experience, and greater riches remain than those I have held up to the light. Journeying through the labyrinth of Warren's mind, one encounters horror and fear—much of the way is darkness—yet calmness and light await at the end, and peace beyond all reasonable expectation. In consummating his search for identity with the vision of oneness of Flesh and unity of Time, Warren gives all that poetry can offer. This is not just poetry of therapy, seeking to assuage—if just for a moment—the ruined heart's rage; it is poetry of vision, intended to transfigure Reality by a glimpse of its ultimate meaning. Regathering the fragments of self and time, it seeks to make man whole.

CHAPTER FOUR

You, Emperors, and
Others: A Culmination

UNLIKE FAULKNER and Hemingway, whose greatest artistic success happened in their earlier careers, Warren's talent has developed into its fullest maturity only within the last two decades, as the writer has moved through his forties and fifties. In poetry, at least, this judgment is supported both externally—by the lavish praise given *Brother to Dragons* and *Promises*—and internally, by critical analysis of the poetry itself. In these works, certain trends both of theme and of technique come into full maturity, as we have seen.

To judge from Warren's most recent book of poems, *You, Emperors, and Others* (1960), the major trends in the earlier verse, far from weakening as the years go on, are, rather, culminating. Even a cursory analysis of the title will reveal this tendency with respect to Warren's subject matter. The "you" of direct address, which we first saw emerge into prominence in *Eleven Poems* and "The Ballad of Billie Potts," becomes overtly a major theme in Warren's latest book, where Warren flagrantly tramples upon modern theories of the impersonality of art. When T. S. Eliot felt compelled to address the reader directly in *The Waste Land*, he at least retained the minimal protective armament of using a foreign language—"You! hypocrite lecteur!—mon semblable,—mon frère!" Not so with Warren: his first line in *You, Emperors* is relentlessly simple, straightforward English: "Whoever you are, this poem is clearly about you." As for the "emperors," whom we might (if we did not know Warren) expect to appear clothed in some kind of esthetic distance or impersonal dignity, they are merely the culmination of Warren's long and intimate scrutiny of history, his transformation of dead past into living present. Lest we should mistake his intention, in fact, he explicitly transforms one of these "emperors" into the "you" which is ever his true subject in the "Apology for Domitian": "Let's stop horsing around—it's not Domitian, it's you / We mean." The "others," needless to say, follow the same lead, all filing down through the inward caverns of self or plumbing the outer darkness in search of identity.

In technique, too, Warren's latest book shows a roughened, crudely finished verse that stands in contrast to the finely wrought lines of many of Warren's contemporaries. This is not to say that Warren's latest work is by any means carelessly or haphazardly executed; on the contrary, these coarsening effects are carefully calculated. But the directness and vigor of tone in this work, coupled with its bold, original, sometimes parodic experimentations with form, whether free verse, *terza rima,* "ballad," dramatic monologue or even nursery rhyme, may give the book as a whole an appearance of being out of step with the times. In *Eleven Poems,* where, as we remember, Warren's distinctly original voice and vision first began to come forward with consistency, their effect was to estrange Warren from the schools, conventions, and critical attention of his contemporaries. In connection with that initial appearance of Warren's true "voice," W. P. Southard made a comment, using a passage from "End of Season" as illustration, that could well apply to most of Warren's subsequent poetry, and to *Promises* and *You, Emperors, and Others* in particular:

> "Summer's wishes, winter's wisdom—you must think
> On the true nature of Hope, whose eye is round and does not wink.

"That loose line is his favorite, and his best. His tight metrics mostly don't come off, they're too tight, a strain. . . . He gets an easy effect, of a voice admirably accenting its various speeches, and I have a hunch he writes it that way: just talks it out, to see how the diction hits the ear. . . . Mr. Winters wouldn't like that, but you know what Mr. Winters does like." [1]

Two pertinent observations may be drawn from this statement. First, Southard's opinion that Warren's "loose line is his favorite, and his best" appears to be confirmed by the loose line's creator, Robert Penn Warren. Although Southard probably oversimplifies the creative process involved (I doubt that Warren "just talks it out, to see how the diction hits the ear"), he certainly seems in retrospect to have been an accurate, if unwitting, prophet, for Warren's lyric verse has grown increasingly loose and informal in recent years, almost to the point of being (in a poem like "He Has Fled") Whitmanesque. In most of his poems, however, we should note that Warren has retained much of the formal discipline of popular convention, including a fairly strict rhyme scheme and a repeating stanza pattern. Indeed, even in his most recent works Warren can sometimes be remarkably faithful to complex, difficult stanza patterns while at the same time giving no appearance of constraint or awkwardness. "The Letter about Money, Love, or Other Comfort" is a good example of this subtle, almost unnoticeable adherence to form. Together with his vigorous, personal tone, his power and originality of imagery, and his penchant for experimentation, this subtle mastery of form should eventually gain for Warren considerable recognition as a craftsman.

The other pertinent remark of Southard's is his reference to Yvor Winters as someone who would not like Warren's relatively loose, direct manner of expression. This reference to Winters, a foremost defender of "reason," esthetic distance, and formal discipline in art, brings up another point which, in retrospect, gives Southard's statement a prophetic air. In discussing *Promises*, I took note of how the split between Redskins and Palefaces has affected Warren's reception adversely so far as the Redskins, represented by Kenneth Koch and his "New Romanticism," are concerned.[2] Ironic as it seems, the Palefaces also have given Warren a hostile reception. He has been getting rough treatment, in short, from both of these warring factions, by whose standards (in either case) he has been tried and found wanting.

The chief spokesman for the Paleface, or academic, attitude towards Warren's recent verse is John Edward Hardy, whose review of *You, Emperors, and Others* is based on principles that Yvor Winters, one might presume, would

warmly endorse. Hardy's indignation is kindled not by Warren's personal subject matter, which he approves in general,
but by Warren's appalling attempt to bring "you," the reader,
directly into his text. Such a rape of the reader's sanctity, in
Hardy's estimation, not only reveals the insolent bad taste of
its perpetrator but also, what is worse, calls his sincerity into
question: "Warren (as lyric poet) . . . does not
know . . . or indeed, I suspect, care . . . anything
about mice, travelling salesmen, ladies with cancer, or you. He
has written a book, apparently, out of some obscure feeling
that he *ought* to know and care, of regret that he
doesn't; . . . it is simply the Eliotic posture of universal
benediction (*Cf. Lullaby*, for example—'For I who
bless . . . ,' etc.)"[3] Specifically, Hardy attacks "Nocturne: Traveling Salesman in Hotel Bedroom," "Nightmare of
Mouse," and "Clearly about You" as examples of Warren's
"stale and unconvincing posturings, assumptions of worn-out
disguises," which add up to "seventy-nine pages of poems
largely about nothing in the world, except a desperate striving
for significance. Or, striving for you."[4]

The fact that criticism of Warren's poetry has grown
poorer in recent years, has grown more superficial and even
unfair, is confirmed by a look at some of the other reviews of
You, Emperors, and Others. Even reviewers who classify themselves as admirers of Warren's earlier work express strong
support of Hardy's judgment that the latest poems are "largely
about nothing in the world." John Thompson, who gives *You,
Emperors, and Others* one paragraph in his "Catalogue of
Poets," dismisses the volume with a joke: "His first poems
sounded sometimes like a fierce Marvell; these newest ones
sound, sometimes, like a fierce Ogden Nash."[5] Although Dud-
ley Fitts, writing for the New York *Times,* is not so flippant,

calling Warren's latest work "an exercise in metrical high
jinks," his well-meaning apology on Warren's behalf may be
even more damaging than John Thompson's sarcasm: "All in
all, and in spite of a handful of poems that seem to be clear
about the point they want to make, Mr. Warren's new book is
an exercise in metrical high jinks. Fairly high jinks. There's no
law against a poet's taking an artistic vacation, and this binge
was obviously fun." [6]

Appearing at the zenith of Warren's artistic reputation,
these are remarkable criticisms indeed. If Warren has in fact
become "a fierce Ogden Nash" in his latest work, has indeed
taken "an artistic vacation" by writing "poems largely about
nothing in the world," this must truly be a most inexplicable
development for a poet who has hitherto spent all his powers
in a deadly serious probing of inner and outer darkness,
endlessly seeking a final identity. Although there are precedents for this sort of development (T. S. Eliot's book of "cat"
poetry is lighter than his usual work, for example), those
precedents usually bear lucid testimony to their playful intention. One wonders, however, how poems about the death of
one's father, about the mangling of a fellow wayfarer beneath
train wheels, about a woman doomed with cancer, about
slaughter of man, mouse, and insect, or about the "half-
destroyed bodies" of old people at a health resort can possibly
be construed as a "binge" that is "obviously" in "fun."

The truth is, of course, that behind his facade of grim
humor, his parodying of nursery rhymes and the like, Warren
has never been more serious in his life. Indeed, the roughening
and deliberate disruption of form that led critics to call his
latest work metrical high jinks worthy of Ogden Nash has
quite possibly resulted from the increased violence of Warren's subject matter, the content of these verses. It is as though

the violence of Warren's vision of things has found an appropriate vocal outlet at last in the far-ranging extremities of tone, pitch, and meter evident in this latest collection.

The major critical problem concerning *You, Emperors, and Others*, to sum up the situation, has been the same as that which Southard observed in connection with Warren's first major publication, *Selected Poems:* "Robert Penn Warren . . . has been so badly read, when read at all, that [his latest volume] may really need . . . a little elementary unheroic plumbing." [7] The reviewers we have been looking at, I feel, simply have not understood the content of *You, Emperors, and Others.* Even Hardy's fairly extensive treatment reveals this weakness inadvertently when Hardy makes what I would consider an erroneous distinction between *You, Emperors* and its predecessor, *Promises.* Whereas in *Promises* the "motivating and shaping power was affection," Hardy asserts, "the family and friends are largely missing from the latest collection." [8] I think Hardy is wrong here. If anything, *You, Emperors, and Others* arises more directly and frankly than ever out of its author's personal experience, not only in such obvious instances as the extended sequence on his father or on the fellow crushed under the boxcars, but also in the sequence about "You," where the "I" and the "Thou" of speaker and reader blend gradually into a unified "we." Warren obviously includes himself in the "You" to whom he addresses a series of questions in "Arrogant Law" and "The Self That Stares": "Have you crouched with rifle, in woods, in autumn . . . ?" "Have you stood beside your father's bed / While life retired . . . ?" "Have you seen that brute trapped in your eye . . . ?" Since these are clearly Warren's own experiences (the second question above, for example, provides the subject matter for the five lyrics on his deceased father), Warren's unconventional intimacy with his reader must be read not as presumption and insolence, I think, but rather as an urgent, forthright attempt to share his experience with his reader, a striving to get the reader to participate. Warren's effect in this artist-audience relationship is quite analogous, I should say, to Thornton Wilder's effect in extending the playing area of his drama out into the audience itself, so that, for example, the bride and groom in *Our Town* run up the middle aisle of the auditorium, and various members of the audience stand from time to time to take part in the proceedings.

As a misunderstanding of content seems to be the major critical problem concerning Warren's latest volume, and as, also, this content happens to offer satisfactory material for my concluding remarks, I think we may proceed now to analyze in more detail Warren's aims and achievement in *You, Emperors, and Others*. The motif of the dark night of the soul, with its inner and outer dimensions of darkness, continues to provide the central structure of Warren's poetry, I feel. In *You, Emperors, and Others*, Warren goes once again "naked into the pit . . .   to make the same old struggle for his truth," to use Warren's own description of "the philosophical novelist, or poet." [9]

The exploration of the darkness within the human psyche, the theme which was at the heart of *Eleven Poems* and *Brother to Dragons*, occupies the center of the series of poems which begins *You, Emperors, and Others*. These eight poems, entitled "Garland for You," are especially concerned with the recognition of the deeper self, the undiscovered self who, though scorned and shunned by the conscious mind, holds the secret of ultimate identity. We may recognize throughout this sequence a number of familiar phrases and images that recur from earlier poems. In the first poem of the book, "Clearly about You," there is the "face drowned deep under water, mouth askew," at which Billie Potts once stared in perplexity as he leaned to drink of his deep identity. There is also in this poem the "innocent" conscious self whose primary need is to recognize its complicity in the general pollution, to acknowledge its relationship to the collective dark shadow of mankind. The humiliating irony which Warren directed at the surface self in *Eleven Poems* and which the guide similarly directed at the initiate in "Ballad of a Sweet Dream of Peace" (in *Promises*) reappears as forcefully as ever in "Clearly about You." Specifically, the surface self finds whoredom and thievery in its immediate ancestry ("Your mother preferred the more baroque positions. / Your father's legerdemain marks the vestry accounts"), and so the issue of self-knowledge has assumed some disturbing complications: "So you didn't know? Well, it's time you did—though one shuns / To acknowledge the root from which one's own virtue mounts."

What differentiates the "you" in this poem from Billie Potts is his advanced age and greater sophistication. "In the age of denture and reduced alcoholic intake," this character, unlike Billie, may turn consciously to religion and psychology for relief from his uneasiness: "You will try the cross, or the couch, for balm for the heart's ache." Like Billie, however, the "you" in this poem will find all evasions of the inner confrontation to be unavailing: "But that stranger who's staring so strangely, he knows you are you." By reason of advancing old age, moreover ("Things are getting somewhat out of hand now—light fails on the marshes"), this character must feel an additional urgency to know himself that Billie Potts would not have felt.

The lack of identity continues to constitute the central

problem in the second poem, "Lullaby: Exercise in Human Charity and Self-Knowledge." The headnotes of both the first and second poems in the book emphasize the basic theme of anonymity, of lack of identity. "Clearly about You" mentions the epitaph of a "Roman citizen of no historical importance," which is Warren's way of assailing the oversimplifications necessary to the historian's craft; the "Lullaby" draws its headnote from a contemporary manifestation of anonymity, Walter Winchell's fictitious "Mr. and Mrs. North and South America," a euphemism of the press that must cover millions of "citizens of no historical importance." To Warren, of course, either everything and every self is of "historical importance" or else nothing is, including you, emperors, and others. To establish *real* historical importance, however, identity must be redefined, in terms that neither the historian nor the journalist would recognize.

Three commonplace modes of ascertaining identity (name, face, and sex) are rendered meaningless by sleep in the first three stanzas of "Lullaby." Supplanting those superficial credentials of identity, now that the conscious self has subsided into oblivion, are assurances of a subconscious identity, which has no sex, face, or name. What the subconscious identity does have, however, is a permanent affinity with its environment that gives it some kind of immortality. This idea has been stated or implied in a number of Warren's poems, as I have previously indicated. There was the resurrected self, whose "cold heart" heaved like a toad in the cellar in "Crime," and there was the submission of the conscious self to the father's hatchet-blow in "The Ballad of Billie Potts." In *Brother to Dragons*, we may remember, there was similarly the catfish image and the vision of the serpent self, "looped and snug" in the underground dark, safely hibernating through naturalism's winter. In *Promises*, too, there were intimations of a new, immortal identity, having nothing to do with the conscious self (represented by the initiate and by granny before the hogs got her), in the "Ballad of a Sweet Dream of Peace."

The particular contribution of "Lullaby" to this series of images is the affinity with the entire cosmos that appears to exist, in sleep, between the deeper self and its surroundings. Though "Galactic milk spills down light years," the deeper self is perfectly at ease in infinity: its "personal fame is / Sung safely now by all the tunèd spheres," and its "sweet identity / Fills like vapor, pale in moonlight, all the infinite night sky." Although of course one may feel that Warren is deriding such notions of self as delusions of grandeur, I think we may infer from evidence in this poem and elsewhere that Warren actually considers such subconscious intuitions, per- ceived in sleep or otherwise, to have serious truth-value, partic- ularly since the perceptions of the conscious mind may have such distorted, unreliable truth-value. In connection with the search for identity, the subconscious perceptions in sleep may fill our deepest need, as Warren construes it: "For you to yourself, at last, appear / Clearly, my dear." A state of blessed- ness may attend such a perception, in Warren's estimation; at any rate, he concludes the poem by blessing the "nameless- ness" of the deeper self. Its very anonymity, we might suppose, is the source of its potentiality; because it lacks all the distinc- tions of name, face, and sex upon which the conscious identity prides itself, it may transcend those distinctions at the last and contribute to the oneness of Flesh that culminates Warren's apocalypse in "Ballad of a Sweet Dream of Peace." The beginning of such a vision of unity is seen in the dual anonym- ity at the end of the "Lullaby," where the speaker and sleeper both lack identity alike: "Whoever I am, what I now bless / Is your namelessness."

The theme of identity takes an unexpected twist in "Man in the Street," where the title figure, dressed in apparel suggesting absolute conformity ("gray flannel suit, knit tie, and Brooks Brothers shirt"), turns out to be a Christ-figure. The headnote to this poem, taken from the pseudepigraphic Sayings of Jesus, should prepare us for the unexpected, it is true, but it is nevertheless a bit startling to hear Jesus' promise of immortality restated by so unlikely a messiah as this "nice young man" with "face flour-white as a miller's": "And I go to prepare a place for you, / For this location will never do." Like the "cranky old coot" who insisted on following the King's practice in "Friends of the Family, or Bowling a Sticky Cricket" in *Promises,* this Christ-figure represents Warren's attempt to reconceptualize the stale, etherealized stereotypes of orthodoxy (as he would apparently construe them) into a dramatic, here-and-now level of apprehension. The original Christ, after all, had hardly any greater external credentials to distinguish him than has the "nice young man" in this poem. As far as the surface-self is concerned, Jesus himself would have ranked as "a citizen of no historical importance" in the eyes of his more eminent contemporaries. Warren's purpose in presenting this off-beat Christ-figure is apparently indicated in his headnote, attributed to the Sayings of Jesus: "Raise the stone, and thou shalt find Me, cleave the wood, there am I." Warren's poetry has, in fact, constituted an attempt to "raise the stone" and "cleave the wood" in the pursuit of identity; this poem in particular seems intended to offset the implication that only a darker, more sinister reality may be uncovered by such searching. Irrational, unexpected benediction, as we have seen in earlier poems, may also befall the seeker, even in the nearly ludicrous context of "Man in the Street."

"Switzerland," "A Real Question Calling for Solution," and "The Letter about Money, Love, or Other Comfort, If Any" are poems that work out the familiar Warren theme of moral and psychological unease in persons trying to evade the inner and outer darkness of their existence through flimsy, sometimes desperate measures. Chief among those measures is the simple device of escape, or running away to a hypothetical Shangri-La such as Switzerland, "world-mecca for seekers of pleasure and health." Here a pathetic assortment of seekers have gathered, including the old, with "half-destroyed bodies," the young, whose bodies perform perfectly their digestive and reproductive functions, and the in-between, such as the "lady theologian" whose needs are not exclusively metaphysical ("for therapy now trying a dago"). Despite the new and costly environment, these people find out (like Billie Potts) that they really have not escaped a thing; here they meet "old friends" known from "long, long back," and here they discover that, after all, "there's little difference . . . between different places."

At the end of "Switzerland" an abrupt shift in tone takes place when the narrator, after asserting that all these moral derelicts reside, in fact, "in that high, highly advertised Switzerland of your own heart," invokes a prayer on behalf of the naked ego, in all its "pain, need, greed . . . and spasm":

> O God of the *steinbock's* great sun-leap—Ice-spike in ice-
> chasm—
> Let down Thy strong hand to all whom their fevers destroy
> And past all their pain, need, greed, lip-biting, and spasm,
> Deliver them all, young and old, to Thy health, named joy.

The need for "joy," here described as a gift of God, was, as we remember, a primary theme in *Promises*, especially in the

Rosanna sequence. Apparently, Warren is now attaching increasingly theological significance to this state of being, comparable to the orthodox state of grace, which he calls "joy." Such joy, it appears, is the emotional means of emerging out of the dark night of the soul. Viewed in this light, joy does become a religious value of very high importance.

In "A Real Question Calling for Solution," the "Question" involves the relationship between subjective and objective reality, or between the unconscious self (the soul) and the conscious, which inhabits the objective, temporal world. As we might suppose from Warren's earlier verse, the conscious self comes away the worse in this situation. Its form of reality begins to crumble in the very first line of the poem, where ironically disturbing assurance is given ("Don't bother a bit, you are only a dream you are having"), and it disintegrates even more under the stress of the moral and intellectual chaos that follows—the failure of love and of self-understanding. (The failure of "you" to learn Greek apparently ties in with the headnote from Aristotle's *Psychology*, which itself may bring to mind the ancient Greek admonition, so ironic in this context, "Know thyself.") The final stanza of this poem shows an ironic capitulation to the unconscious mode of reality, the "logic of dream," which alone (to a self as divided as "you") can offer coherence, meaning, and identity:

> There is only one way, then, to make things hang together,
> Which is to accept the logic of dream, and avoid
> Night air, politics, French sauces, autumn weather,
> And the thought that, on your awaking, identity may be
> destroyed.

"The Letter about Money, Love, or Other Comfort, If Any" is a strangely obscure poem about the pursuit of an alter ego by the recipient of the "letter" (in the title). The pursuing self in this case appears to be, in some complicated way, the poet himself, the one who has "accepted the trust so many years back" and who has "discovered I had small knack / for honesty, but only a passion, like a disease, for Truth." (These characteristics, I think, describe Warren as poet quite accurately, particularly since the speaker claims a "small knack for honesty" as one of his virtues but feels unable to describe his perceptions as absolute "Truth.") The self whose name is on the special delivery letter ("By Hand Only"), the letter which has rendered the speaker's life a "metaphysical runaround," is described in terms suggesting the beast imagery in *Brother to Dragons* or the imagery of slaughter in *Promises*. In pursuing the other self, so as to deliver the letter, the speaker finds evidence of utterly amoral living: "you had blown, the rent in arrears, your bathroom a sty," "and at the delicious New England farmhouse your Llewellin setter / was found in the woodshed, starved to death," "and you fooled with the female Fulbrights / at the Deux Magots and the Flore, / until the police caught you dead to rights."

What makes the other self redeemable, despite his sins and flight from responsibility, is his relentless search for identity, which is always a heroic undertaking in Warren's art. The speaker feels "moved nigh to tears" by "the tale you'd been caught / crouched in the dark . . . [near] the orphanage where it appears / you were raised—yes, crooning among the ruined lilies to a teddy bear." (We may recall granny's sawdust doll in *Promises* in connection with this scene; she, too, was seeking a "poor self she'd mislaid.") The final scene of this poem occurs in a setting that should remind us of "Colder Fire" in *Promises*. The pursuit of the other self, in the attempt to deliver the letter, has led the speaker at last to austere,

lonely heights, where, according to "peasant hearsay," that
other self now abides:

> . . . I will go up, and beyond the north face,
> find that shelf where a last glacial kettle, beck, or cirque glints
> blue steel to sky in that moon-place,
> and there, while hands bleed and breath stints,
> will, on a flat boulder not
> far from the spot where you at night drink, leave the
>   letter.   .   .   .

Unlike the ascent in "Colder Fire," unfortunately, the ascent
of this mountain by the other self has been obligatory. He has
been hunted there ("by dog and gun   .   .   .   hunted to the
upper altitudes") because of his complete devolution into
animalism: "you, like an animal, / will crouch among the
black boulders   .   .   .   , for you are said to be capable now
of all bestiality, and only your age / makes you less dangerous."

Perhaps because he has found the other self at last, and has
accepted him in his full bestiality ("though I've never seen
your face" I "have fulfilled / The trust"), the speaker sees a
transcendent vision with the coming of dawn as the poem
ends:

> [I] see, in first dawn's drench and drama, the snow peak go
>   gory,
> and the eagle will unlatch crag-clasp,
> fall, and at the breaking of wing-furl, bark glory,
> and by that new light I shall seek
> the way, and my peace with God.   .   .   .

Once again, in this reference to "my peace with God," Warren
gives evidence that he is becoming more explicitly theological,
though not more orthodox, in these later poems. A sense of joy

and vision of glory seem to be gaining increasing importance as a counterweight to the great darkness that still pervades much of the poetry.

"Arrogant Law" and "The Self That Stares," the final two poems in "Garland for You," explore the inner darkness with increased urgency. In part, this urgency derives from a sense of isolation. The deeper self of the lover who lies sleeping or of the father who lies dying will not reveal itself to the speaker, who longs for communication: "But desolate, desolate, turned from your love, / Knowing you'd never know what she then thought of." The other reason for urgency seems to be the imminence of death, an imminence which, according to Warren's nearly surrealistic image, makes time appear greatly accelerated: "Time unwinds like a falling spool." The withdrawal of the deeper self into eternity after "Time's spool" has run out is apparently what constitutes the "arrogant dispensation, and law" which the speaker complains of. Both lover's sleep and father's death in turn invoke that "arrogant law," leaving the speaker to contemplate his own inner darkness in isolation.

In "The Self That Stares" the theme of time and identity culminates in the speaker's wish that "Time's spool" may run out quickly for him so that he might embrace the deeper self ("that brute trapped in your eye") at last. Time, the keeper of all mysteries, has taught so little in its "school," this life, that the seeker of self-knowledge actually pines for "graduation day," though it means death: "No, nothing, nothing, is ever learned / Till school is out and the books are burned." A resemblance to the ending of "The Ballad of Billie Potts" may once again be apparent, for this speaker, like Billie, seems to be yearning for the hatchet-blow that will resolve, once and for all, the problem of ultimate identity. The "sweet lesson" that will follow will grant recognition of identity, or confrontation of the deeper self, at last: "What is that lesson? To recognize / The human self naked in your own eyes." Echoes of *Brother to Dragons* are also evident in this poem, for the nature of the deeper self, the "brute" glimpsed in the eye looking back from the mirror, is described in terms suggesting the serpent seen by R.P.W. Just as the serpent in *Brother to Dragons* looks "benevolent and sad and sage, / As though it understood our human pitifulness" (p. 35), the brute self in "The Self That Stares" looks pityingly out from the mirror, though the surface self thinks that bestowing pity is *his* prerogative: "Yes, pity makes that gleam you gaze through— / Or is that brute now pitying you?"

Most of the other poems in this volume that treat man's inner darkness expand upon the motifs developed in "Garland for You." I have already mentioned how the "Emperors" shed their classic dignity to become identified with "you"; other historical figures likewise descend to the personal, here-and-now level of immediacy. The two "war" poems, taken from classical and American history, give the main characters ample occasion for self-exploration. The "Fatal Interview" between Penthesilea and Achilles almost evokes echoes of the conflict within the divided self, for after Achilles has killed the Amazon warrior he mourns, "But woe is my soul that it's this sweet blood I spill now, / For this is my True Love." The other "war" poem is "Two Studies in Idealism: Short Survey of American, and Human, History." This work, which is one of Warren's very best achievements in the form of the dramatic monologue, works out several motifs that we have encountered before. The "lesson" in "The Self That Stares" ("What is that lesson? To recognize / The human self naked in your own eyes") is precisely what bothers the Confederate soldier in

"Bear Track Plantation" (the first of the "Two Studies in Idealism"). As long as he sees that "naked self" in the eyes of others only, in consequence of his two main pleasures in life ("killing and you-know-what"), he feels secure about his own identity:

> When those eyelids go waggle, or maybe the eyes pop wide,
> And that look comes there. Yeah, Christ, then you know who
>   you are—
> And will maybe remember that much even after you've died.

But having now met his own death, the speaker is no longer so certain about knowing who he is, and he worries about the naked self that may have appeared in his own eye at the last (This passage suggests a parallel with the "blue eyes that, puzzled, stare up at blue sky they lie under" at the end of the earlier "war" poem, "Fatal Interview"):

> But now I lie worrying what look my own eyes got
> When that Blue-Belly caught me off balance. Did that look
>   mean then
> That I'd honed for something not killing or you-know-what?

The Harvard graduate of 1861 who provides the other "Study in Idealism" has no such qualms, even momentarily, about his identity. Like the political millennialist "who wrathless, rose, and robed in the pure / Idea, smote" in "Butterflies over the Map" (*Selected Poems*), this young soldier is assured of his perfect innocence: "I tried to slay without rancor, and often succeeded. / I tried to keep the heart pure, though hand took stain." What this character most needs is an awareness of complicity to counteract his separation (for the sake of "Right") from the oneness of Flesh. The old man whom the speaker slays knows the complicity, his last act being to render forgiveness though his dying is not for "Right": "Son, you look puke-pale. Buck up! If it hadn't been you, / Some other young squirt would a-done it." This spontaneous forgiveness, it may be noted, places the old rebel soldier in the category frequently occupied by the secret inner self, such as the serpent who "forgave all, and asked forgiveness, too" in *Brother to Dragons* (p. 35). In contrast to the "idealism" practiced by Thomas Jefferson and his various followers, such as this Harvard graduate of 1861, the deeper self, whether the serpent or the old man offering forgiveness, practices a true and efficacious virtue that belies its loathesome appearance. Pursuit of such virtue, once the false mantle of purity has been cast off, is the only valid approach to the darkness within the human psyche according to Warren's religious-psychological ethic. Pursued far enough, this spontaneous virtue—this forgiveness and acceptance regardless of "Right"—holds out the promise of an identity beyond the limitations of the conscious self. The end of "He Was Formidable," the second poem of "Ballad: Between the Boxcars (1923)," would appear to imply this hope, at any rate, for it recapitulates, although in question form, the image of the oneness of Flesh (through death) that was so crucial in *Promises:*

> And why should we grieve for the name that boy might have
> made
>
> . . . .
>
> When we cannot even remember his name, nor humbly have
> prayed
> That when blunt grossness, slam-banging, bang-slamming,
> blots black the last blue flash of sky,
> And our own lips utter the crazed organism's cry,
> We may know the poor self not alone, but with all who are
> cast

>To that clobber and slobber and grunt, between the
>boxcars?

An effective transition between the consideration of man's inner darkness and the theme of outer darkness occurs, I think, in the two "Emperor" poems, "Apology for Domitian" and "Tiberius on Capri." As one who would "for hours . . . lock himself up to pull wings from flies," Domitian initially seems to embody the theme of the monster-self within, suggesting an analogy to the bestial figure in "The Letter about Money" who starved his dog, fooled with the female Fulbrights, and eventually took on a completely animal nature after being hunted to the top of the mountain. Domitian's motive for bestiality, however, is not so much a monstrous impulse from within as it is a frenzied response to outer darkness, the fear of extinction. Unlike the old rebel soldier in "Harvard '61," Domitian lacks the grace to die virtuously. Beset by nasty omens, "Fear the fifth hour" and so on, Domitian finds (as will "you," says Warren) that "virtue comes hard in face of the assigned clock," and when he dies, "he claws like a cat."

Tiberius, called "cruel" in "Apology for Domitian," is far too sane a man to indulge in Domitian's frenzied cruelties. In fact, he appears in "Tiberius on Capri" to be something of a philosopher, in the Stoic-nihilist tradition. Counterbalancing his philosophical pessimism, however, as he hears the sea sing "All is nothing, nothing all," is an ethic of hedonism. His very presence on Capri, indeed, is explained as a retirement into unbounded self-indulgence, on an island renowned for its beauty and promise of pleasure. Here, like the mecca-seekers in "Switzerland," Tiberius may enjoy a lifelong orgy, using his imperial power to fulfill all "his Eastern lusts and . . .

Egyptian fantasies." Here, perhaps, an emperor can forget the less enticing realities.

Unfortunately for Tiberius, however, he could forget nothing. Instead, he found that the sea of eternity, singing about nothing being all, encircles even the finest pleasure island. And if that should fail to affect him, there was another symbol of nothingness, encroaching nightfall, to remind him recurrently of what he would rather forget: "Tiberius, / Sea-sad, stares past the dusking sea-pulse . . . darkward he stares in that hour. / Blank now in totality of power." At such a moment, even a Roman emperor might well consider John Henry's remark to the Captain, in the headnote to "The Self That Stares," "A man ain't nothing but a man." Warren himself, who appears as central character in the last two stanzas of "Tiberius on Capri," feels the oppressiveness of that great dark even as Tiberius had. His last act, as he sniffs the "night air of autumn," is to make "outcry / At the paradox of powers that would grind us like grain, small and dry." The form of this "outcry," the throwing of "a small stone from that ruin" into the sea, suggests Warren's conception of the efficacy of his art, I believe. Whether the "ruin" refers to the house of Tiberius, to Lilburn's house in *Brother to Dragons*, or to the abode of the "citizen of no historical importance," the fact remains that art may avail something even in the face of naturalistic darkness: "Dark down, the stone, in its fall, / Found the sea: I could do that much, after all." This gesture could just as well, perhaps, be interpreted as purely futile, with "that much" being ironic, but it seems to me that the impulsive throwing of the stone serves some function of value, if only to release, through this "outcry," the intolerable sense of tragedy that the speaker feels. The throwing of the stone is, moreover, an assertion of self, of the will, and as such it may affirm, in defiance of darkness and time, the artist's identity. If this reading is accurate, Warren's image should remind us of Faulkner's description of the artist making "a scratch on the face of anonymity" in his Nobel Prize Address. Warren can make a small splash in the sea of eternity.

The outer darkness deepens in the very tender and personal series of poems called "Mortmain," a legal term literally meaning "dead hand." The dead hand in the first poem of this sequence may remind us a bit of the "supplication of a dead man's hand / Under the twinkle of a fading star" in Eliot's "The Hollow Men," for the hand of Warren's father "rose cold from History / To claw at a star in the black sky, / But could not reach that far—oh, cannot!" It would seem, though, that rather than trying to reach towards an afterworld, Warren's father is reaching towards this one, in a vain last attempt to make contact with his son in the realm of the living. The blackness of the sky that surrounds that star, whether the star represents this world or another, would imply that Warren is contending with the outer darkness of naturalism in this poem, especially since the father's hand could not make contact with the star ("in darkness the wax-white clutch could not / Reach it").

On behalf of his father, who is certainly as deserving as Domitian or Tiberius, Warren makes another small splash in the sea of eternity in the remaining poems of "Mortmain." Although Warren does not subscribe to the absolute despair of philosophic naturalism, he does, as we have seen, appear to consider the conscious identity consigned to ultimate oblivion to be supplanted by a new identity, an all-embracing universal selfhood that is recognizable now only in the unconscious. In order to compensate for this loss of conscious identity, Warren recreates his father's image, and very movingly, in these lyrics.

Most memorable among these probings of time past, I feel, is
the last one, "A Vision: Circa 1880," where Warren looks
"Down the tube and darkening corridor of Time" to see his
father as a young boy. To conceive of one's father as younger
than oneself must be psychologically startling, to say the least,
but to see him crossing "that sunlit space" as vividly as Warren
sees his father is more than startling; it is agonizing. Past and
present are as cleft asunder as life and death, with no communication between them:

> . . . I strive to cry across the dry pasture,
> But cannot. . . .
> .   .   .   .
> . . . The boy,
> With imperial calm, crosses a space, rejoins
> The shadow of woods, but pauses, turns, grins once,
> And is gone.

Some of the most powerful images of outer blackness in
You, Emperors, and Others occur in the experimental poems
towards the end of the volume. The "Nursery Rhymes" have a
particularly bizarre effect because of this intrusion of naturalistic chaos into a little child's outlook. In "Knockety-
Knockety-Knock" death comes to take the little boy's mother.
Since "the strange foot came in," she who had "held me tight"
is now "deader than mackerel," while father, who used to ride
the speaker on his knee, has taken to drink to ease his
sorrow:

> . . . Ma's deader than mackerel,
> And Pa pickled as pickerel,
> And oh! knockety-knockety-knock,
> God's red eyes glare
> From sockets of dark air—
> Knockety-knockety-knock.

Death comes knocking for various other characters before the volume ends, including Little Boy Blue, Mouse, Man, and Cricket. Death comes calling for "you" also, though his immediate victim is a lady with cancer, in "Prognosis: A Short Story, the End of Which You Will Know Soon Enough." The "Prognosis," of course, is that you must die; and life is the "Short Story," the end of which is death. There is plenty of concrete experience, in short, to justify the speaker's "Obsession," in the poem of that name, that makes the speaker dread to awake in the naturalistic dawn ("when dawn brings only dawn"), with "Sweat cold now on pillow, before the alarm's *burr*." He has little heart now to give up "the logic of dream," as Warren called the lapse into unconsciousness in "A Real Question Calling for Solution," and to confront once more his "Obsession," the "old thought for the new day" that bedevils all his waking hours.

But despite the darkness within mankind and surrounding him in *You, Emperors, and Others*, I think it must be said of this volume, as of *Promises*, that the most important element in the book is its imagery of affirmation. Even in the darkest places, there is some hint of redemption. I have already mentioned, in this regard, the supplication for "Thy health, named joy," that ends "Switzerland," and the resolve to "seek / the way, and my peace with God" at the conclusion of "The Letter about Money." That affirmation gathers strength, I think, in the "Mortmain" sequence, and especially in the fourth of these lyrics on his father, "In the Turpitude of Time." The concept of all nature striving towards some "far-off divine event, / To which the whole creation moves," as Tennyson expressed it in "In Memoriam," seems to have been central in Warren's vision of life, at least since the ending of "The Ballad of Billie Potts." In this poem about the "Turpitude of Time," it appears that only man, because of his perversely skeptical mind, fails to respond to this innermost urge and aspiration. Man's lack of belief—which ties in with his separation from the unconscious—has tragically cut him off from a potentially transfiguring source of sustenance:

> Can we—oh, could we only—believe
> What annelid and osprey know,
> And the stone, night-long, groans to divulge?
> If we could only, then that star
> That dawnward slants might sing to our human ear,
>
> And joy, in daylight, run like feet,
> And strength, in darkness, wait like hands.   .   .   .

Although they do not ascend to this level of mystic possibility, the "Quiet, Plain Poems" at the center of the volume seem calculated to buttress the theme of faith, hope, and joy. The first such poem, "Ornithology in a World of Flux," pretty well describes in its title the hope for spiritual sustenance that undergirds these lyrics. As a traditional symbol of mystic expression, the bird may offer a valid refuge, unlike Switzerland or Capri, from the naturalistic "world of flux." The moment of stillness which this poem describes likewise suggests mystic possibilities, a way of transcending the world's meaningless flux. "In Moonlight, Somewhere, They Are Singing" tells also of a moment of enchantment, a time of perfect human communion that bound singers and listeners magically together. That remembered harmony—and it continues yet, the title says—suffices to sustain in the speaker "Some life-faith yet, by my years, unrepealed."

Even the drabbest, grisliest circumstances may not withhold the possibility of glory, according to Warren's outlook.

"Nocturne: Traveling Salesman in Hotel Bedroom" provides one of the most unpromising scenes in the whole volume. The salesman in this case could well have stepped from the pages of James Joyce's *Ulysses*: there is even the soap and the tooth-brush and the call to stool that Leopold Bloom built his life around. But even in this shabby setting, Warren insists as the poem ends, ". . . vision is possible, and / Man's meed of glory not / Impossible—oh remember / Remember—in life's upshot."

"Prognosis: A Short Story," certainly one of the grimmest poems in this collection, offers its hope and promise as well. In contrast to the disappointing human elements in this poem—the drunkard son-in-law, the daughter who commits whoredom and bitchery, the husband who rapes ("by blunt bruteness") his cancerous wife—the natural elements, i.e., sand and joree bird, give sustenance of spirit. Through lapsing into the unconscious world of dream, the doomed woman gains participation, joy, and identity in the final two subpoems. She hears "the grain of sand say: I know my joy" and she hears the joree sing "his sweet sadness of self" literally in the shadow of the grave ("where the cedar leans / Black on white lime-stone"). Although she loses her conscious identity in this experience ("the enormity of sun-blaze consumed her name"), she gains her true identity at last, and so, in "What the Sand Said," she fears nothing: ". . . if I dream, I shall be real, or really / myself . . . and I do not grieve to be lost in whatever / awfulness of dark the / world may be, and love is. . . ." Though the surrealistic atmosphere of this poem renders interpretation uncertain, I think we may begin to see now why the unconscious self, despised, ignored, and repudiated in various poems, looks in pity at the temporal self. The resources of the deeper self, it would seem, are so rich as to make the conscious self by contrast look pitiable: the husband, daughter, and son-in-law are more to be pitied in the end than the woman with cancer, who (like the catfish and serpent in *Brother to Dragons*) does "not grieve to be lost in whatever / awfulness of dark."

Perhaps the most effective of all the images of affirmation are those which occur side by side with horrifying glimpses into outer darkness. As was the case in *Promises*, the two modes of vision have to coexist in a kind of spiritual dialectic. Warren makes this idea explicit in his last two nursery rhymes, "Mother Makes the Biscuits" and "The Bramble Bush." The first of these juxtaposes the vision of glory and the vision of horror in consecutive stanzas, linking them by a cause-and-effect sequence which asserts that the vision of glory, perceiving nature in rapturous harmony, is possible only because of the view of ultimate nothingness beyond the last star:

> For the green worm sings on the leaf,
> The black beetle folds hands to pray,
> And the stones in the field wash their faces clean
> To meet break of day.
>
> But we may see this only
> Because all night we have stared
> At the black miles where stars are
> Till the stars disappeared.

"The Bramble Bush" likewise tells of seeing ultimate reality in both its horror and its glory. What seems especially significant about this poem is that the glory comes last—it follows the harrowing vision of space-time immensity that might reasonably be expected to swallow into oblivion all human potentiality:

And I now saw past the fartherest stars
   How darkness blazed like light,
And the sun was a winking spark that rose
   Up the chimney of the night,

And like petals from a wind-torn bough
   In furious beauty blown,
The stars were gone—and I heard the joy
   Of flesh singing on the bone.

What these remarkable passages point to, finally, is an end, by means of mystic perception, to the dark night of the soul. With the subconscious offering unexpected riches inwardly and with the outer darkness giving way now to images of redemption for man and nature ("the joy / Of flesh singing on the bone" as "the stones in the field wash their faces clean / To meet the break of day"), both the inner and outer dimensions of the soul's dark night would appear to be coming to some mystical dawn at last. But it is important to realize that if such a dawn may now be conceivable, it is by no means as yet realized. Warren is quite serious, I think, when he suggests that only the hatchet-blow, death (or the departure from "Time's school" in "The Self That Stares"), can conclusively resolve the problem, one way or the other.

In the meantime, he leaves us, as the book ends, in the position of the grasshopper trying to "Break Solipsism," as he puts it in the title of the final poem. The "solipsism," or the theory that the self is the only existent thing (all reality being therefore subjective), must indeed be broken if an end to the inner and outer darkness of man is ever to be realized. We have seen in a number of Warren's poems, especially in *Promises*, how important it is to find some reality beyond the self to which the self may commit its identity. Without self-transcendence, seen in the grasshopper's faith and love towards God ("For God is light, oh I love Him"), all is lost, including God's own purpose for existence, it would seem: "I sing, for I must, for God, if I didn't, would weep, / And over all things, all night, His despair, like ice, creep." This is Warren's final word in the poem, and in *You, Emperors, and Others*. He has presented, as clearly and forcefully as he can, the alternatives: self-transcendence or self-annihilation, faith or despair. Knowing too well the weight of evidence that lies with either alternative, he does not try to force the reader's judgment, does not lapse into didacticism. But he does consider the attempt to break the solipsism worth making, apparently. Although there is no guarantee of success and the grasshopper's summer will not be long, he may as well spend it at this undertaking as any other, singing "*summer, summer*, . . . summerlong." Besides—and this may be important—the grasshopper is responding to a deep, innermost compulsion ("oh I love Him, love is my song. / I sing, for I must. . . ."). In accordance with Warren's synthesis of religion and psychology, as we know, that innermost instinct should settle the issue, logic and conscious reasoning notwithstanding. On these grounds, Warren's final word in his latest volume may be considered a religious affirmation.

By way of conclusion, I think we may say that Warren's whole career as a poet has been evolving towards some kind of religious affirmation. Even in the early poems of naturalistic despair, as we remember, there were occasional glimpses of the religious attitude. There were the trees in "The Last Metaphor" that reared "not up in strength and pride" but lifted "unto the gradual dark in prayer." There was also the insistence on the necessity of hope and courage in "Letter to a Friend," and more importantly, there were mystic intimations concerning the vanished self in "Eidolon" and in "Kentucky

Mountain Farm," where the spirit that "moves and never sleeps" received all the produce of time into the "absolute deeps" of eternity.

In the more recent poems, such as *Promises* and *You, Emperors, and Others*, the religious attitude has been gaining ascendancy, I think, largely through Warren's portrayals of the unconscious mind, which—unlike the conscious, temporal self—lives in perfect affinity with its environment, unperturbed by the awesome immensity of space and time and darkness. To an orthodox reader, this reliance on the unconscious as the primary source of religious experience may seem to classify Warren as a psychological rather than religious writer, for it is true that the forms and doctrines of religious orthodoxy have almost no place in his poetry. (A Christ-figure such as the "Man in the Street" does little to alter this impression.) Ultimately, however, Warren's interest in psychology, in confronting man's inner darkness, is subordinate to his intensely religious concerns: knowledge of self, of the meaning of existence, of man's fate.

Although Warren's perceptions of inner and outer darkness are original, profound, and vividly presented, I feel that his poetry will be most highly valued, in the long run, for its moments of mysticism, such as the glimpse of all creatures moving "home" at the end of "The Ballad of Billie Potts" or such as the induction into ultimate reality, where "all Time is a dream, and we're all one Flesh, at last," in "Ballad of a Sweet Dream of Peace." Such insights, strengthened, as we have seen, in *You, Emperors, and Others*, constitute Warren's original contribution to poetry and to psychological-religious experience, it seems to me. Considered in relation to his vision of darkness, "past the fartherest stars" as he says in "The Bramble Bush," Warren's final affirmation, his hearing "the joy / Of flesh singing on the bone," marks a quite considerable triumph of the human spirit against the "bramble bush" of worldly experience and tragedy.

Because it has been an arena for spiritual experience, both suffering and triumph, both naturalistic despair and mystical joy, I would definitely consider Warren's poetry to be of first importance when judged on thematic grounds. Warren's consistent preoccupations from his earliest verse to his most recent have been with problems central to our age. Despite his increasingly independent "voice," or manner of presentation, Warren stands in the mainstream of modern literature in his strongly honest and searching confrontation of naturalism and in his attempt to find alternatives other than despair in response to that spiritually paralyzing philosophy. Whether considering man's outer darkness (the fear of naturalistic oblivion predominant in *Thirty-six Poems, Promises,* and *You, Emperors, and Others*) or searching man's inner darkness (as he does in *Eleven Poems* and *Brother to Dragons*), Warren has been concerned with the major issues of our time.

The leading reason why Warren's poetry has been so largely neglected, I feel, is simply that its "vision," its concern with these central issues of our age, has not been understood adequately. The concept of an inner, subconscious self, and the theme of the relationship between this inner self and the conscious identity—these have been Warren's main concerns with respect to man's inner darkness. Perhaps because of the special demands of this subject matter, which requires some rather special knowledge of modern psychology, or perhaps—and more likely—because of the obscure, original imagery with which Warren represents this material, critical recognition and understanding of these concerns have come rather slow and late, or so my study of the matter would

indicate. The theme of outer darkness, or the threat of extinction of the self in naturalistic oblivion, has not been quite so
troublesome, since it is more obviously attuned to the general
literary and ideological currents of our time, but Warren's
response to this outer darkness, through mystical or subconscious perceptions of unity and design in creation, has again
caused some difficulties in interpretation. Such misunderstanding of theme, I think, has caused Warren's poetry to be
inadequately and sometimes unfairly criticized.

Whether Warren's themes have been so effectively embodied in form and structure as to exert the maximum persuasive
power that is always one of the artist's objectives is, as we have
seen, subject to critical controversy, and no doubt will long
continue so. It seems to me, however, that in the matter of
form as well as of content, critics have often gone somewhat
amiss in their process of judgment. Readers who are too
narrowly committed to any specific basis of judgment, whether
it is the New Critical doctrine of the impersonality of art or the
New Romanticist idea of art as spontaneous expression, accordingly limit their access to what poetry can offer. To
reprimand Warren for writing about "you" or to call his
experiments with form "metrical high jinks" is to comment
primarily on one's own limitations of preference, I should
think. Such commentaries surely cannot be accepted as abso-
lutes in our final evaluation of this poet. Warren's growing
disregard for the formal discipline of the New Criticism—his
increasingly personal approach and subject matter and his
sometimes Whitmanesque freedom of form—ought to be
regarded as within the artist's prerogative. Warren, after all,
has never agreed to be limited by *any* point of view, or by any
set of strictures laid down by one or another school of esthet-
ics. In neglecting this fact, Warren's critics more often than

not have revealed their own lack rather than Warren's. Perhaps he should rather be admired for his continual launching out into technical innovations, for his reluctance to confine himself to the old established formulas in which he had already demonstrated (most critics agree) high technical competence as early as *Thirty-six Poems.*

There is, moreover, another side to this argument about Warren's technical competence. Even if we should agree that Warren has excessively violated modern formal conventions, I think there still remains in his verse much that should gratify contemporary tastes. Even during his period of boldest experimentation, in *Promises* and *You, Emperors, and Others,* Warren simultaneously produced poems that may be considered perfect triumphs in the mode of traditional forms. The first three poems in *Promises,* for example, adhere quite strictly to the stanza pattern of a very respectable tradition, the Shakespearean sonnet form. In *You, Emperors, and Others* Warren shows his versatility by adhering remarkably well to such varied forms, of several centuries' standing, as the nursery rhyme and the neoclassic grand style. The rhyme, rhythm, and stanza pattern of his "Nursery Rhymes," with their simple diction and sentence structure, are in marked contrast with the verse texture in the "classical" poems, those treating Tiberius, Domitian, or Achilles, where the sentences often embrace five or ten lines of poetry. The traditional form of the dramatic monologue, too, finds perfect expression in the "Two Studies in Idealism."

On the grounds of both form and content, then, but especially because of his freshness and depth of vision in encountering problems central to our age, Robert Penn Warren deserves more critical respect and attention than he has been getting. It is my contention that if and when he does get such notice he will probably be ranked as one of the major poets of our time, for he is one of the few (to requote James Dickey's review of *Promises*) "to give you the sense of poetry as a thing of final importance to life."

Notes

INTRODUCTION

[1] *Kenyon Review,* I (Autumn 1939), 391.

CHAPTER ONE

[1] (Modern Library edition; New York, 1951), p. xxxvi.
[2] (Modern Library edition; New York, 1946), p. 303.
[3] W. P. Southard's "The Religious Poetry of Robert Penn Warren," an essay that ridicules *Selected Poems,* and John Hardy's "You, Robert Penn Warren," a disparaging review of *You, Emperors, and Others,* effectively represent the chronological range of such critical hostility, from early poems to the most recent. Southard's article appeared in *Kenyon Review,* VII (Autumn 1945), 653–76, and Hardy's in *Poetry,* XCIX (October 1961), 56–62.
[4] Casper, *Robert Penn Warren: The Dark and Bloody Ground* (Seattle, 1960), p. 81; Matthiessen, "American Poetry Now," *Kenyon Review,* VI (Autumn 1944), 691; Southard, *Kenyon Review,* VII, 665.
[5] Jung, *The Undiscovered Self* (Mentor Books edition; New York, 1959), pp. 107–108.
[6] Jung, p. 93.
[7] Nor is it what Southard thinks it is: "The original sin . . . is naked science." *Kenyon Review,* VII, 663.
[8] Let me stress here that other interpretations of individual poems

are certainly possible. My Jungian reading arises from a study of Warren's whole body of poetry rather than from what many readers would consider presumptions concerning this or that individual poem.

⁹ Jung, p. 110.

¹⁰ Jung, pp. 102–103.

¹¹ *Kenyon Review,* VI, 691; VII, 668.

¹² "The Phoenix in the World," *Furioso,* III, no. 3, p. 36.

¹³ It is worth noting that Warren and Jung seem to agree on the ambiguous nature of the shadow-self, which is both the repository of collective human evil and the source of religious intuition. This ambiguity appears even more explicitly in *Brother to Dragons,* where at one point the shadow-self is depicted as a catfish having both good and evil properties—whose "brute face / Is the face of the last torturer" but who "under the ice . . . [is] at one with God." This idea bears an obvious parallel to religious orthodoxy, in which recognition of vicarious guilt correlates with the hope of attaining oneness with God.

¹⁴ Casper, p. 70.

¹⁵ *Kenyon Review,* VI, 690.

¹⁶ *Kenyon Review,* VII, 658.

¹⁷ See, for example, Casper, p. 73.

CHAPTER TWO

¹ "On the Underside of the Stone," New York *Times Book Review,* August 23, 1953, p. 6.

² "The Dragon of Guilt," *New Republic,* CXXIX (September 14, 1953), 17.

³ *PMLA,* LXX (September 1955), 565–86.

⁴ Garrett quotes this passage from McDowell as the starting point for his "The Function of the Pasiphae Myth in *Brother to Dragons,*" *Modern Language Notes,* LXXIV (April 1959), 311–13.

⁵ Robert Penn Warren, *Brother to Dragons* (New York, 1953), pp. 32–33. Hereinafter I shall note the page references to this book in parentheses within my main text.

⁶ *The Undiscovered Self,* p. 101.

⁷ In his study of archetypes Joseph Campbell, like Warren and like Jung, declares the cleavage within the self to be modern man's most serious problem. In *The Hero with a Thousand Faces* (New York, 1953), p. 388, Campbell says: "The lines of communication

between the conscious and unconscious zones of the human psyche have all been cut, and we have been split in two."

CHAPTER THREE

[1] "Poets and Peasants," X (Winter 1957–1958), 608.

[2] "In the Presence of Anthologies," LXXI (Spring 1958), 298–314. The review of *Promises* is on pages 307–309.

[3] "The Battle of the Bards," IV, 116–21. The Paleface-Redskin metaphor derives, as most readers know, from Philip Rahv's famous essay.

[4] A prime example of Warren's suiting of sound to sense is his shift in form during the Rosanna sequence: the first three poems, those showing the narrator's melancholy, are sonnets, whereas the last two poems indicate through freer style a movement away from constriction and despair. The fourth poem, "The Flower," for example, uses a simple rhyme scheme (*aabb*) and fast-breaking trimeter to support its projected heart-lift, and the more meditative concluding poem, "Colder Fire," frames its contemplations within a dozen quatrains of *abab* rhyme in dignified iambic pentameter.

[5] Nature's "geometry," we may note in passing ("the glade was geometric, circular . . ."), appears to impress Warren more favorably than the human geometry, employed for military purposes, in "Sirocco."

[6] Casper, p. 81.

[7] Casper, p. 84.

CHAPTER FOUR

[1] *Kenyon Review*, VII, 653.

[2] See my introductory remarks on *Promises*.

[3] *Poetry*, XCIX, 62.

[4] Hardy, p. 60.

[5] *Hudson Review*, XIII (Winter 1960–1961), 619.

[6] "Exercise in Metrical High Jinks," New York *Times Book Review*, October 23, 1960, p. 32.

[7] *Kenyon Review*, VII, 653.

[8] *Poetry*, XCIX, 59.

[9] Introduction to Joseph Conrad, *Nostromo* (New York, 1951), p. xxxviii.

Index